HTML5 Multimedia Developer's Guide

About the Authors

Ken Bluttman is the author of more than a dozen computer books, including those on aspects of web development. Coming from a business background primarily in Fortune 500 companies, Ken approaches development from the point of usage, rather than making the fancy become more important than the need—a form-follows-function approach. Ken has developed sophisticated corporate intranets, and has mentored and led teams of developers. For the past several years, Ken has been working independently, building web sites and writing books (with an occasional nap). He often consults for businesses in areas of analytics, traffic generation, and search engine optimization (SEO). When Ken gets some rare free time, you might find him playing a myriad of musical instruments, hiking up a small mountain, out on a photo shoot, or taking care of his variety of animals, and family, too!

Lee Cottrell is the Program Manager for Computer Programming and Networking at Bradford School in Pittsburgh, Pennsylvania. He completed a Masters in Information Science from the University of Pittsburgh in 2001. He has been creating web pages with HTML since 1993, primarily for nonprofit and community organization web pages. As HTML changed, Lee kept pace, working with early versions of HTML5 and CSS3.

HTML5 Multimedia Developer's Guide

Ken Bluttman and Lee Cottrell

New York   Chicago   San Francisco
Lisbon   London   Madrid   Mexico City
Milan   New Delhi   San Juan
Seoul   Singapore   Sydney   Toronto

The McGraw·Hill Companies

Cataloging-in-Publication Data is on file with the Library of Congress

McGraw-Hill books are available at special quantity discounts to use as premiums and sales promotions, or for use in corporate training programs. To contact a representative, please e-mail us at bulksales@mcgraw-hill.com.

HTML5 Multimedia Developer's Guide

1234567890 QFR QFR 1098765432

ISBN 978-0-07-175282-4
MHID   0-07-175282-X

Sponsoring Editor   Roger Stewart
Editorial Supervisor   Janet Walden
Project Manager   Aloysius Raj, NewGen Publishing and Data Services
Acquisitions Coordinators   Joya Anthony and Ryan Willard
Technical Editor   Thomas Powell
Copy Editor   Marilyn Smith
Proofreader   Emily Rader
Indexer   Jack Lewis
Production Supervisor   James Kussow
Composition   NewGen Publishing and Data Services
Illustration   NewGen Publishing and Data Services
Art Director, Cover   Jeff Weeks
Cover Designer   Ty Nowicki

Dedicated to my wonderful family—my loving wife Gayla and my awesome son Matthew. Let's not forget our several nonhuman family members, too!

–Ken Bluttman

As always, this book is dedicated to my incredible family. Without my family's support, I would not accomplish anything.

–Lee Cottrell

Contents at a Glance

Contents

Acknowledgments

Special thanks to my coauthor Lee! Lee gave 110% at times when I couldn't make my 100%. Whew! It's a finished product now. Thanks to our technical editor, Thomas Powell—great job! Thanks to Roger Stewart (a man of incredible patience), Ryan Willard, Joya Anthony, and all the other people involved in making this book who I didn't get to know, but do know they are there.

Thanks to Neil Salkind and Studio B. Most important, thanks to all the web developers pushing the new technology envelope.

Readers, visit me at http://www.kenbluttman.com.

–Ken Bluttman

They say no man is an island, and it takes a village to raise a child. Extrapolating this, then, it certainly takes a platoon of people to write a book. The author gets the credit for the accomplishment, while behind the scenes, editors, testers, and designers toil away thanklessly.

I would like to take this opportunity to thank everyone who contributed to this book. First, I need to thank the excellent staff at McGraw-Hill. Roger Stewart invited me on board this project. His trust in my abilities enabled this project to be completed. Ryan Willard, while late to the project, did a fabulous job of coaxing the last pieces of work from my stubborn fingers. Lastly, Joya Anthony, while no longer with McGraw-Hill, supported my every request.

Outside of McGraw-Hill, I need to thank my technical editor, Thomas A. Powell, and his staff at Pint.com. I have been an educator my entire life, and Thomas a professional programmer. I did not always like what he had to say about my code, or how he said it, but he made my part of this book much better.

Ken Bluttman, the first author on the book, needs my thanks as well. Ken was doing an admirable job of writing the book when life intervened, and he had to step away. Ken, this is your book. I just helped you to finish it. Ken, I would love to work with you again.

I need to thank my students at Bradford School in Pittsburgh. Many of them checked my code, provided feedback, and even supplied a screenshot or two. While all of them remain in my heart, Dave Losket, Roti Midani, and Chris Alderson provided the most feedback and help with this project.

Finally, I need to thank you, the reader. Without your desire to better yourself, this book would never have happened. Please accept my most sincere gratitude for your purchase of this book. If I can help you with your understanding of the book, you can e-mail me at lee@leecottrell.com.

–Lee Cottrell

Introduction

HTML5: What It Is and Why It Is Important to Learn

Web sites over the timeline of the Internet have evolved from simple one-pagers of static text and pictures to sites with thousands of pages, features, personalization, and more. In the present day, a decent web site is expected to have an appealing graphic appearance and easy navigation, and provide visitors with the information—textual or visual—for which they came to the site. Perhaps they came to research something, to make a purchase, or for some entertainment.

To offer the plateful of varied experiences, web technologies have sprung up, matured, and either kept evolving or were put to pasture. Early web sites used Common Gateway Interface (CGI) scripts to offer back-end processing. Today, a plethora of technologies is available, as well as sophisticated database usage, analytics (tracking visitor behavior), and targeted content based on location and previous browsing efforts.

The Internet started out as a somewhat idealistic and pure platform to impart information, without advertising or any other impurity to detract from the focus of web site visits. Well, progress can be delayed but rarely stopped. Marketing and advertising are common Internet realities, and have been for many years. With that comes technology to support the marketing efforts. The new geolocation feature in HTML5, which pinpoints the user's location, will no doubt be used for many marketing campaigns. To a marketer, that means sending you targeted, focused local enticements. Figure 1 shows that I have been found!

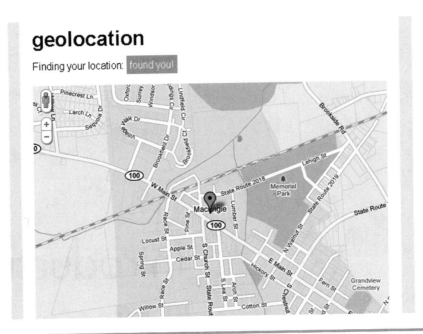

Figure 1 Geolocation is used to locate the browser.

What We Have So Far

Web pages are built with HTML (or variations, such as XHTML). Styling is provided via Cascading Style Sheets (CSS). Back-end processing is accomplished using server-side languages, primarily PHP and ASP.NET. Animation is accomplished with Adobe Flash or through JavaScript manipulation. This tool set has been the staple of web development for many years. Some changes have occurred along the way, such as to remove HTML tags that offered style attributes instead of content or organization. The style-centric tags became incorporated into CSS. Content management systems became popular to use as the backbone for web sites, as they combine many of the essential elements in an easy-to-use package.

Animation provided by Flash provides a rich and sometimes amazing visual experience. Really a sort of art-based tool, Flash became so popular that browsers began supporting it without requiring people to go out of their way to download the Flash Player, which is essentially a browser plug-in. Flash has a powerful programming language of its own: ActionScript.

Unfortunately for Flash aficionados, the nature of Flash, essentially being a movie, cannot be properly indexed by search engines. This presents a conflict many developers have needed to wrestle with: You can have a beautiful web site, and that beauty reduces the ability to get higher up in search engine results.

Clarifying All the Terms

We're barely into the introduction of the book and have already mentioned a good number of technologies, and more will be coming. It seems that here at the start is a good place to define these acronyms and tools—the lingo used by web designers and developers. The list is by no means exhaustive. A glossary of several pages might do justice to the world of web lingo.

NOTE

Not all of the items listed here are covered in the book, as this book focuses on multimedia and not the whole kitchen sink.

HTML and XHTML   Hypertext Markup Language (HTML) is the basic web page programming language. As far as true programming languages go, HTML is not quite one at all. Comprehensive languages have the ability to repeat sections of code (looping), do conditional testing (with `if` and `while` statements), and much more. HTML does not have these capabilities.

HTML's primary purpose is to have content appear on a web page. This is done via *tags*, which are ways to tell the web page what it is supposed to show or do. The tags are rendered sequentially as they appear in the code. In other words, there is no going up and down through the code (JavaScript is used for that).

XHTML is a variation of HTML. The *X* indicates XML (Extensible Markup Language).

CSS   Cascading Style Sheets (CSS) is used for styling content. For example, a line of text might be italicized, be larger than surrounding text, or have any number of other treatments applied to it. All these visual options are of the styling camp. The text is still the text, or content. The text says the same thing, regardless of what it looks like.

CSS is applied to parts of the HTML. How this is done is shown in this book.

JavaScript   JavaScript is a full-fledged programming language—looping and all—that runs in the web browser. This distinction is important. It means that the JavaScript running in my browser might be doing something different than the JavaScript running in your browser, even though we are viewing the same web page. JavaScript is arguably one of the most important items in modern web development.

AJAX   Asynchronous JavaScript and XML (AJAX) is a mixed set of technologies that provides the answer to a key web need. The use of AJAX is to refresh a section of a web page without needing to reload the entire page in the browser.

PHP and ASP/ASP.NET   PHP and ASP are server-side programming languages. They are mostly used to output the HTML that shows up in a web browser. They handle various server-based necessities, such as reading data from a database to present on a web page. Other server-side technologies—Perl, ColdFusion, and JSP—are also common, to a degree.

Flash   Flash is an application used to make web-based movies. That simple description does not do justice to how powerful Flash is. It could be debated that much of the Web's appeal has been based a fair amount on the visuals that Flash provides on web pages.

CMS The goal of a content management system (CMS) is to organize pages of content. Blogs are the common CMS. WordPress is the biggie in this arena.

Tag A tag is a building block of HTML and its variations. A tag is structured such that it is enveloped by the less-than and greater-than symbols (< >). For example, the body tag looks like this: `<body>`. Most tags require (or at least should have) a closing one, such as `</body>`.

Tags can have attributes. For example, the form tag often comes with the action attribute: `<form action="process.php">`.

Canvas Tag Canvas is a new HTML5 tag. It is essentially a drawing platform, but one on which a great amount of creative endeavors can be realized. JavaScript is used extensively with the canvas tag.

Audio Tag Audio is a new HTML5 tag. As is obvious by its name, it is used to have audio played in the browser. Previously, this was accomplished by third-party solutions, such as an audio player built with Flash. Now, HTML gains a native audio player.

Video Tag Video is a new HTML5 tag. The use of video has become a primary means of communicating to the masses. YouTube (www.youtube.com) is the leading video repository. In the past, using YouTube, a video would appear in a web page either by having code generated by YouTube embedded within the HTML code or by having an HTML link point to the video on the YouTube site. The new video tag provides a way to play video via a native core tag. The source of the video can be anywhere—most likely on your web server.

On the Horizon

HTML5 is the next-generation HTML. It is not a complete overhaul by any means. However, it does bring the over-mature HTML4 up to the needs of today. HTML5 provides functionality that was not even a consideration just a handful of years ago. An item such as client-side storage (local storage) had no place or need in the HTML years of yore. The new geolocation feature, mentioned earlier, is useful for providing location-centric features, such as suggesting a restaurant in your neighborhood.

This book introduces a variety of HTML5 features, predominantly those for multimedia, such as audio, video, and animation. A few other key features are showcased as well to make your new HTML5 endeavors a rewarding experience.

NOTE
There are endless issues with finding perfect conformance among the various available web browsers. Browser support changes often, so specific browser details become quickly outdated. In this book, the approach is to present the material and let you, the reader, experiment. Certain browsers will be named as applicable to the material, but the recommendation is to keep up with the latest!

In regard to media presentation, three new tags—audio, video, and canvas—are meant to replace third-party tools that do the same tasks. However, this is a subjective statement, as the

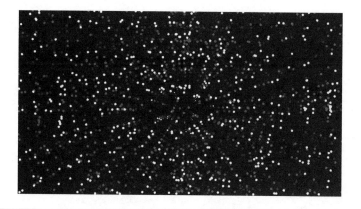

Figure 2   The canvas tag displays a JavaScript-run animation.

popular third-party tools will be around for a long time to come. Just because HTML5 is available doesn't mean web sites must be updated to this new standard. Also, even as new sites are developed, those who put these together will naturally want to stick with the tools they are the most familiar with. A sticky side to this is the use of JavaScript as the main programming language for new web development—on the browser side anyway.

Keep in mind that a web page is served from a web server. There are server-side languages to help render the pages that appear in a web browser. But once in the browser, JavaScript becomes key, as it is a programming language that runs in the browser, or the client side of the web experience.

Historically, JavaScript was the baby of the languages. It was used to provide simple actions such as image rollovers (an image can change when the mouse moves over it). A few years ago, a new use of JavaScript, named AJAX, became the rage and brought JavaScript to the attention of the developer community.

In today's development arena, JavaScript is a very important piece. JavaScript is not a particularly easy language to learn. A background with a traditional object-oriented language such as C++ will help make JavaScript easier to learn. If your cup of tea has been drag-and-drop tools, such as Dreamweaver, well, cook up a pot of coffee, roll up your sleeves, and take it at a comfortable pace.

Now, let's get to the fun! To get excitement started, Figure 2 shows the canvas element displaying an exploding star field effect. Stick around—you will soon be creating dazzle like this.

About the Code in this Book

Typing code is the best way to learn a language. If, however, you find yourself with code that refuses to work after you've typed it in, you can download all of the code from www.webbingways.com or www.mhprofessional.com/computingdownload.

Part I

Overview

Chapter

New Features of HTML5

HTML5 contains quite a number of new tags and approaches to building web pages. The doctype has been simplified. Audio, video, and drawing have become native. Even the way data is handled via local storage has changed how web pages can behave. But this version of HTML offers more than these features. HTML5 takes into account the problems designers and developers have experienced in conforming to standards.

Before delving into the intricacies of HTML5 code, let it be clear that the first new feature is at the top of every page. The doctype is now simply as follows:

```
<!doctype html>
```

Gone are the transitional and strict doctypes. I, for one, will not miss them.

HTML5 Is a Kinder, Gentler HTML

The World Wide Web Consortium (W3C) is the source for web standards (see www.w3.org). HTML is one of the technologies maintained by the W3C. Web developers, subjectively based on their programming chops, have followed the requirements of HTML to a varying degree of compliance. Mistakes with HTML such as the following have crept into many web sites:

- Improperly nested tags

- Unclosed tags

- Mismatched or missing quotation marks ("quotes") around attributes

- Missing tags

Let's examine some of these errors as they are coded, beginning with Code Listing 1-1.

Code Listing 1-1   Incorrectly nested <p> and <span> tags

```
<!doctype html>
<html>
<head>
<title>HTML5</title>
</head>
<body>
<p>
<span style="color:#0000ff;">
I am a paragraph with an incorrect nested span
</p>
</span>
<p>I am another paragraph, and proper in all respects!</p>
</body>
</html>
```

The code in Code Listing 1-1 has a mismatched nesting of HTML tags. In particular, the first paragraph starts with the `<p>` tag, followed by a `<span>` tag: `<p><span></p></span>`. The code construct should end in the reverse of this structure: `<p><span></span></p>`.

No matter! In a web browser, nothing appears awry, as shown in Figure 1-1.

Code Listing 1-2 shows a paragraph tag (`<p>`) left unclosed.

Code Listing 1-2   An unclosed `<p>` tag

```
<!doctype html>
<html>
<head>
<title>HTML5</title>
</head>
<body>
<p>I am inside a paragraph tag that does not close
<p>I am a properly tagged paragraph</p>
</body>
</html>
```

The result of this problematic unclosed tag is—business as usual. Figure 1-2 shows the expected browser output.

HTML tags can have attributes, which are additional snippets of settings for the particular tag to make use of in presenting itself. Code Listing 1-3 shows an `<img>` tag with a `height` attribute that is missing a closing quote.

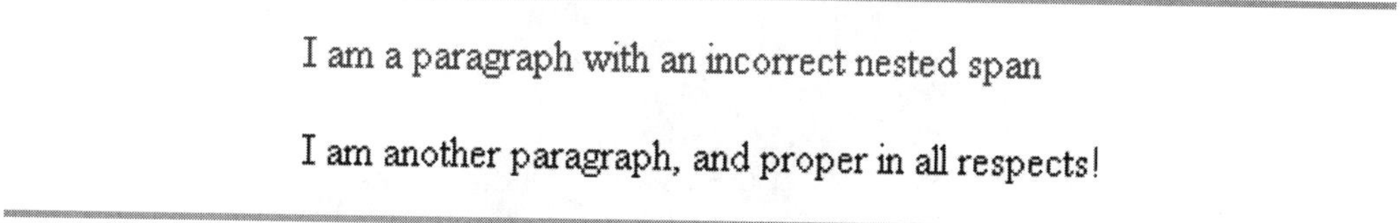

I am a paragraph with an incorrect nested span

I am another paragraph, and proper in all respects!

Figure 1-1   Incorrectly nested tags do not prevent the browser from finding the correct interpretation.

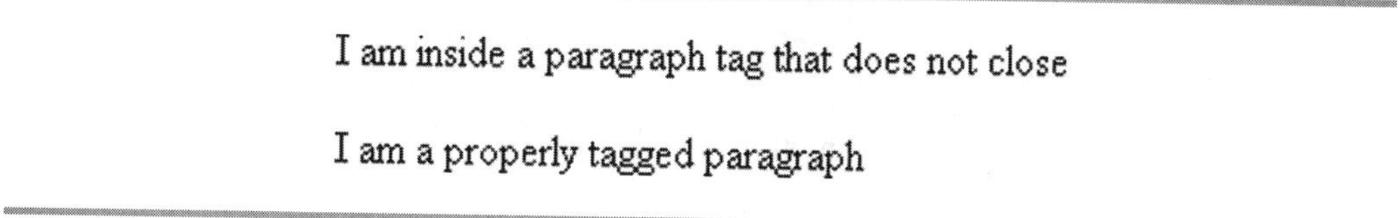

I am inside a paragraph tag that does not close

I am a properly tagged paragraph

Figure 1-2   An unclosed tag does not phase the browser.

Code Listing 1-3   <img> height attribute not properly enclosed in quotes

```
<!doctype html>
<html>
<head>
<title>HTML5</title>
</head>
<body>
<img src="tree.jpg" height="300px />
<p>A tree in Winter</p>
</body>
</html>
```

Even with the missing quote, the browser overlooks this issue and shows the picture at the height indicated by the attribute. Figure 1-3 shows the image at the intended 300-pixel height.

Code Listing 1-4 points out what would appear to be a serious coding error: The body tag (<body>) is not matched with its closing tag, which should appear near the bottom of the code.

A tree in Winter

Figure 1-3 Missing quotes around an attribute value present no problem.

Code Listing 1-4   A <body> tag that does not close

```
<!doctype html>
<html>
<head>
<title>HTML5</title>
</head>
<body>
<p>My body does not end!??</p>
</html>
```

Web browsers—regardless of the issues you might hear about developers needing to deal with each vendor's peculiarities—can overcome serious coding errors. Figure 1-4 attests to this. Even with the missing </body> closing tag, no sweat over what is shown.

Web browsers have been forgiving of such errors. That's lucky for web designers and developers! Yet, trying to force perfection onto those who do web site work, a new standard known as XHTML arose, and a doctype designated as strict came into being. This corrected some problems but created some others. Whereas strict conditioning of HTML became all the rage for a while, validators (web sites that examine other web sites for errors) reported errors and would drive webmasters bananas trying to achieve perfection. The best-known validator is on the W3C web site at http://validator.w3.org/.

Figure 1-5 demonstrates just how batty validation has placed its veil on web design. It shows that a leading web site—Yahoo—fails validation. I'm sure Yahoo knows this, and I can only imagine that its developers don't care. It hasn't stopped Yahoo from being a web leader.

As seen in Figure 1-5, Yahoo's main web page has 158 errors, and uses the strict doctype to boot! No matter—if you visit the Yahoo site, you are guaranteed a rich and rewarding experience, regardless of validation errors.

Yahoo is a bit more of an involved site than most of us work on. If Yahoo, with a team of developers, doesn't validate, why should you or I? Rather than discuss the philosophical issues, here's what has become of the fact that web pages have HTML errors: The W3C decided this can't be a forced issue. A result of this is that HTML5 has been steered away from the strict concept, and instead embraces (well, at least puts up with) such validation errors and warnings.

By the way, Google gets validation errors, too. As shown in Figure 1-6, Google has 35 errors, and is using HTML5 to boot.

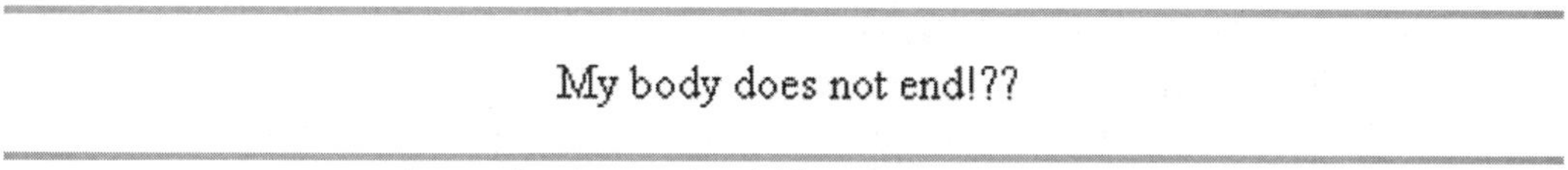

My body does not end!??

Figure 1-4   A missing closing body tag should be a major error, but is not.

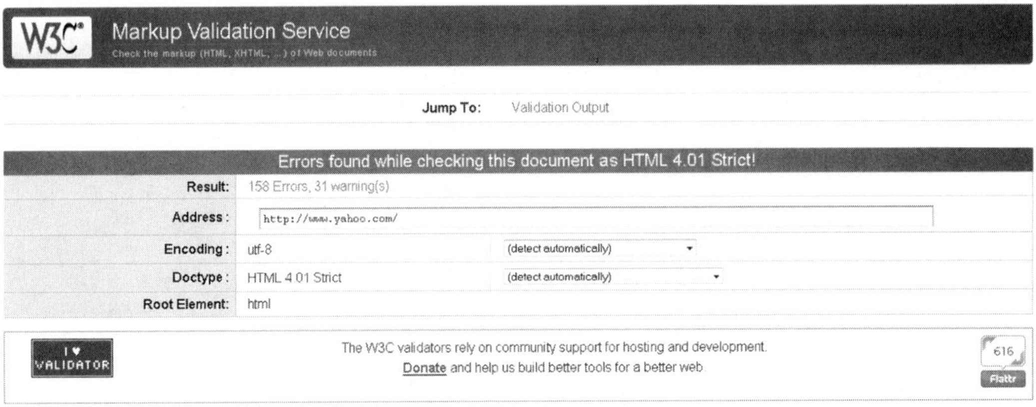

Figure 1-5   Yahoo fails validation and keeps on ticking.

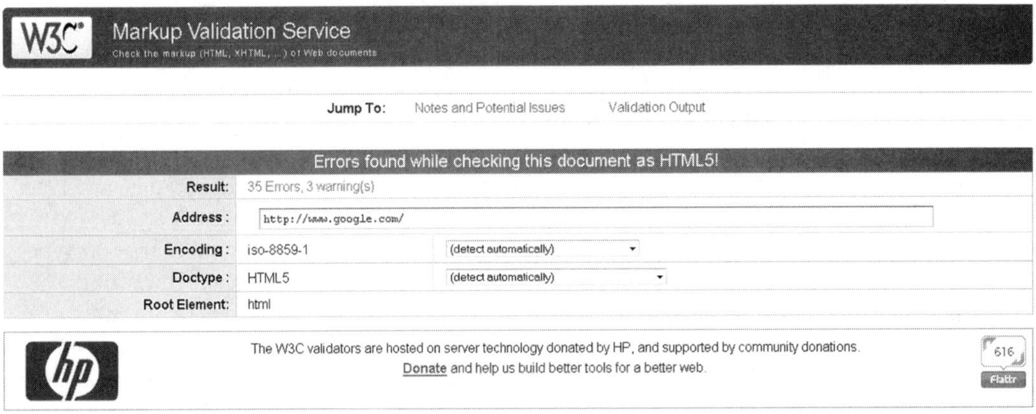

Figure 1-6   Google does not validate, but who cares?

Many HTML coders are self-taught. Some HTML coders are comfortable with a certain style of coding that suits them best, even as the rules are broken. The point to all this is that an attitude shift exists in the HTML5 specification, in that HTML coding errors are forgiven, and browsers should make their best attempt to display the web page the developer intended.

TIP

HTML5 specifies that web browsers provide internal mechanisms to handle poorly written HTML code.

HTML5 and CSS

Cascading Style Sheets (CSS) and the specifications that go along with the various versions (currently the shift from CSS2 to CSS3 is underway) don't particularly have any effect on HTML5. Rather, it is the fact that new HTML tags such as video can be treated with CSS in the same manner as the old tag standbys of body, list, div, and so on.

Figure 1-7 shows a web page with a video tag. The included video is of an octopus at an aquarium. Around the video, the border has been treated with CSS to have a black, 20-pixel border. The CSS is in the head of the page, like this:

```
<style>
video { border-style:solid;
       border-width:20px;
       border-color:black;
    }
</style>
```

Most HTML coders use CSS as part of their strategy of making web pages, but how much CSS and at what level varies widely.

CSS freed HTML from being the tool of choice to provide the presentation aspects of a web page. In plain language, this means that when examining a web page, if coded to modern accepted practices, the look is handled with CSS.

NOTE
The specification upgrade from CSS2 to CSS3 is ongoing and not universally applicable among all the various browsers. This transformation will take a while to play out.

Figure 1-7   The new video tag is treated with CSS.

New HTML5 Tags

Let's get down to the nitty-gritty. Just what is new in HTML5? First, consider the importance that HTML5 usage remains compatible with HTML4. So, right off the bat is the fact that HTML5 is HTML4 with some new tags. In other words, most of HTML5 is the same as HTML4. Older browsers that do not support new HTML5 tags will have a problem, but looking at it from the other side, newer browsers that handle HTML5 will not have a problem with HTML4.

The new HTML5 tags apply to various parts of the web page and browser usage. Table 1-1 lists many of the new tags and what they do.

Additionally, HTML5 includes the canvas, video, and audio tags, which much of this book is about.

HTML5 and HTML4 Comparison

So HTML5 has new tags, but what else has changed? Some HTML tags have been deprecated or their syntax has been altered. Many tag attributes have changed as well. Here is a list of some tag updates:

- The a element without an href attribute now represents a placeholder for where a link otherwise might have been placed.

Tag	Description
section	Represents a generic document section
article	Represents an independent piece of content of a document, such as a blog entry or newspaper article
aside	Represents a piece of content that is only slightly related to the rest of the page
header	A section to be used near the top of a page to show a page title and/or other introduction based content
footer	A section to be used at the bottom of web pages to show copyright information and other typical items found in page footers
nav	Used for setting up a navigation area on a page
figure	Represents a piece of self-contained content that can stand out from the rest of the content
progress	Shows progress of a task, such as downloading a file
meter	Represents a measurement, such as sales revenue generated on the site
time	Represents a date and/or time

Table 1-1   Some New HTML5 Tags

- The `cite` element now represents just the title of a content-based work (such as a book, a paper, an essay, a poem, and so on). The HTML4 usage where `cite` is used to mark up the name of a person is no longer considered the proper use of `cite`.

- The `hr` element now represents a paragraph-level break, instead of the standard use of creating a horizontal rule, although in appearance it is the same.

- The `i` element now represents text offset from the normal prose. In practice, no doubt it will still be used to italicize text.

- The `menu` element has been updated to be a help in structuring toolbars and context menus.

- The `small` element now represents small print (for side comments and legal print). It is no longer meant to indicate a font size attribute. This holds true with the related size attributes of `x-small`, `xx-small`, `large`, and so on.

- The `strong` element is no longer to be used to simulate a bold text look. Instead, the intent is to indicate importance. Subjectively, this is hardly a difference at all.

- The `head` element no longer allows the `object` element as child.

Perhaps more relevant are the attribute changes. The following are some of those changes:

- The `type` attribute on script and style tags is no longer required if the scripting language is ECMAScript (JavaScript) and the styling language is CSS, respectively.

- The `border` attribute on img tags is required to have the value 0 when present. Better still, the border should be set with CSS.

- The `language` attribute on script tags can be omitted.

- Authors should use the `id` attribute, rather than the `name` attribute, on anchor <a> tags.

Bear in mind that the HTML5 overall specification is a work in progress. It is evolving as this book is being written, and can even seem to contradict itself. The source for these comprehensive usage changes is the W3C. For details of these changes and much more, visit www.w3.org/TR/2010/WD-html5-diff-20101019/.

Some attributes are no longer in the picture. In HTML5, the attributes listed in Table 1-2 are not used.

Attribute	No Longer Used On
align	caption, iframe, img, input, object, legend, table, hr, div, h1, h2, h3, h4, h5, h6, p, col, colgroup, tbody, td, tfoot, th, thead, and tr
alink, link, text, and vlink	body
background	body
bgcolor	table, tr, td, th, and body
border	table and object
cellpadding, cellspacing	table
frame	table
frameborder	iframe
height	td and th
hspace, vspace	img and object
marginheight, marginwidth	iframe
noshade	hr
nowrap	td and th
scrolling	iframe
size	hr
type	li, ol, and ul
valign	col, colgroup, tbody, td, tfoot, th, thead, and tr
width	hr, table, td, th, col, colgroup, and pre

Table 1-2 Attributes That Are Not in HTML5

Keep in mind that the loss of these attributes does not mean you can no longer accomplish what they did. The goal is to move these attributes to being handled with CSS. CSS is a wonderful evolvement in web design. Perhaps it is new and scary to some. My best advice is take the time to learn it and apply it. Consider it necessary (a subjective opinion, of course, but shared by many).

The nested div structure that has been the common web organization approach now gains additional tags to help with layout, as shown in Table 1-1. Code Listing 1-5 is an example of the header, section, article, and aside tags put to use.

Code Listing 1-5   Page layout using new HTML5 tags

```html
<!doctype html>
<html lang="en">
<head>
<meta charset="utf-8">
<title>html5 layout with new tags </title>
<meta name="description" content="HTML5 demo" />
<style>
body { background-color:#eeeeee; }
header { border-style:solid;
         border-width:3px;
         border-color:black;
         text-align:center;
         width:410px;}
.section1 {border-style:solid;
         border-width:3px;
         border-color:blue;
         width:400px;
         font-size:1.2em;
         text-align:center;
         padding:5px;}
.section2 {border-style:solid;
         border-width:3px;
         border-color:red;
         width:400px;
         font-size:1.2em;
         padding:5px;}
.aside1  {margin-left:180px;
         border-style:dotted;
         border-width:2px;
         border-color:black;
         padding:5px;}
footer {font-size:.1.1em;
         font-weight:bold;
         color:blue;}
</style>
</head>
<body>
<div id="outer" style="margin-left:50px;margin-top:50px;">
<header>
<h1>This is H1 inside the header</h1>
<h2>This is H2 inside the header</h2>
</header>
<br>
<section class="section1">
This is a section
<article>
```

```
<p>This is an article. Here is the meat of the story.</p>
</article>
</section>
<br>
<section class="section2">
This is another section
<aside class="aside1">
And here is an aside inside the second section
</aside>
<br>
</section>
<br><br>
<footer>
Always a good idea to have a footer - like this one!
</footer>
</div>
</body>
</html>
```

Figure 1-8 shows the page generated by this code listing.

NOTE
Nearly 20 years into the Web being a public entity, we still need to deal with browser differences. The layout shown in Figure 1-8 is how the page appears in the Google Chrome browser. Other browsers may or may not display the page in the same way.

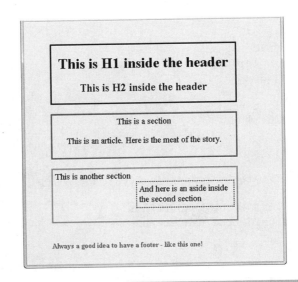

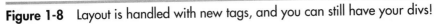
Figure 1-8 Layout is handled with new tags, and you can still have your divs!

The Latest in Multimedia the HTML5 Way!

The Web is far and away a visual place to visit. Sure there is text, for without it, only so much can be conveyed. But graphics, movies, and sound are the vehicles to deliver content. A modern web site should have in its realm ways for visitors to have rich and exceptional experiences and interactions with the site. Multimedia usage is imperative for this. If as the old saying goes, "A picture is worth a thousand words," what is a video worth?

Much of the attention-getting focus is not just that there are visual entities on the page, but also that they are animated. Figure 1-9 shows a rotating image. Of course, you can't tell that it's rotating here—you need to see it for yourself.

The image in Figure 1-9 is created with the code in Code Listing 1-6.

Code Listing 1-6   Code to create the rotating image

```
<!doctype html>
<html lang="en">
<head>
<meta charset="utf-8">
<title>twister</title>
<style>
body {background-color:black}
canvas { margin: 0 auto; display: block; padding: 1px; }
</style>
</head>
<body>
<canvas id="canvas1" width="420" height="420">
Your browser doesn't support the canvas! Try another browser.
</canvas>
```

Figure 1-9 A rotating image

```
<script>
var mycanvas=document.getElementById("canvas1");
var cntx=mycanvas.getContext('2d');
cntx.lineCap = 'round';
cntx.strokeStyle = '#ffff00';
cntx.lineWidth = 4;
function turn_it(){
  cntx.beginPath();
  cntx.moveTo(0, 0);
  // How far to move from center
  move_num =2; // try different numbers for unique appearances
  // How far to rotate around center
  rotate_num = 0.1;  // between 0 and 1
  // convert to radians.
  rads = rotate_num * 2 * Math.PI;
  // calculate positioning around center
  for (i=1; i<=100; i++){
    distance = i * move_num;
    turn = i * rads;
    // position point to draw from
    x = Math.cos(turn) * distance;
    y = Math.sin(turn) * distance;
     // draw line
    cntx.lineTo(x, y);
  }
}
cntx.translate(cntx.canvas.width/2, cntx.canvas.height/2);
setInterval(
  function () {
  cntx.clearRect(-cntx.canvas.width/2, -cntx.canvas.height/2,
 cntx.canvas.width, cntx.canvas.height);
  cntx.rotate(.01);  //controls rotation speed
  turn_it.apply();
  cntx.stroke();
  }, 10);
</script>
</body>
</html>
```

Summary

Sights, sounds, colors! HTML5 is making the Web an exciting place to visit—again. The first iteration of the Web, say circa 1996 or so, got us displayed static content, with some animation. It was good for the times. In the 2000s, web sites evolved to be much more detailed and interactive. That was a big step from the first Web of the last century. Now, HTML5 is set to take the web experience to new heights. And it isn't just on your computer—HTML5 is revolutionizing how smart devices are interacting with web pages. All (well, for all practical purposes, all) tablets, cell phones, and other carry-out gadgets can browse the Web, and they all support HTML5, JavaScript, and CSS. As such, the rich experiences HTML5 offers can be viewed from just about anywhere. Coming up—how to implement much of these multimedia initiatives.

Chapter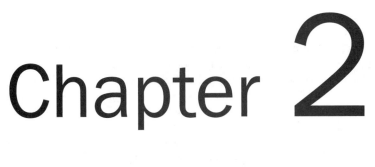

JavaScript and CSS in HTML5 Web Development

HTML is the basic web page language, but on its own, it does nothing much more than lay out items on the page. It does not offer any inherent power to process routines or crunch numbers. HTML does not loop (meaning you can't create a reusable HTML code snippet). HTML structures the page. That is its role. The rest is up to other technologies.

JavaScript adds the punch to the page. Quite powerful, JavaScript can do many things, from move an item on the page to sophisticated calculations. With its conditional statements (if, for, switch, and so on), JavaScript can be coded to make decisions and branch out in a specific area of processing based on other variables.

CSS, like HTML, is not a language with processing power. What it does excel at is making a page look pretty much any way you might imagine it should. CSS3 is the latest standard, and its implementation will be great once all the browsers catch up with what it can do. The progress toward this goal is continuing. Until there is uniformity, certain code structures of CSS3 are not supported across all major browsers.

JavaScript Is Integral to Web Development

Prior to coverage of what can be achieved with JavaScript, it's prudent to first explain how JavaScript runs in the first place. When a web page is served (rendered in the browser from what is sent by the web server), the activity is sort of "first come, first served." When there is JavaScript in-line with HTML code, the JavaScript will run as it is assembled in the browser. This might be what is needed, or it might be adverse to what is needed.

Two ways to control when JavaScript code runs are to place JavaScript in a function and to make use of the onload event of the body tag. An example is the best way to show this. First, note that all JavaScript goes within script tags, as shown in Code Listing 2-1.

Code Listing 2-1   A script section from a web page

```
<script>
//JavaScript code put here runs as soon as it can
    var d1=document.getElementById("div1")
    d1.style.color="#0000ff";
    d1.style.fontWeight = "bold";
function waitawhile() {
  //JavaScript code in here does not run until called
  //by some action, such as a button click, or the
  //firing of an event
  alert ("I've been alerted!");
}
</script>
```

In Code Listing 2-1, note an action that occurs immediately: changing the font color and weight used in div1 to blue and bold. The waitawhile() function would display an alert popup box, but only if the function is called in some way.

Let's go a step deeper. Code Listing 2-2 shows a full page of code, including the part shown in Code Listing 2-1.

Code Listing 2-2   A web page with a script section

```
<!doctype html>
<html lang="en">
<head>
<meta charset="utf-8">
<title>javascript example 1</title>
<meta name="description" content="HTML5 demo" />
<script>
//JavaScript code put here runs as soon as it can
    var d1=document.getElementById("div1");
    d1.style.color="#0000ff";
    d1.style.fontWeight = "bold";
function waitawhile() {
//JavaScript code in here does not run until called
//by some action, such as a button click, or the
//firing of an event
 alert ("I've been alerted!");
}
</script>
</head>
<body>
<div id="div1">
<p>This is the content of div 1</p>
</div>
<div id="div2">
<p>This is the content of div 2</p>
</div>
</body>
</html>
```

When the web page represented as code in Code Listing 2-2 appears in the browser, the wording "This is the content of div 1" does not appear as blue and bold. Why? The JavaScript is entered correctly; however, it is accessed before `div1` is rendered in the page. In other words, the script attempts to change the font appearance of a page element that has not yet appeared. Figure 2-1 shows the result. All of the text is plain.

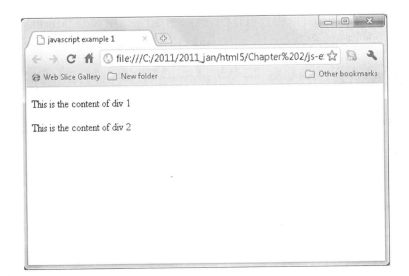

Figure 2-1 The page text is plain.

Placing a Script at the End of a Page

Code Listing 2-3 contains the same code as Code Listing 2-2, except the script section has been moved to the end of the code, just before the closing body tag (</body>).

Code Listing 2-3   Changing the text in div1

```
<!doctype html>
<html lang="en">
<head>
<meta charset="utf-8">
<title>javascript example 2</title>
<meta name="description" content="HTML5 demo" />
</head>
<body>
<div id="div1">
<p>This is the content of div 1</p>
</div>
<div id="div2">
<p>This is the content of div 2</p>
<p><a href="javascript:waitawhile()">Click me for the alert</a></p>
</div>
<script>
//JavaScript code put here runs as soon as it can
    var d1=document.getElementById("div1");
```

```
    d1.style.color="#0000ff";
    d1.style.fontWeight = "bold";
function waitawhile() {
//JavaScript code in here does not run until called
//by some action, such as a button click, or the
//firing of an event
 alert ("I've been alerted!");
}
</script>
</body>
</html>
```

Since the page code is rendered sequentially, `div1` exists prior to the JavaScript attempting to change its text. In this case, the font is blue and bold, as shown in Figure 2-2. So, by moving the JavaScript to the bottom of the code, or at least to a point after `div1` is rendered, you can have JavaScript create the intended change.

Also in this page, an extra paragraph within `div2` presents a link. Rather than the link navigating to a different web page or web site, the link calls the `waitawhile()` JavaScript function. Clicking the link causes the alert message to appear, as shown in Figure 2-3.

TIP

A JavaScript function must be called by an action—a click or some other activity or event. In Code Listing 2-3, the anchor tag is used to call a function, instead of the anchor tag's typical use to navigate to another page or a bookmarked part of the current page. In the code listing, the syntax `<a href="javascript:waitawhile()">` calls the function.

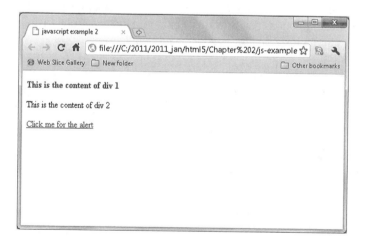

Figure 2-2   The text in div1 is blue and bold.

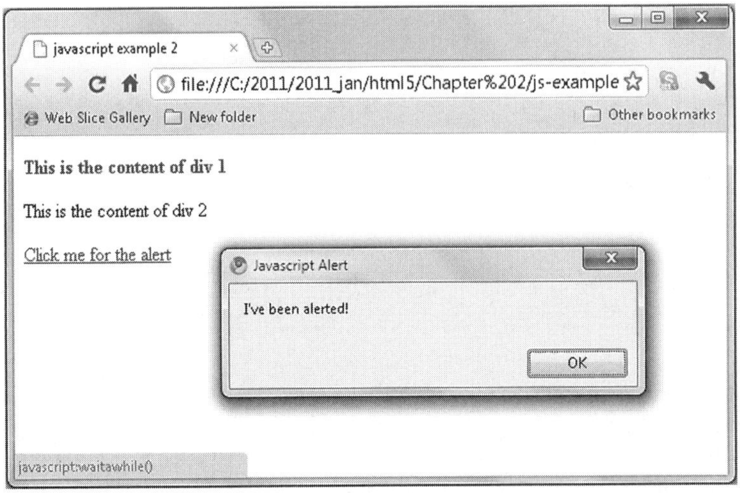

Figure 2-3 Clicking the link calls the JavaScript function.

Mentioned earlier is the option to call the JavaScript function by using the `onload` event. To do this, the body tag is given the instruction, like this:

```
<body onload="javascript:waitawhile()">
```

Loops and Conditional Tests

JavaScript provides looping and conditional testing that interact with activities in the browser. This is key to creating actions that provide a unique experience. Code Listing 2-4 shows the HTML and JavaScript for a sample loop and conditional test.

Code Listing 2-4   A loop and a test

```
<!doctype html>
<html lang="en">
<head>
<meta charset="utf-8">
<title>javascript example 4</title>
<script>
function loop_and_decide() {
  for (i=0;i<=10;i++) {
    document.write(i + '<br>');
  } // this curly brace matches the start of the for statement
  var d= new Date();
```

```
switch (d.getDay().toString()) {
  case "0":
   document.write('<br><br>Today is Sunday');
   break;
  case "1":
   document.write('<br><br>Today is Monday');
   break;
  default:
   document.write('<br><br>Today is neither Sunday nor Monday');
  } // this curly brace matches the start of the switch statement
} // this curly brace matches the start brace of the function
</script>
</head>
<body onload="javascript:loop_and_decide()">
</body>
</html>
```

NOTE
Curly braces ({ }) are used to designate blocks of JavaScript code. They are necessary for many JavaScript statements to indicate the start and end of the statement.

The script in the page first performs a loop that counts from 1 to 10. Then conditional testing—using the switch statement—tests if the day is Sunday, Monday, or neither one. The appropriate answer is written out on the page, as shown in Figure 2-4.

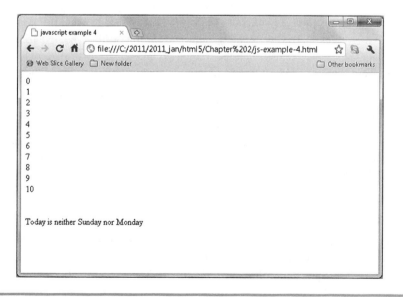

Figure 2-4   Loops and testing with JavaScript

The `for` statement facilitates the loop. The code sets a starting count, a value to reach to stop looping, and the increment. In this example, 1 is the starting value, and the counter increments by 1 until 10 is reached. As this occurs, the `write` method is used to create the output on the page, which is simply outputting the value of the counter (the variable `i` holds the value):

```
function loop_and_decide() {
  for (i=0;i<=10;i++) {
    document.write(i + '<br>');
  } // this curly brace matches the start of the for statement
```

Whatever code is placed within the curly braces ({ }) is run each time the loop increments. After the code, the `switch` statement is used to test the date. A series of `if` statements could have been used instead. It's a matter of programming style. Finally, note that all this activity occurs only because of the `onload` event within the body tag:

```
<body onload="javascript:loop_and_decide()">
```

JavaScript in an External File

JavaScript is often linked into a web page. In other words, the JavaScript code resides in an external file on the web server, rather than being written directly into the page. The script tag includes a source (`src`) attribute that points to the file. Here is an example:

```
<script src="js/common.js"></script>
```

Using JavaScript from an external file makes for easy changes when the JavaScript routines are used by numerous web pages. If any JavaScript needs to be updated, it is done in one place: in the external file. Then all the web pages that reference the external file will have the update. This beats the alternative of needing to update every page individually.

TIP

Serious web development requires a good understanding of JavaScript. There is much more to the language than is included in this book. Find books or online resources that appeal to you. One very well-designed site for learning JavaScript is the W3Schools site at www.w3schools.com.

CSS Overview

Cascading Style Sheets (CSS) has made the Web much more manageable and design-friendly since entering the mainstream. You may wonder about the name—what is cascading about the style sheets? To understand, consider the three ways CSS can be incorporated into a web page:

- From an external file

- From a block of style instructions in the head section of the HTML (also known as an *internal style sheet*), which will be inside a set of style tags

- In-line—written as an attribute of a single HTML tag

The hierarchy, or priority, of how these three methods of CSS are used can be said to *cascade*. Styling set at the tag level overrides styling found within a style tag in the head section. Styling in the head section overrides styling from an external file, assuming the external file is referenced before the style tag in the head section. If the external file is referenced after the style tag, then the styling in the external file overrides the styling set in the style tag. Note that it is not required to have all of the styling types present. Often, referenced external files are used without any head style tag or in-line styling.

CSS works via a system of *selectors*, which are identifiers used to match page elements. A selector will have one or more *declarations*. A declaration consists of a property and a value. A colon sits between the property and the value, and a semicolon sits at the end of the value. The selector has a section of one or more property-value pairs, and the entire section is within curly braces. An example serves best here:

```
p {border-style:solid;}
```

Here, the paragraph element (p) is the selector. Assigned to the selector is a declaration. The declaration gives the value `solid` to the property `border-style`. Assuming there is no other influencing CSS (as demonstrated later), all paragraphs in a web page will appear with a border. This affects only text within a set of paragraph tags. Consider this section of a web page:

```
<p>I am text within a paragraph tag</p>
I am another paragraph but I do not sit in a paragraph tag.
 Therefore I am not affected by CSS applied to paragraph tags.
<p>I am another paragraph. My border is kinda neat, don't ya think?</p>
```

Figure 2-5 shows what the CSS treatment of the <p> tag causes to appear on the page.

The appearance of the text shown in Figure 2-5 is not aesthetically pleasing. A particular thorny issue is that the text within the borders is butting up against the border. Also, the border is much wider than the text it contains. These issues are fixed with the `padding` and `width` properties, by giving them reasonable values for the intended visual presentation, as follows:

```
p {border-style:solid;
   padding:10px;
   width:500px;}
```

This example shows how multiple property-value pairs follow one another. Often, you will see them on separate lines. This is not a requirement; it is done for easy readability.

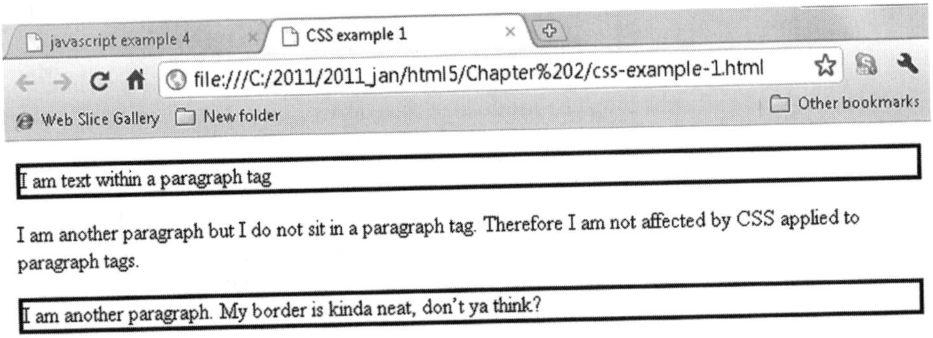

Figure 2-5 Paragraph-tagged text has a border around it.

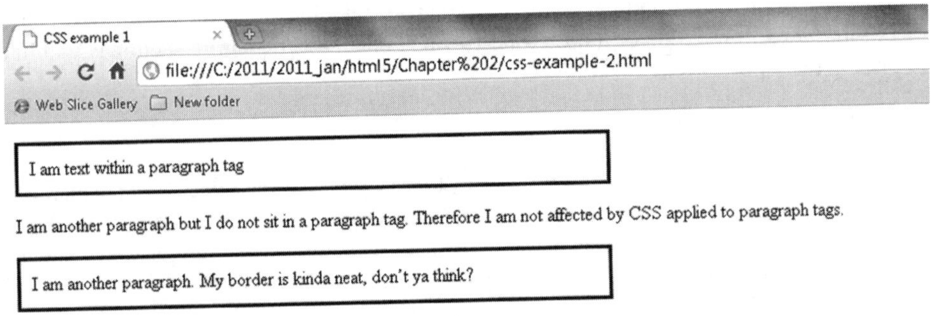

Figure 2-6 The page style has a better look when the padding and width properties are used.

Figure 2-6 shows how the sample page looks with the padding and width properties. Code Listing 2-5 is the complete code for the page shown in Figure 2-6.

Code Listing 2-5 A web page with a style section in the head section

```
<!doctype html>
<html lang="en">
<head>
<meta charset="utf-8">
<title>CSS example 1</title>
<style>
  p {border-style:solid;
      padding:10px;
      width:500px;}
```

```
</style>
</head>
<body>
<p>I am text within a paragraph tag</p>
I am another paragraph but I do not sit in a paragraph tag.
Therefore I am not affected by CSS applied to paragraph tags.
<p>I am another paragraph. My border is kinda neat, don't ya think?</p>
</body>
</html>
```

Now about that cascading effect. Consider the paragraphs in the example shown in Figure 2-7. What is going on here? Every paragraph looks different. Code Listing 2-6 shows the code for this page.

Code Listing 2-6   A web page with external, internal, and tag-specific CSS

```
<!doctype html>
<html lang="en">
<head>
<meta charset="utf-8">
<title>CSS example 3</title>
<link rel="stylesheet" href="style.css" type="text/css" />
<style>
p {border-style:solid;padding:10px;width:500px;}
</style>
</head>
```

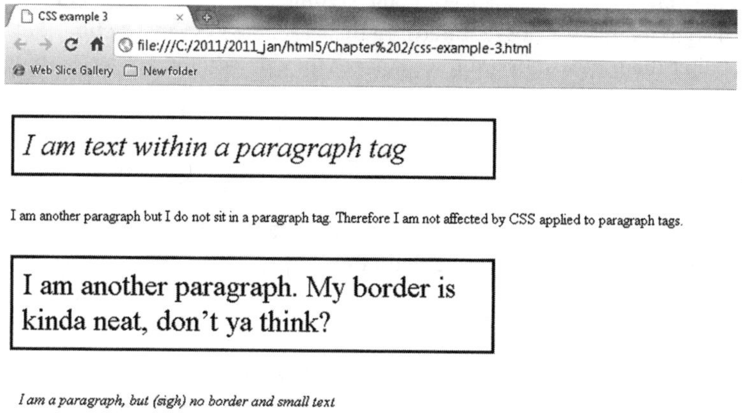

Figure 2-7   Various paragraph CSS treatments

```
<body>
<p>I am text within a paragraph tag</p>
I am another paragraph but I do not sit in a paragraph tag.
Therefore I am not affected by CSS applied to paragraph tags.
<p style="font-style:normal;">I am another paragraph.
My border is kinda neat, don't ya think?</p>
<p style="border-style:none;font-size:1em">
I am a paragraph, but (sigh) no border and small text
</p>
</body>
</html>
```

First, an external style sheet is referenced with this line:

```
<link rel="stylesheet" href="style.css" type="text/css" />
```

The style.css file contains the following:

```
/*
This is a CSS external file
*/
p {
  font-size:2em;
  font-style:italic;
  }
```

Since this is the external CSS file, any styling rules in here apply to the entire page, or more particularly, to the elements that are specified in the file—in this case, the paragraph tag. This means all text inside <p> and </p> tags is set to a large font size and italic. These rules apply until they are altered or enhanced by the styling set in the style tags in the head section (if there is a style there—it's not required). In this case, the CSS instructions at the top of the page do not alter the font size or italic setting, but they do add the border, padding, and width:

```
p {border-style:solid;
  padding:10px;
  width:500px;}
```

However, a couple of individual paragraph tags override the top of the page styling. One paragraph overrides the font italic effect with this:

```
<p style="font-style:normal;">
```

Also, the last paragraph of the page overrides the font size and removes the border, with this:

```
<p style="border-style:none;
font-size:1em">
```

TIP

In-line CSS is managed by using the `style` attribute. The structure is `style="CSS info goes here".`

ID Selectors: Targeting Specific Page Sections

CSS can be applied to all visual HTML tags. In other words, it makes sense to apply CSS to the body, tables, lists, paragraphs, images, and so on. However, it does not make sense to apply CSS to the script tag, since this does not produce anything visual on the web page.

Besides the appropriate HTML tags, you can target specific page areas—areas that are typically segregated as divs or spans. In a web page, an area can be represented as a div. In fact, it is quite normal for a page to have several divs and nested divs. Each div tag can be given an identifier.

A single div is identified so CSS treatment will apply to it without affecting other div tags. This same approach applies to the all visual HTML tags, but in practice, divs seem to be the ones that are most likely to receive treatment using identifiers. (Classes, explained later in the chapter, tend to be applied to the typical page elements, but even this is a subjective observation.)

Code Listing 2-7 shows a portion of the markup of a page that uses divs to arrange the page layout.

Code Listing 2-7   Div tags with identifier attributes

```
<div id="header">
  <div id="logo">
  </div>
  <div id="tagline">
    A resource for writers and fans of the written word<br /><br />
  </div>
  <div id="menu">
       <a href="http://www.shakespearesplayground.
com">Home</a>
          |   
     <a href="fiction.php">Fiction</a>
          |   
     <a href="nonfiction.php">Non-Fiction</a>
          |   
     <a href="editing.php">Editing/Grammar</a>
          |   
     <a href="publishing.php">Getting Published</a>
          |   
    <a href="resources.php">Resources</a>
  </div>
</div>
```

This code contains four divs. Each has an identifier (id=). They are named header, logo, tagline, and menu. The logo, tagline, and menu divs are nested inside the header tag.

The purpose of the naming is to give each div its own CSS treatment. Code Listing 2-8 shows a portion of the CSS file that is linked into the HTML page. Note that each of the four divs is represented in the CSS by its identifiers, which begin with a pound sign, as in #header {.

Code Listing 2-8   Identifiers in a CSS file

```
/*Shakespeare's Playground
author: Ken Bluttman
 */
#header {
 height:128px;
 background-color:#ffffff;
 margin-left:15px;
 clear:both;
 width:1065px;
}
#logo {
 margin-left:0px;
 margin-right:0px;
 height:65px;
 background: url(images/sp_logo_1.gif) 0 0 no-repeat;
 background-position:center;
}
#tagline {
 text-align:center;
 vertical-align:center;
 height:32px;
 font-size:1.2em;
 font-family:Arial,sans-serif;
 font-style:italic;
 background-color: #ffffff;
}
#menu {
 text-align:center;
 width:1065px;
 height:30px;
 font-weight:bold;
}
```

In this example, the tagline presents italic centered text, the menu occupies a height of 30 pixels, and the text is bold. (Actually, the text in the menu is mostly hyperlinks, which have additional styling not shown here.)

$\mathfrak{S}$hakespeare's $\mathfrak{P}$layground

A resource for writers and fans of the written word

<u>Home</u> | <u>Fiction</u> | <u>Non-Fiction</u> | <u>Editing/Grammar</u> | <u>Getting Published</u> | <u>Resources</u>

Figure 2-8   The appearance of a web site styled with CSS

TIP

As with all live sites on the Internet, you can use the View Source feature in the browser to view any and all HTML, CSS, and JavaScript.

Figure 2-8 shows the web page styled with the HTML and CSS shown in Code Listings 2-7 and 2-8.

CSS Classes

Identifier selectors are used to apply CSS to a particular page element. *Classes* are used for applying the same CSS to multiple tags. This is for efficiency. The CSS is written once and applied multiple times. If something needs to be changed, it is changed once in the class declaration.

Classes start with a period (.). Unlike straight tag names or identifier selectors, class names are not tag names. For example, a class might be called ad_section, product, or anything that makes for a sensible name. Code Listing 2-9 is a portion of a CSS file that shows a couple of classes.

Code Listing 2-9   Classes in a CSS file

```
.articletitle1 {
  font-size:1.4em;
}
.spacer1 {
  height:4px;
}
```

Any page element given a class designation of articletitle1 has a large font size. Any page element given a class designation of spacer1 will have a height of 4 pixels. Considering these names, it's easy to surmise that there likely are several articles and several areas on the page to add a bit of space. Indeed, the two lines shown next are used multiple times in the page markup.

```
<span class="articletitle1">(Article name goes here)</span>
<div class="spacer1"> </div>
```

How CSS Is Applied to New HTML5 Multimedia Tags

Actually, there is nothing new in the application of CSS to any of the new HTML5 tags. The reason? Because they are true HTML tags. This means that they are treated in the same manner as any other HTML tags. The intent isn't for this to sound like plain-old business. It's quite the opposite. This treatment makes it easy to create visually appealing—dare I say stunning—visual renderings of these tags.

One tag that on the surface seems to have little visual impact is the audio tag. This tag plays audio, aimed to and for the ears, not the eyes. But the native audio player that is now part of HTML can take on a variety of looks. Figure 2-9 shows three audio players, all the same, rendered from the audio tag, but styled differently.

NOTE

The appearance of the players in Figure 2-9 is how they render in one browser: Chrome. The same page displayed in other browsers may yield a different visual result.

Code Listing 2-10 shows the page code for the example in Figure 2-9.

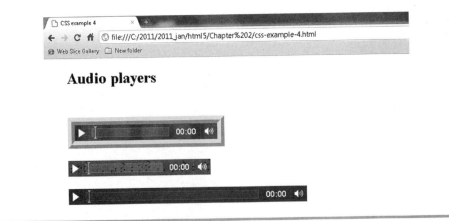

Figure 2-9   Applying CSS to the audio tag

Code Listing 2-10   Styling the audio tag

```
<!doctype html>
<html lang="en">
<head>
<meta charset="utf-8">
<title>CSS example 4</title>
<style>
#audio1 {border-style:ridge;
         border-color:#c3eefd;
         border-width:15px;
         background: url(gradient1.jpg);
  }
#audio2 {background: url(musicstaff.jpg);}
#audio3 {background-color:red;width:500px;}
</style>
</head>
<body>
 <div style="margin-left:40px;">
  <h1>Audio players</h1>
  <br><br>
  <audio id="audio1" src="guitar1.ogg" controls="true">
<b>Your browser does not support the audio tag.</b>
</audio>
  <br><br>
  <audio id="audio2" src="guitar1.ogg" controls="true">
<b>Your browser does not support the audio tag.</b>
</audio>
  <br><br>
  <audio id="audio3" src="guitar1.ogg" controls="true">
<b>Your browser does not support the audio tag.</b>
</audio>
 </div>
</body>
</html>
```

The CSS is set in the style tag in the head section. The audio players are named `audio1`, `audio2`, and `audio3`, and each has a corresponding CSS identifier.

Note that if there were just the tag name of `audio` in the CSS, then any of its properties would apply to all the audio players. However, when a single player is identified as, for example, `audio1`, its CSS treatment applies to just that one player. So, in this example, the audio players are styled individually by using their identifiers.

To close out this chapter, let's consider CSS applied to the canvas element. The next chapter covers the canvas in detail, so this is a taste of what's to come. Figure 2-10 shows a canvas element displaying a radial green and black image. The canvas, in the middle, is given a red border, via CSS.

Figure 2-10 Styling the body and the canvas together

An interesting point here is that the background image of the body (the page itself) is a .jpg file. The imagery in the canvas is created with JavaScript. Using CSS, the canvas element is positioned on the page in such a way that the radial imagery looks continuous from the center on out to the edges of the page. Techniques like this are possible with CSS by using positional properties such as `top` and `left`. The sophistication of JavaScript to create the dynamic imagery within the canvas is explained in the next chapter. For now, Code Listing 2-11 shows the CSS used for the image.

Code Listing 2-11   Applying CSS to create a continuous appearance of two separate page items

```
<style>
body {background: url(radialbackground.jpg);
     background-repeat:no-repeat;
     }
#myCanvas {border-style:solid;
          border-width:30px;
          border-color:red;
          position:relative;
          left:70px;
          top:40px;
          }
</style>
```

Summary

Whew! We covered a lot here. As HTML5 is put to use, the integration with JavaScript becomes quite a nice thing to do. Is that integration essential? You can code HTML5 pages without JavaScript, but those pages will be missing a lot of the excitement that occurs as a result of JavaScript making the pages jump.

Unlike HTML/HTML5, JavaScript follows handle coding techniques that all proper programming languages do—loops, conditional branching, and such. Therefore, incorporating JavaScript is essential in order to have your web pages become more than static.

CSS is the icing on the cake, and that's not a bad metaphor. CSS provides the look, polish, and visual pizzazz. Good usage of CSS and JavaScript carries HTML to new heights. To wow your audience, take the time to become proficient in these technologies.

Part II

Graphics and Media

Chapter 3

Getting Creative with the Canvas

The canvas is one of the most exciting new elements in HTML5—perhaps the most exciting. Not only does it provide a powerhouse of visual specialties, but it is also competition for Adobe Flash. I say that with a grain of salt (and a slice of lemon). Flash is a monster of a tool/ utility/product—call it what you will. Flash has brought the web site experience to new heights for those sites that make use of it.

However, the use of Flash has been sidetracked with a whammy of a dilemma. At the time of this writing, Flash does not work in Apple mobile devices: the iPad and iPhone. Is this a good or bad thing for Apple? For Adobe (which makes Flash), it is clearly a negative. As developers, we can stay out of the way of that business entanglement and deal with it on our level by using HTML5 in place of Flash. With the canvas in HTML5, we can skirt the issue. The canvas is native HTML. It is not a plug-in, add-on, or something that you must download.

At some point, all browsers will fully support the canvas (yes, a rub on Internet Explorer here). The canvas is core to HTML5 and raring to go. So let's get to it.

Introducing the Canvas

As with any introduction to a technology, the old standard "Hello World" is typical to see. Here, I'll show you the equivalent. You will not see the words "Hello World." You will not see any words at all. What you will see is a canvas sitting on a web page. It has a border and a background color, but is essentially blank and unexciting, yet it *is* there, or rather here—in Figure 3-1.

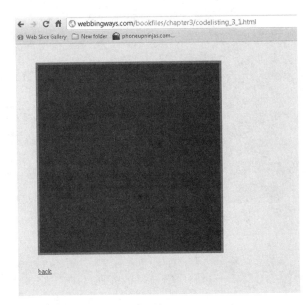

Figure 3-1 Say hello to the canvas

This plain canvas does nothing other than be visible. In this chapter and the next, we will add drawing, animation, and event usage. To get started, we'll simply display the canvas, as in Figure 3-1. Code Listing 3-1 shows the source code that presents the canvas on the web page.

Code Listing 3-1   Displaying a canvas element

```
<!doctype html>
<html lang="en">
<head>
<meta charset="utf-8">
<title>canvas example 1</title>
<style>
body { background-color:#eeeeee; }
#canvas1 {width:400px;
          height:400px;
          background-color:blue;
          border: 5px red solid; }
#outer {margin-left:40px;
        margin-top:40px;
        }
</style>
</head>
<body>
<div id="outer">
<canvas id="canvas1">
Your browser doesn't support the canvas! Try another browser.
</canvas>
</div>
</body>
</html>
```

A simple code construct is all it takes to display a canvas:

```
<canvas id="canvas1">
Your browser doesn't support the canvas! Try another browser.
</canvas>
```

As with other HTML elements, you use an opening tag and a closing one. In the case of the canvas, a line of text informing the user that the browser does not support showing the canvas is placed between the opening and closing tags. This informative line appears when the canvas itself cannot be displayed (as we wait for all browsers catch up with technology). Otherwise, the canvas will appear.

NOTE

NOTE

A line of text stating that a browser does not support the canvas will appear when that case is true; otherwise the canvas will appear. The text statement goes in between the opening and closing tags of the canvas.

The canvas is styled a bit with a red border and a blue interior, as well as given a width and height:

```
#canvas1 {width:400px;
          height:400px;
          background-color:blue;
          border: 5px red solid; }
```

Drawing on the Canvas

Common among drawing programs is the ability to place shapes, free-form lines, and usually something along the lines of layering. The canvas makes use of the Red, Green, Blue (RGB) model of color representation, which has been around for a long time. It also has a variation that includes the alpha channel, for setting transparency. The acronym now becomes RGBA. It is not required to include the fourth (alpha) component to indicate color; in other words, RGB and/or RGBA can be used.

Code Listing 3-2 displays a few rectangles on the canvas. One rectangle does not use transparency, and the rest do use it.

Code Listing 3-2   A canvas showing rectangles

```
<!doctype html>
<html lang="en">
<head>
<meta charset="utf-8">
<title>canvas example 2</title>
<style>
body { background-color:#eeeeee; }

#outer {margin-left:40px;
        margin-top:40px;
        }
</style>
</head>
<body>
<div id="outer">
<canvas id="canvas1" width="400" height="400"
    style="border: 10px yellow solid">
Your browser doesn't support the canvas! Try another browser.
</canvas>
```

```
</div>
<script>
var mycanvas=document.getElementById("canvas1");
var cntx=mycanvas.getContext('2d');
//draw solid rectangle
cntx.fillStyle='rgb(255,0,255)';
cntx.fillRect(30,30,400,400);
//draw rectangle with 50% transparency
cntx.fillStyle='rgba(0,255,255,0.5)';
cntx.fillRect(60,60,200,200);
//draw rectangle with 75% transparency
cntx.fillStyle='rgba(0,0,0,0.25)';
cntx.fillRect(90,90,400,400);
</script>
</body>
</html>
```

So, what does it look like? See Figure 3-2.
First, the canvas element is coded as follows:

```
<canvas id="canvas1" width="400" height="400"
    style="border: 10px yellow solid">
```

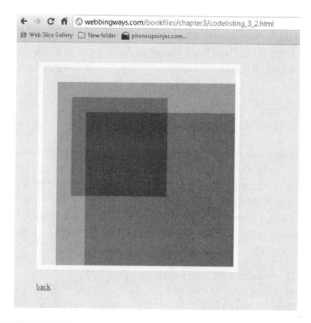

Figure 3-2 A canvas displaying rectangles

In this case, the width and height are put directly in-line with the element tag.

Displaying the canvas is pretty much just a line of code, as you've seen. The action is in the use of JavaScript. An application programming interface (API) is built into the canvas. It needs to be declared, and is known as the *context*. Indeed, the code that brings it to the plate is getContext:

```
var mycanvas=document.getElementById("canvas1");
var cntx=mycanvas.getContext('2d');
```

Currently, there is one type of context, which sets up a two-dimensional drawing surface. An approach to simulate 3D is shown in the book's last chapter.

Once the canvas and the context are established, which is done here with variables (mycanvas and cntx), other activities, such as drawing, can occur. The context provides the hook to the API, which has methods for image manipulation on a two-dimensional plane.

Two approaches are available for putting shapes on a canvas:

- Stroke is used for creating the edges of a shape.

- Fill is used to fill the interior.

In the example in Figure 3-2, the rectangles are filled. So, using the established context variable (cntx in this case), the fillStyle and fillRect methods are used. The first sets the color using RGB, and the second sets the position and size of the rectangle. The background color of the canvas is gray, as indicated for the overall page color (given to the body tag) A solid purple rectangle is placed on top of this, beginning at a top and left position of 30 pixels offset from the canvas border, and extending to the bottom-right corner, indicated by the 400,400 setting. The size of the canvas is 400 × 400, so this rectangle is taken to that lower-right corner:

```
cntx.fillStyle='rgb(255,0,255)';
cntx.fillRect(30,30,400,400);
```

Note that when either rgb or rgba is used, the setting is enclosed in either single quotes or double quotes.

Next, a rectangle is drawn with full green and blue, which results in a green-blue color. However, here the alpha channel is used to set the transparency at 50%. Therefore, the color of the rectangle is altered by both the purple one under it and the black one over it. The black rectangle does not look black at all, but more on that in a moment. Here is the code for the 50% transparent rectangle:

```
//draw rectangle with 50% transparency
cntx.fillStyle='rgba(0,255,255,0.5)';
cntx.fillRect(60,60,200,200);
```

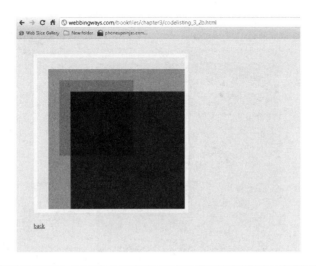

Figure 3-3 The rectangle's transparency setting is changed.

TIP
Transparency is set by placing a value between 0 and 1 in the RGBA construct. The use could seem backward. The setting is not actually an indication of the transparency percent, but rather of the solidity percent. For example, 0.2 indicates just 20% is visible, not that 20% is transparent.

This rectangle is smaller based on the dimensions given. The next rectangle is larger. It is set to black—an RGB of 0,0,0 (`'rgba(0,0,0,0.25)'`); however, the transparency is set to just 25%, which can be confusing. This really means it's 75% transparent. As such, its black color does not have the rectangle clearly cover the large portion of the canvas. At best, it just makes the other rectangles a bit darker in the converged area. To make this clear, the canvas shown in Figure 3-3 is altered to have the rectangle appear with just 25% transparency (the amount in the RGBA is set to .75). The rectangle is now much darker and covers up much more of the underlying rectangles.

Using Gradients

Gradients are visuals that mix two or more colors. The colors don't mix in the sense that red and blue make purple. Instead, the colors are set at points, and the variation of the mix smoothly transitions from one color to the other, similar to how a rainbow appears. For example, picturing a square, red could be on one side and blue on the other. Along the width of the square (or the height, depending on the orientation), the coloring is seen as smoothly changing from red to blue. Figure 3-4 illustrates this with a square that is all red on the left and all blue on the right.

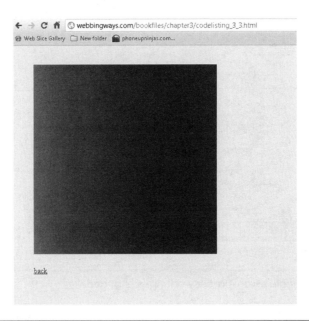

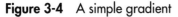

Figure 3-4   A simple gradient

Gradients are established by using a method that creates the gradient along with color stops. The gradient has four settings: the left, top, bottom, and right points (relative to the canvas). A color stop has two parts: a positional offset relative to the coordinates established by the gradient method and the color setting itself. Two gradient types are available: linear and radial.

Code Listing 3-3 shows the code that creates the image in Figure 3-4.

Code Listing 3-3   A simple gradient

```
<!doctype html>
<html lang="en">
<head>
<meta charset="utf-8">
<title>canvas example 3</title>
<style>
body { background-color:#eeeeee; }
#outer {margin-left:40px;
        margin-top:40px;
        }
</style>
</head>
<body>
```

```
<div id="outer">
<canvas id="canvas1" width="400" height="400">
Your browser doesn't support the canvas! Try another browser.
</canvas>
</div>
<script>
  var mycanvas=document.getElementById("canvas1");
  var cntx=mycanvas.getContext('2d');
  var mygradient=cntx.createLinearGradient(0,200,400,200);
  mygradient.addColorStop("0","#ff0000");
  mygradient.addColorStop("1.0","#0000ff");
  cntx.fillStyle=mygradient;
  cntx.fillRect(0,0,400,400);
</script>
</body>
</html>
```

Here are the lines of code that create the gradient:

```
var cntx=mycanvas.getContext('2d');
var mygradient=cntx.createLinearGradient(0,200,400,200);
mygradient.addColorStop("0","#ff0000");
mygradient.addColorStop("1.0","#0000ff");
cntx.fillStyle=mygradient;
cntx.fillRect(0,0,400,400);
```

The context to the API is set (cntx). Then a variable (mygradient) is set to one of the gradient types. Here, it is the linear gradient. Using the variable, the color stops are added. The addColorStop method is applied to the gradient variable, once for each color stop. The color stop takes two parameters. First is a positioning in the gradient, using a value between 0 and 1. The second parameter sets the color. You can use any number of color stops, although practical use should keep the number to something subjectively reasonable. A gradient with an excessive amount of color stops will likely appear as a squeezed bunch of colors without smooth transitions.

Finally, the fill style (fillStyle) method of the context is applied to the variable holding the gradient settings, and a fill method (fillRect) is used to complete the rectangle. If it helps, think of this as "create gradient, set colors, and fill it."

Linear Gradients

Linear gradients follow a straight path from one color to another. A linear gradient can have several colors, each set with a different position along the way. This provides numerous possibilities for how a linear gradient will appear. Figure 3-5 shows a linear gradient with five color stops. Code Listing 3-4 shows the code used to create this figure.

Figure 3-5 A linear gradient with five color stops

Code Listing 3-4 A complex linear gradient

```
<!doctype html>
<html lang="en">
<head>
<meta charset="utf-8">
<title>canvas example 4</title>
<style>
body { background-color:#eeeeee; }
#outer {margin-left:40px;
        margin-top:40px;
        }
</style>
</head>
<body>
<div id="outer">
<canvas id="canvas1" width="400" height="400">
Your browser doesn't support the canvas! Try another browser.
</canvas>
</div>
<script>
  var mycanvas=document.getElementById("canvas1");
```

```
    var cntx=mycanvas.getContext('2d');
    var mygradient=cntx.createLinearGradient(30,30,300,300);
    mygradient.addColorStop("0","#ffdd30");
    mygradient.addColorStop(".40","#3de6a6");
    mygradient.addColorStop(".57","#003333");
    mygradient.addColorStop(".82","#00ccee");
    mygradient.addColorStop("1.0","#333333");
    cntx.fillStyle=mygradient;
    cntx.fillRect(0,0,400,400);
</script>
</body>
</html>
```

Each of the five color stops is sequentially in position from 0 to 1, along with its associated color. The gradient itself is created with the `createLinearGradient` method:

```
    var mygradient=cntx.createLinearGradient(30,30,300,300);
    mygradient.addColorStop("0","#ffdd30");
    mygradient.addColorStop(".40","#3de6a6");
    mygradient.addColorStop(".57","#003333");
    mygradient.addColorStop(".82","#00ccee");
    mygradient.addColorStop("1.0","#333333");
```

Even with the the color stops set to span from 0 to 1, the gradient is also set to sit at coordinates 30, 30 to 300, 300 on top of a canvas that is 400 × 400 pixels. The four linear gradient coordinates are set in the `createLinearGradient` method. The first color stop establishes a yellow color (#ffdd30), and the last color stop establishes a gray color (#333333). Logically then, the canvas is filled with these colors from its corners to where these color stops sit.

TIP
If the coordinate system in unfamiliar, think of graph paper. In some systems, the center point would relate to position 0, 0. Here the 0, 0 position is the upper-left corner.

Radial Gradients

Radial gradients appear to spread from a point outward. The method to make one, `createRadialGradient`, takes six parameters, unlike the `createLinearGradient` method, which takes only four parameters. The six parameters of the radial gradient are best thought of as two sets of three parameters, with each set establishing the starting point and the radius of a circle. By setting the circles with different parameters, the radial effect is created, as shown in Figure 3-6.

Notice how the radial gradient can appear to not fit completely on the canvas. This effect is caused by the parameter used to create the gradient. Code Listing 3-5 shows the code used to create the radial gradient shown in Figure 3-6.

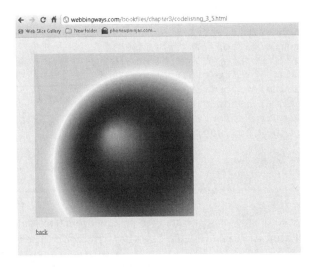

Figure 3-6 A radial gradient

Code Listing 3-5 A radial gradient

```
<!doctype html>
<html lang="en">
<head>
<meta charset="utf-8">
<title>canvas example 5</title>
<style>
body { background-color:#eeeeee; }
#outer {margin-left:40px;
        margin-top:40px;
        }
</style>
</head>
<body>
<div id="outer">
<canvas id="canvas1" width="400" height="400">
Your browser doesn't support the canvas! Try another browser.
</canvas>
</div>
<script>
  var mycanvas=document.getElementById("canvas1");
  var cntx=mycanvas.getContext('2d');
  var mygradient=cntx.createRadialGradient(200,200,10,300,300,300);
  mygradient.addColorStop("0","#00ccee");
  mygradient.addColorStop(".25","blue");
  mygradient.addColorStop(".50","green");
```

```
      mygradient.addColorStop(".75","yellow");
      mygradient.addColorStop("1.0","#00ff00");
      cntx.fillStyle=mygradient;
      cntx.fillRect(0,0,400,400);
</script>
</body>
</html>
```

As with linear gradients, color stops are used as points to vary the color. The parameters used to create this gradient set up two circles. One is centered at the coordinates 200, 200 with a radius of 10, and the other is centered at the coordinates 300, 300 with a radius of 300. Since the second circle starts in the lower-right quadrant of the canvas (which itself is 400 × 400), and the circle has the radius of 300, it is larger, at least based on its starting place, to fit on the canvas.

NOTE
A radius is a straight line extending from the center of a circle to the edge of the circle.

Understanding Paths

You can draw on a canvas by using one or more drawing methods. The examples shown so far in this chapter required the appropriate method, such as `fillRect` or `createRadialGradient`. These methods are straightforward in that they create the item along with taking a parameter for size or placement.

Other drawing methods make use of paths. Paths have a beginning and end based on code statements (`beginPath` and `closePath`). These are best described as organizational points that provide a way to make distinctive blocks of drawing statements. In some cases, they are necessary, as a drawing method may continue to draw from where the last drawing method left off. This becomes obvious in drawing lines, especially when several lines are combined to make a custom shape or other visual. Here's a quick example of a code construct to draw a circle:

```
cntx.beginPath();
cntx.arc(200, 200, 100, 0, Math.PI * 2, true);
cntx.closePath();
```

Drawing Circles and Arcs

Circles and arcs are both created with the same method: `arc`. The parameters make the difference for how the shape appears. Here's an example that creates a circle:

```
cntx.arc(200, 200, 100, 0, Math.PI * 2, true)
```

The following creates an arc (in this case, a semicircle):

```
cntx.arc(200, 350, 100, 0, Math.PI, true);
```

The parameters, in order, are the left position, the top position, the radius, the start angle, the end angle, and the direction. Left and top together indicate a point, or coordinate position. The radius controls how large the arc will be. Concerning the two angle settings, consider that a circle has 360 degrees. If you were to put a pen on paper and draw a quarter-circle, you would be completing an arc covering 90 degrees. However, did you draw this quarter-circle from a true 0-degree position (for example, the 12:00 position on a clock) to a true 90-degree position (for example, the 3:00 position on a clock)? Or did you draw it from, say, the 250-degree position to the 340-degree position? Either approach would account for a coverage of 90 degrees. The angle settings determine where the drawing of the arc starts and stops using this methodology.

However, the start angle and end angle settings work with radians, not degrees. Radians are an alternate measurement system. How many radians make a complete circle? The answer is 2 times pi, or approximately 6.28. Therefore, the start and end angles should be from 0 to 6.28. A start of 0 and an end of pi times 2 creates a complete circle. A shorter range (for example, 0 and 4) creates a portion of a circle. A start angle value of 0 actually indicates starting at the 3:00 position (not the probably assumed 12:00 position). It is perfectly fine to indicate starting at 1 or another number.

The last parameter indicates whether the arc is drawn clockwise or counterclockwise. False (the default if left out) draws in a clockwise direction. True draws in a counterclockwise direction. Experimenting with different values for the start and end angles, and toggling true and false of the last parameter will show how it comes together.

Code Listing 3-6 shows the circle (angles range of 0 to pi times 2), semicircle (angles range of 0 to pi), and the use of beginPath and closePath.

Code Listing 3-6   A circle and an arc

```
<!doctype html>
<html lang="en">
<head>
<meta charset="utf-8">
<title>canvas example 6</title>
<style>
body { background-color:#eeeeee; }
#canvas1 {background-color:white;
          border: 5px orange solid;

             }
#outer {margin-left:40px;
        margin-top:40px;
        }
</style>
</head>
<body>
```

```
<div id="outer">
<canvas id="canvas1" width="400" height="400">
Your browser doesn't support the canvas! Try another browser.
</canvas>
</div>
<script>
var mycanvas=document.getElementById("canvas1");
var cntx=mycanvas.getContext('2d');
// draw black circle
cntx.beginPath();
cntx.arc(200, 200, 100, 0, Math.PI * 2, true);
cntx.closePath();
cntx.lineWidth="4";
cntx.strokeStyle="black";
cntx.stroke();
// draw red semi-circle
cntx.beginPath();
cntx.arc(200, 350, 100, 0, Math.PI, true);
cntx.closePath();
cntx.lineWidth="2";
cntx.strokeStyle="red";
cntx.stroke();
</script>
</body>
</html>
```

TIP

To draw a circle, multiply pi x 2, as in the following:

```
cntx.arc(200, 200, 100, 0, Math.PI * 2, true)
```

Code Listing 3-6 draws a circle. It is a complete circle, since pi is doubled in the appropriate parameter:

```
cntx.arc(200, 200, 100, 0, Math.PI * 2, true);
```

Conversely, a semicircle is created when pi is the value used:

```
cntx.arc(200, 350, 100, 0, Math.PI, true);
```

Of course, seeing it makes it clear. Figure 3-7 shows the circle and semicircle created with Code Listing 3-6.

Figure 3-8 illustrates what happens when the beginPath and endPath statements are removed. As you can see, the use of the path statements affect how an image is drawn. Code Listing 3-7 is the source for the image in Figure 3-8.

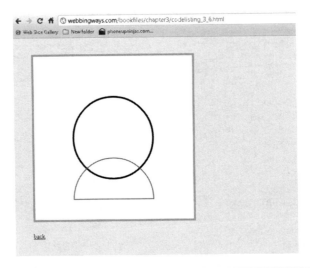

Figure 3-7 Drawing circles and arcs

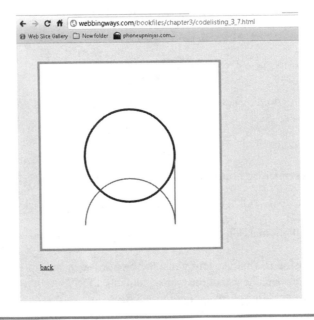

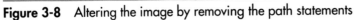

Figure 3-8 Altering the image by removing the path statements

Code Listing 3-7   An altered arc

```
<!doctype html>
<html lang="en">
<head>
<meta charset="utf-8">
<title>canvas example 7</title>
<style>
body { background-color:#eeeeee; }
#canvas1 {background-color:white;
         border: 5px orange solid;


         }
#outer {margin-left:40px;
      margin-top:40px;
      }
</style>
</head>
<body>
<div id="outer">
<canvas id="canvas1" width="400" height="400">
Your browser doesn't support the canvas! Try another browser.
</canvas>
</div>
<script>
var mycanvas=document.getElementById("canvas1");
var cntx=mycanvas.getContext('2d');
// draw black circle
cntx.arc(200, 200, 100, 0, Math.PI * 2, true);
cntx.lineWidth="4";
cntx.strokeStyle="black";
cntx.stroke();
// draw red semi-circle
 cntx.arc(200, 350, 100, 0, Math.PI, true);
 cntx.lineWidth="2";
cntx.strokeStyle="red";
cntx.stroke();
</script>
</body>
</html>
```

Trying different values for the parameters in the `arc` method provides different shapes. They will still have the circle/part-circle appearance, but with some experimentation, you can achieve some interesting variations, as shown in Figure 3-9.

Code Listing 3-8 shows the source for the image in Figure 3-9. Note the varied parameters in each `cntx.arc()` statement.

Figure 3-9 Arc variations

Code Listing 3-8 Varied circular shapes

```
<!doctype html>
<html lang="en">
<head>
<meta charset="utf-8">
<title>canvas example 8</title>
<style>
body { background-color:#eeeeee; }
#canvas1 {background-color:white;
          border: 5px orange solid;


          }
#outer {margin-left:40px;
        margin-top:40px;
        }
</style>
</head>
<body>
<div id="outer">
<canvas id="canvas1" width="400" height="400">
Your browser doesn't support the canvas! Try another browser.
</canvas>
```

```
</div>
<script>
var mycanvas=document.getElementById("canvas1");
var cntx=mycanvas.getContext('2d');
cntx.lineWidth="4";
cntx.strokeStyle="black";
cntx.beginPath();
cntx.arc(50, 50, 30, 0, Math.PI * 2, true);
cntx.closePath();
cntx.stroke();
cntx.beginPath();
cntx.arc(100, 100, 30, 0, Math.PI * 1.2, true);
cntx.closePath();
cntx.stroke();
cntx.beginPath();
cntx.arc(150, 150, 30, 0, Math.PI * 0.5, true);
cntx.closePath();
cntx.stroke();
cntx.beginPath();
cntx.arc(200, 200, 30, 2, Math.PI * 2, true);
cntx.closePath();
cntx.stroke();
</script>
</body>
</html>
```

Working with arcs, you can also show the image as one continuous line by removing the path statements. The middle section of code in Code Listing 3-8 becomes this:

```
cntx.arc(50, 50, 30, 0, Math.PI * 2, true);
cntx.stroke();
cntx.arc(100, 100, 30, 0, Math.PI * 1.2, true);
cntx.stroke();
cntx.arc(150, 150, 30, 0, Math.PI * 0.5, true);
cntx.stroke();
cntx.arc(200, 200, 30, 2, Math.PI * 2, true);
cntx.stroke();
```

NOTE

The output is identical if you do not have any `beginPath` ... `closePath` statements *or* if you enclose the entire middle section in one `beginPath` ... `closePath` statement.

Figure 3-10 shows the change in the image after removing the path statements.

Figure 3-11 shows a canvas filled with small circles. If each were individually coded within a path block, it would be a rather long listing of code. The point here is not the drawing technique (they are just circles), but rather it's the JavaScript used to do this. JavaScript

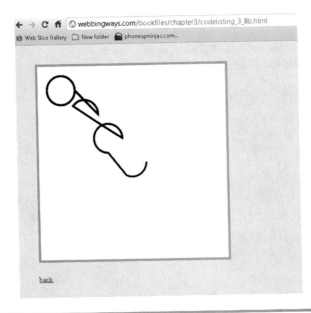

Figure 3-10 Continuous line arcs

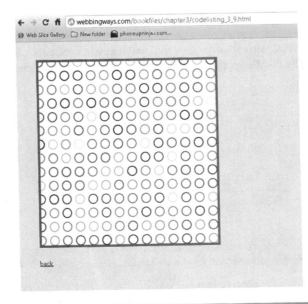

Figure 3-11 Many circles on a canvas

looping is put to work to make the circles. The full code for this example is shown in Code Listing 3-9.

Code Listing 3-9   Using JavaScript looping to make circles

```html
<!doctype html>
<html lang="en">
<head>
<meta charset="utf-8">
<title>canvas example 9</title>
<style>
body { background-color:#eeeeee; }
#canvas1 {background-color:white;
          border: 5px red solid; }
#outer {margin-left:40px;
        margin-top:40px;
        }
</style>
</head>
<body>
<div id="outer">
<canvas id="canvas1" width="400" height="400">
Your browser doesn't support the canvas! Try another browser.
</canvas>
</div>
<script>
var mycanvas=document.getElementById("canvas1");
var cntx=mycanvas.getContext('2d');
cntx.lineWidth="2";
for (i=0;i<=400;i=i+30) {
 for (a=0;a<=400;a=a+30) {
  cntx.beginPath();
  cntx.arc(i, a, 10, 0, Math.PI * 2, true);
  rndcolor1=(Math.floor(Math.random()*255));
  rndcolor2=(Math.floor(Math.random()*255));
  rndcolor3=(Math.floor(Math.random()*255));
  cntx.strokeStyle='rgb(' + rndcolor1 + ',' +
    rndcolor2 + ',' +  rndcolor3 + ')';
    cntx.closePath();
    cntx.stroke();
 }
}
</script>
</body>
</html>
```

The pertinent part of the code used to make the circles is this:

```
for (i=0;i<=400;i=i+30) {
 for (a=0;a<=400;a=a+30) {
  cntx.beginPath();
  cntx.arc(i, a, 10, 0, Math.PI * 2, true);
  rndcolor1=(Math.floor(Math.random()*255));
  rndcolor2=(Math.floor(Math.random()*255));
  rndcolor3=(Math.floor(Math.random()*255));
  cntx.strokeStyle='rgb(' + rndcolor1 + ',' +
      rndcolor2 + ',' +  rndcolor3 + ')';
   cntx.closePath();
   cntx.stroke();
 }
}
```

What you see here is a set of loops, one nested in the other. One loop sets the left parameter, and one sets the top parameter. The order in which these loops occur in this example is not important, since they are both the same size; in other words, they each iterate the same number of times. Also, they increment by the same amount (30). Within the nest of loops, a beginPath method is stated, and then the arc method is used with PI * 2 (to make the arc a circle). Next, three random colors are established to use in the RGB color construct, which happens next in the strokeStyle method. This method is used to set the color. Then the path is closed. Finally, the circle is drawn with the stroke method.

This occurs repeatedly until the loops run out. On the canvas, 196 circles are placed—or about 196, since the increment of 30 does not fit exactly with the 400 × 400 dimension of the canvas. This results in some circles being cut off.

Since the colors are selected using JavaScript's random method, each refresh of the browser shows a different spread of color among the circles. Later in the chapter, you will see these circles again in a way that uses an animation technique to continuously change the colors.

Drawing Lines

Rectangles, circles, arcs, and other predefined shapes are great, yet when it comes to drawing, the ability to create a line is paramount. The two main methods for drawing lines are moveTo and lineTo. Imagine a pen pressed down on a piece of paper. If you move the pen, a line is drawn; if you keep the pen down but draw in a different direction, another line is drawn, and it is connected to the first line. What if you need to start a new line somewhere else that is not connected? Then you need to lift the pen and move it. The lineTo and moveTo methods are how you achieve these actions.

Figure 3-12 shows a house drawn with a number of lines, connected and not connected, as well as a round doorknob to boot (made with the arc method).

The code used to make this image uses reusable JavaScript functions and a number of techniques. An overview of the code is shown in Code Listing 3-10.

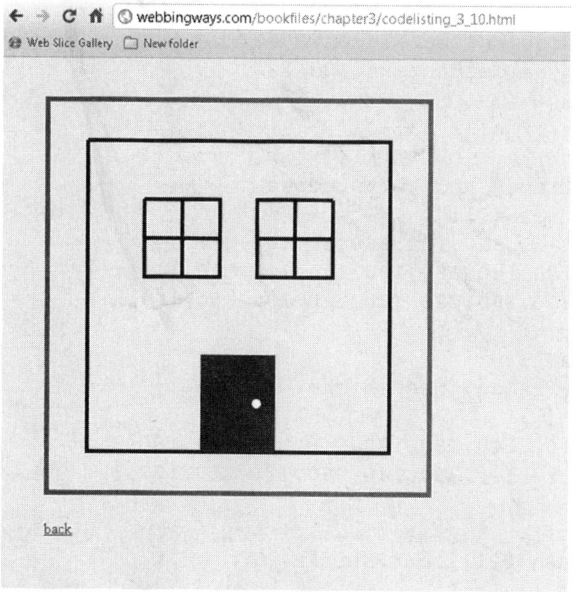

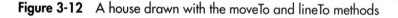

Figure 3-12 A house drawn with the moveTo and lineTo methods

Code Listing 3-10   Drawing lines

```
<!doctype html>
<html lang="en">
<head>
<meta charset="utf-8">
<title>canvas example 10</title>
<style>
body { background-color:#eeeeee; }
#canvas1 {background-color:#eeeeee;
          border: 5px blue solid; }
#outer {margin-left:40px;
        margin-top:40px;
        }
</style>
</head>
<body>
<div id="outer">
<canvas id="canvas1" width="400" height="400">
Your browser doesn't support the canvas! Try another browser.
</canvas>
</div>
```

```
<script>
var mycanvas=document.getElementById("canvas1");
var cntx=mycanvas.getContext('2d');
cntx.lineWidth = 4;
cntx.fillStyle='rgb(33,33,33)';
cntx.beginPath();
//draw house frame, and two windows
//use stroke, not fill
draw(40,40,40,360,360,360,360,40,40,40);
draw(100,100,100,180,180,180,180,100,100,100);
draw(300,100,300,180,220,180,220,100,300,100);
cntx.stroke();
cntx.closePath();
//draw window frames, use stroke, not fill
cntx.beginPath();
windowframes(100,140,180,140,140,100,140,180);
windowframes(220,140,300,140,260,180,260,100);
cntx.stroke();
cntx.closePath();
//draw door, use fill, not stroke
cntx.beginPath();
draw(160,360,160,260,240,260,240,360,160,360);
cntx.fill();
cntx.closePath();
//draw doorknob (a white circle)
cntx.beginPath();
cntx.arc(220, 310, 5, 0, Math.PI * 2, true);
cntx.closePath();
//change color to white, use fill, not stroke
cntx.fillStyle="#ffffff";
cntx.fill();
function draw(m1,m2,l1,l2,l3,l4,l5,l6,l7,l8) {
   cntx.moveTo(m1,m2);
   cntx.lineTo(l1,l2);
   cntx.lineTo(l3,l4);
   cntx.lineTo(l5,l6);
   cntx.lineTo(l7,l8);
}
function windowframes(m1,m2,l1,l2,m3,m4,l3,l4) {
   cntx.moveTo(m1,m2);
   cntx.lineTo(l1,l2);
   cntx.moveTo(m3,m4);
   cntx.lineTo(l3,l4);
}
</script>
</body>
</html>
```

Keep in mind that a line has a starting position and an ending position. The coordinate system is in play here. The starting position has two numbers (left and top), while the ending has another two (also left and top).

The starting position can be determined either by the moveTo method or by being implied by where the drawing last took a pause, which must be at some set of coordinates. The only difference is whether you first lifted the pen. If so, you used the moveTo method. Therefore, moveTo(100,150) places the pen down at a position of 100 pixels in from the left and 150 pixels down from the top. If this were followed by a lineTo(200,200), a line would be drawn from the designated position to the 200, 200 spot. If this were then followed by lineTo(320,380), a line would be drawn from 200, 200 to 320, 380. That second draw action assumed the last stopped spot of 200, 200 as the place to start from. Had there been another moveTo (which is like lifting the pen), it would designate the starting point. But as described here, there was no second moveTo. So, here is what we have from this example:

```
moveTo(100,150);
lineTo(200,200);
lineTo(320,380);
```

Besides this, no lines are drawn unless there is a stroke method used.

Let's dissect the code in Code Listing 3-10 (no, not quite like a biology class). First, a line width and color are selected. The 'rgb(33,33,33)' sets a fairly dark color, approaching black. Then a beginPath statement is put in.

```
cntx.lineWidth = 4;
cntx.fillStyle='rgb(33,33,33)';
cntx.beginPath();
```

After the path is opened, drawing is performed. In this example, a function named draw() is used. This function accepts a slew of variables to do the work. It takes ten parameters. The first two are used for the moveTo method, and the other eight are actually four sets of two parameters used with four successive lineTo methods. Thinking this through, imagine a pen is put down on a piece of paper, and a square is drawn. A square has four sides—the four successive lineTo iterations.

```
//draw house frame, and two windows
//use stroke, not fill
draw(40,40,40,360,360,360,360,40,40,40);
draw(100,100,100,180,180,180,180,100,100,100);
draw(300,100,300,180,220,180,220,100,300,100);
cntx.stroke();
cntx.closePath();
```

Notice that after the beginPath started a path block, the draw method is called three times in a row. Then a single stroke method call draws all three squares, and a final closePath is stated. The draw method is shown in the following code.

```
function draw(m1,m2,l1,l2,l3,l4,l5,l6,l7,l8) {
   cntx.moveTo(m1,m2);
   cntx.lineTo(l1,l2);
   cntx.lineTo(l3,l4);
   cntx.lineTo(l5,l6);
   cntx.lineTo(l7,l8);
}
```

First, for clarity, the eight parameters are each the letter l (for line), followed by a number. The first two parameters place the pen using moveTo, and then following are the four iterations of lineTo. If you closely follow the parameters sent to the function, like this:

```
draw(40,40,40,360,360,360,360,40,40,40);
```

you'll see a square is drawn. The three successive calls to the draw method draw the large frame around the house (not to be confused with the border of the canvas), and also draw the two windows—just squares for the moment, without cross frame lines in them.

Next, the crosses on the windows are drawn in much the same way as the squares; that is, parameters are sent to a function, named windowframes() in this case.

```
//draw window frames, use stroke, not fill
cntx.beginPath();
windowframes(100,140,180,140,140,100,140,180);
windowframes(220,140,300,140,260,180,260,100);
cntx.stroke();
cntx.closePath();
```

The windowsframe function has fewer parameters. The first pair are moveTo coordinates, the second pair are for a lineTo, the third pair is for another moveTo, and the last pair is for another lineTo. Here is the actual function:

```
function windowframes(m1,m2,l1,l2,m3,m4,l3,l4) {
   cntx.moveTo(m1,m2);
   cntx.lineTo(l1,l2);
   cntx.moveTo(m3,m4);
   cntx.lineTo(l3,l4);
}
```

Rounding out the picture are the door and doorknob. The door is drawn with the draw function. However, upon returning from the function, a fill is used instead of a stroke. This means the drawn rectangle of the door is filled in, not outlined like the windows. Finally, an arc method places the doorknob—a small, white circle—and it becomes visible with a fill. Just prior to the fill, the color is changed to white with the fillStyle method.

```
//draw door, use fill, not stroke
cntx.beginPath();
draw(160,360,160,260,240,260,240,360,160,360);
```

```
cntx.fill();
cntx.closePath();
//draw doorknob (a white circle)
cntx.beginPath();
cntx.arc(220, 310, 5, 0, Math.PI * 2, true);
cntx.closePath();
//change color to white, use fill, not stroke
cntx.fillStyle="#ffffff";
cntx.fill();
```

This one comprehensive example of drawing a house should suffice for demonstrating how drawing works. You've seen how it relates to what you do when drawing on a piece of paper.

Using Multiple Canvases

This is fun—a page filled with multiple canvases, each doing its own thing. Since each canvas can be named individually, each can be treated separately with CSS and JavaScript. Figure 3-13 shows four canvases on a single web page.

Code Listing 3-11 shows how each canvas is inside its own div, as well as being uniquely named. CSS is applied to both the divs and the canvases. CSS is used for page placement and canvas border colors.

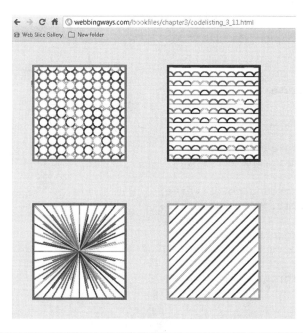

Figure 3-13 Multiple canvases on a single web page

Code Listing 3-11   Multiple canvases

```
<!doctype html>
<html lang="en">
<head>
<meta charset="utf-8">
<title>canvas example 11</title>
<style>
body { background-color:#eeeeee; }
#outer {margin-left:40px;
        margin-top:40px;
}
#c1 {
position:absolute;
top:50px;
left:50px;
}
#c2 {
position:absolute;
top:50px;
left:350px;
}
#c3 {
position:absolute;
top:350px;
left:50px;
}
#c4 {
position:absolute;
top:350px;
left:350px;
}
#canvas1 {background-color:white;
          border: 5px red solid;
}
#canvas2 {background-color:white;
          border: 5px blue solid;
}
#canvas3 {background-color:white;
          border: 5px green solid;
}
#canvas4 {background-color:white;
          border: 5px orange solid;
}
</style>
</head>
<body>
<div id="outer">
```

```
<div id="c1">
<canvas id="canvas1" width="200" height="200">
Your browser doesn't support the canvas! Try another browser.
</canvas>
</div>
<div id="c2">
<canvas id="canvas2" width="200" height="200">
Your browser doesn't support the canvas! Try another browser.
</canvas>
</div>
<div id="c3">
<canvas id="canvas3" width="200" height="200">
Your browser doesn't support the canvas! Try another browser.
</canvas>
</div>
<div id="c4">
<canvas id="canvas4" width="200" height="200">
Your browser doesn't support the canvas! Try another browser.
</canvas>
</div>
</div>
<script>
var mycanvas1=document.getElementById("canvas1");
var cntx1=mycanvas1.getContext('2d');
cntx1.lineWidth="2";
var mycanvas2=document.getElementById("canvas2");
var cntx2=mycanvas2.getContext('2d');
cntx2.lineWidth="2";
var mycanvas3=document.getElementById("canvas3");
var cntx3=mycanvas3.getContext('2d');
cntx3.lineWidth="2";
var mycanvas4=document.getElementById("canvas4");
var cntx4=mycanvas4.getContext('2d');
cntx4.lineWidth="2";
function animate() {
 for (i=0;i<=200;i=i+20) {
 for (a=0;a<=200;a=a+20) {
  cntx1.beginPath();
  cntx2.beginPath();
  cntx3.beginPath();
  cntx4.beginPath();
  cntx1.arc(i, a, 10, 0, Math.PI * 2, true);
  cntx2.arc(i, a, 10, 0, Math.PI, true);
  cntx3.moveTo(a,i);
  cntx3.lineTo(100,100);
  cntx4.moveTo(i,a);
  cntx4.lineTo(a,i);
  rndcolor1=(Math.floor(Math.random()*255));
```

```
    rndcolor2=(Math.floor(Math.random()*255));
    rndcolor3=(Math.floor(Math.random()*255));
    cntx1.strokeStyle='rgb(' + rndcolor1 + ',' +
      rndcolor2 + ',' +  rndcolor3 + ')';
    cntx2.strokeStyle='rgb(' + rndcolor1 + ',' +
     rndcolor2 + ',' +  rndcolor3 + ')';
    cntx3.strokeStyle='rgb(' + rndcolor1 + ',' +
     rndcolor2 + ',' +  rndcolor3 + ')';
    cntx4.strokeStyle='rgb(' + rndcolor1 + ',' +
     rndcolor2 + ',' +  rndcolor3 + ')';
    cntx1.closePath();
    cntx2.closePath();
    cntx1.stroke();
    cntx2.stroke();
    cntx3.stroke();
    cntx4.stroke();
   }
  }
}
//this sets the animation speed
setInterval(animate, 100);
</script>
</body>
</html>
```

This code uses many techniques already discussed in this chapter. Of note is the large function (`animate`) in the middle. What is different here is how the function is called. The JavaScript `setInterval` method is used to repeatedly call the function:

```
//this sets the animation speed
setInterval(animate, 100);
```

A setting of 100 indicates to call the function every tenth of a second. At a fairly fast speed, the canvases are all showing an animated view. To see this in action, visit www.webbingways.com.

Placing Text on a Canvas

So far, you've seen examples of visual images placed on a canvas. What about text? Can words be placed on a canvas? Of course! There are many methods to work with text, including `textAlign`, `measureText`, `textBaseline`, `font`, `fillText`, and `strokeText`. The `fillText` and `strokeText` methods are used to affect whether alphanumeric characters are outlined or filled in.

The example in Code Listing 3-12 shows a technique in which the canvas is filled with a line of text repeatedly.

Code Listing 3-12   Lines of text

```
<!doctype html>
<html lang="en">
<head>
<meta charset="utf-8">
<title>canvas example 12</title>
<style>
body { background-color:#eeeeee; }
#canvas1 {background-color:yellow;
          border: 5px blue solid; }
#outer {margin-left:40px;
        margin-top:40px;
        }
</style>
</head>
<body>
<div id="outer">
<canvas id="canvas1" width="500" height="500">
Your browser doesn't support the canvas! Try another browser.
</canvas>
</div>
<script>
var mycanvas=document.getElementById("canvas1");
var cntx=mycanvas.getContext('2d');
  cntx.font="1em sans-serif";
  cntx.fillStyle="rgb(0,0,0)"
for (i=10; i<=480;i=(i+40)) {
  cntx.fillText("Like magic, text appears on the canvas", 10, i);
}
</script>
</body>
</html>
```

The code in Code Listing 3-12 uses the font setting of the context to declare a sans-serif font sized at the standard 1em. The fillStyle method sets the color to black. The fillText method puts the text on the canvas.

The fillText method takes three parameters: the text, the left position, and the top position. In this example, the top is looped downward to create the effect of filling the canvas with the text, as shown in Figure 3-14.

Vertical Text

Text is placed on the canvas using a method that specifies a coordinate for where the text is to begin. With a little ingenuity, this can be made to accommodate vertical text by placing each letter underneath the one that came before it. Figure 3-15 shows how this looks.

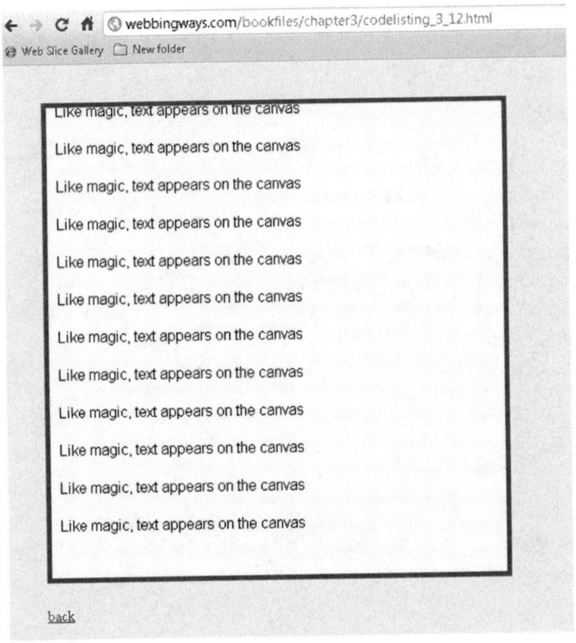

Figure 3-14 Sequential text

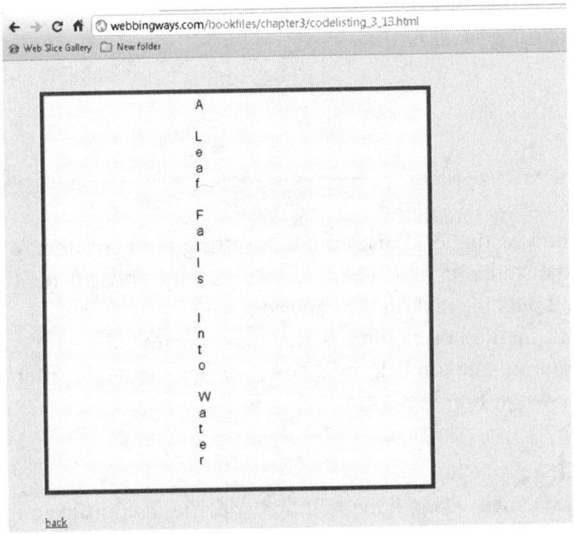

Figure 3-15 Vertically oriented text

Code Listing 3-13 shows the vertical text technique. In the code, a function named `letter()` is used to place the text. Single characters and their vertical position are passed to the function.

Code Listing 3-13   Vertical text

```
<!doctype html>
<html lang="en">
<head>
<meta charset="utf-8">
<title>canvas example 13</title>
<style>
body { background-color:#eeeeee; }
#canvas1 {background-color:yellow;
          border: 5px blue solid; }
#outer {margin-left:40px;
        margin-top:40px;
        }
</style>
</head>
<body>
<div id="outer">
<canvas id="canvas1" width="500" height="500">
Your browser doesn't support the canvas! Try another browser.
</canvas>
</div>
<script>
var mycanvas=document.getElementById("canvas1");
var cntx=mycanvas.getContext('2d');
  cntx.font="1em sans-serif";
  cntx.fillStyle="rgb(0,0,0)"
letter("A", 20);
letter("L", 60);
letter("e", 80);
letter("a", 100);
letter("f", 120);
letter("F", 160);
letter("a", 180);
letter("l", 200);
letter("l", 220);
letter("s", 240);
letter("I", 290);
letter("n", 310);
letter("t", 330);
letter("o", 350);
letter("W", 390);
letter("a", 410);
letter("t", 430);
```

```
letter("e", 450);
letter("r", 470);
function letter(letter, position) {
  cntx.fillText(letter, 200, position);
}
</script>
</body>
</html>
```

The `letter` function in Code Listing 3-13 is passed only two parameters: the alphanumeric character and the vertical position to place it. The horizontal position is fixed at 200 pixels. This forces all letters to be underneath each other in a vertical line.

Shadow Text

Text can be stroked or filled—in other words, be an outline of letters or filled in. This offers possibilities of creating shadow effects with either type of text. It all has to do with placement and transparency. First, text that is outlined by using `strokeText` is placed on the canvas and duplicated with a slight offset to create a shadow. The direction, length, and transparency of the shadow can be controlled with the available features of the various canvas methods. Figure 3-16 shows an example using stroked text. Code Listing 3-14 shows the code used to produce this effect.

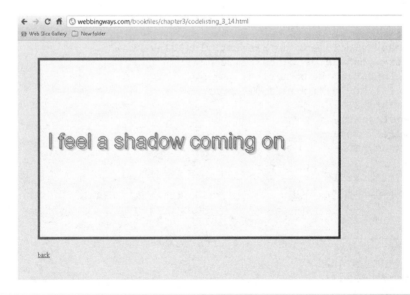

Figure 3-16 Creating a text shadow

Code Listing 3-14   Outlined, shadowed text

```
<!doctype html>
<html lang="en">
<head>
<meta charset="utf-8">
<title>canvas example 14</title>
<style>
body { background-color:#eeeeee; }
#canvas1 {background-color:yellow;
        border: 5px blue solid; }
#outer {margin-left:40px;
      margin-top:40px;
        }
</style>
</head>
<body>
<div id="outer">
<canvas id="canvas1" width="700" height="400">
Your browser doesn't support the canvas! Try another browser.
</canvas>
</div>
<script>
var mycanvas=document.getElementById("canvas1");
var cntx=mycanvas.getContext('2d');
  cntx.font="3em sans-serif";
  cntx.strokeStyle="rgb(0,0,0)";
  cntx.strokeText("I feel a shadow coming on", 20, 200);
  cntx.strokeStyle="rgba(100,100,100,0.5)";
  cntx.strokeText("I feel a shadow coming on", 22, 202);
  cntx.strokeStyle="rgba(100,100,100,0.25)";
  cntx.strokeText("I feel a shadow coming on", 24, 204);
</script>
</body>
</html>
```

This example uses a large text size since it is stroked and not filled. The basic line of text is placed at the coordinates of 20 pixels to the left, and 200 pixels down, relative to the canvas. This line of text has a solid outline. Following this are two more lines of text. The text is identical, however the offsets are sequentially 2 pixels to the bottom and right. With each of the lines, the transparency increases as well, creating the shadow effect.

Filled text can also be shadowed quite effectively. The same approach applies. Display a line of text, and then display and offset with a given transparency. Figure 3-17 shows how this looks with filled text.

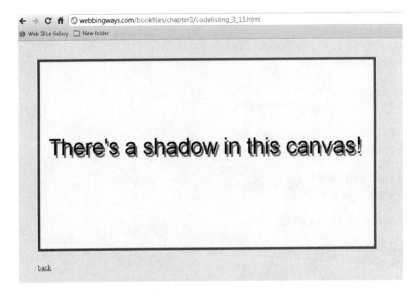

Figure 3-17 Filled, shadowed text

The image in Figure 3-17 displays the shadow with a 4-pixel offset to the bottom and the right. The transparency is slight—just 25% is on the alpha channel. Code Listing 3-15 shows how the image is made.

Code Listing 3-15 Filled, shadowed text

```
<!doctype html>
<html lang="en">
<head>
<meta charset="utf-8">
<title>canvas example 15</title>
<style>
body { background-color:#eeeeee; }
#canvas1 {background-color:yellow;
        border: 5px blue solid; }
#outer {margin-left:40px;
      margin-top:40px;
       }
</style>
</head>
<body>
<div id="outer">
<canvas id="canvas1" width="740" height="400">
Your browser doesn't support the canvas! Try another browser.
</canvas>
```

```
</div>
<script>
var mycanvas=document.getElementById("canvas1");
var cntx=mycanvas.getContext('2d');
  cntx.font="3em sans-serif";
  cntx.fillStyle="rgb(0,0,0)";
  cntx.fillText("There's a shadow in this canvas!", 20, 200);
  cntx.fillStyle="rgba(100,100,100,0.75)";
  cntx.fillText("There's a shadow in this canvas!", 24, 206);
</script>
</body>
</html>
```

You can apply creative techniques with shadows. For example, the shadow can be a different color, or the shadow can use several offsets with increasing transparency until the text completely disappears. Experiment! This is one great way to put pizzazz in your pages.

Summary

The canvas is an exciting and versatile addition to HTML. As a container, in essence, it can display many types of visuals. This chapter has introduced how to work with basic shapes, gradients, ways to draw, and text. But that's not all!

The examples in this chapter have been static for the most part (some animation was demonstrated). In Chapter 4, you'll learn how to use animation and events. If you feel comfortable with what you've seen so far, please dive right in!

Chapter 4

Using Animation and Events with the Canvas

Placing shapes on the canvas, drawing on the canvas, and having text appear on the canvas offer many ways to use the canvas for a variety of image-based applications. However, all these techniques are *static*. You see them, and they can appear very creative or very functional, but they don't move. Animation is a long-time standard item for web pages, and it is imperative that the canvas carries its weight in this arena. And you know what—it does!

This chapter focuses on animation and effects used with the canvas. You can do a lot, and what is shown here is by no means exhaustive. It's more on the side of the tip of the iceberg. The Internet is filled with incredible examples. Searching for "canvas effects" in your favorite search engine is sure to bring up some gems.

Note that the greater the amount of animation, or the more complex the animation, the more JavaScript is involved—perhaps pages of it, including hooks into specialized libraries or even common ones, such as jQuery. The code examples shown here are purposely not overly long. Consider this an exposé of techniques and a guide to get you on your way. That being said, let's go for it.

Circles, Revisited

In Chapter 3, Figure 3-11 shows a field of circles on a canvas. They are stationary. They do change color when you refresh the page, but that's the catch: You need to take an action. What if the color changing just occurred on its own? That's easy enough.

The trick to much animation is that JavaScript has timing statements, the subjective biggie of these being `setTimeout`. This JavaScript goodie repeats a function endlessly, at a pace that is set with a parameter.

Code Listing 4-1 is a variation of Code Listing 3-9. In Code Listing 3-9, the circles are created and randomly colored, once. In Code Listing 4-1, the circles keep changing.

Code Listing 4-1   Animated circles

```
<!doctype html>
<html lang="en">
<head>
<meta charset="utf-8">
<title>canvas example 15</title>
<style>
body { background-color:#eeeeee; }
#canvas1 {background-color:white;
        border: 5px red solid;
        }
#outer {margin-left:40px;
        margin-top:40px;
        }
</style>
</head>
```

```
<body>
<div id="outer">
<canvas id="canvas1" width="400" height="400">
Your browser doesn't support the canvas! Try another browser.
</canvas>
</div>
<script>
var mycanvas=document.getElementById("canvas1");
var cntx=mycanvas.getContext('2d');
cntx.lineWidth="2";
function circles() {
 for (i=0;i<=400;i=i+30) {
  for (a=0;a<=400;a=a+30) {
    cntx.beginPath();
    cntx.arc(i, a, 10, 0, Math.PI * 2, true);
    rndcolor1=(Math.floor(Math.random()*255));
    rndcolor2=(Math.floor(Math.random()*255));
    rndcolor3=(Math.floor(Math.random()*255));
    cntx.strokeStyle='rgb(' + rndcolor1 + ',' +
   rndcolor2 + ',' +  rndcolor3 + ')';
    cntx.closePath();
    cntx.stroke();
   }
  }
}
//this sets the animation speed
setInterval(circles, 100);
</script>
</body>
</html>
```

Code Listing 4-1 is the same as Code Listing 3-9 except that the portion of the code that makes the circles has been put into a function, and `setInterval` repeatedly calls the function:

```
setInterval(circles, 100);
```

TIP

Use `setInterval` to repeatedly call a JavaScript function.

There is no figure to show for the animated circles. A snapshot of the animated circles would look the same as Figure 3-11. You can visit www.webbingways.com to see the example for Code Listing 4-1.

A Moving Gradient

The example in this section shows an interesting radial gradient that moves within the canvas. The gradient appears 3D in a way, as if you're looking into a tunnel. Then with the added motion, the effect is intensified. Figures 4-1 and 4-2 show the gradient at two stages of its animation. The gradient moves up and down, which provides an appearance similar to moving your position around a tunnel opening to get a better look of what is inside it.

In the code for this example, the following `gradient()` function sets a value to the variable z, which is used in the `createRadialGradient` method to alter one coordinate that designates the position of the second circle used in the gradient. The function tests to see if z has been incremented up to a value of 300 or decremented down to a value of 0. When either condition is hit, another variable, `direction`, is given a value of 0 or 1, and this controls whether z is incremented or decremented.

```
function gradient() {
   if (z==0) {
      direction=1;
   }
   if (z==300) {
      direction=0;
   }
   if (direction==1) {
      z=(z+10);
   }
   if (direction==0) {
      z=(z-10);
   }
```

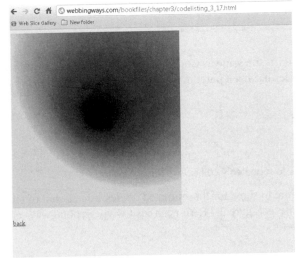

Figure 4-1 Animated gradient, snapshot 1

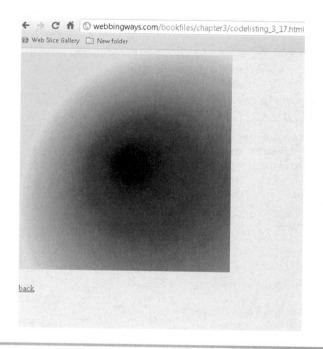

Figure 4-2 Animated gradient, snapshot 2

```
mygradient=cntx.createRadialGradient(200,200,10,300,z,300);
mygradient.addColorStop("0","#000000");
mygradient.addColorStop("1.0","#00ff00");
cntx.fillStyle=mygradient;
cntx.fillRect(0,0,400,400);
}
```

The full code for this example is shown in Code Listing 4-2.

Code Listing 4-2   A radial gradient that looks like a tunnel

```
<!doctype html>
<html lang="en">
<head>
<meta charset="utf-8">
<title>canvas example 17</title>
<style>
body { background-color:#eeeeee; }
</style>
</head>
<body>
<div id="outer">
```

```
<canvas id="canvas1" width="400" height="400">
Your browser doesn't support the canvas! Try another browser.
</canvas>
</div>
<script>
  var z=10;
  var direction=1;
  var mycanvas=document.getElementById("canvas1");
  var cntx=mycanvas.getContext('2d');
  var mygradient=cntx.createRadialGradient(200,200,10,300,300,300);
  function gradient() {
    if (z==0) {
      direction=1;
    }
    if (z==300) {
      direction=0;
    }
    if (direction==1) {
      z=(z+10);
    }
    if (direction==0) {
      z=(z-10);
    }
    mygradient=cntx.createRadialGradient(200,200,10,300,z,300);
    mygradient.addColorStop("0","#000000");
    mygradient.addColorStop("1.0","#00ff00");
    cntx.fillStyle=mygradient;
    cntx.fillRect(0,0,400,400);
  }
  setInterval(gradient, 100);
</script>
</body>
</html>
```

Using Events

So far, you've seen some examples of animation techniques. However, a key piece has not been introduced: the use of events. In a sense, this is a continuation of animation; however, the following examples are not self-running. User interaction is required.

The examples in this section use the click event, as well as three mouse events: mousedown, mouseup, and mousemove. Events are "fired." Many other events are available. Some other common events are fired when an element gets the focus or loses the focus (blur), on the page load, and when a form is submitted. Indeed, the load event happens whenever a page is loaded in your browser; in other words, it is not user-driven.

Mondrian-Inspired Art

Piet Mondrian was an artist who lived and worked in the early part of the twentieth century. He went through periods of different art styles. One of them is quite unique and is instantly recognizable as being his forte. These art pieces typically are on a white canvas, or at least have large light-colored areas. They have solid black lines, both horizontal and vertical, as well as blocks filled with color. The blocks are dimensioned by the black lines.

The example in this section lets you create Mondrian-inspired art. Each click produces a unique mix of lines and filled corner rectangles. Figure 4-3 shows what the canvas might look like after being clicked.

You select the number of black lines from drop-down lists. The code contains a form with two selects (drop-downs): one for setting the number of horizontal lines and the other for setting the number of vertical lines. Here is the code snippet for one of the drop-downs:

```
Enter number of horizontal borders:
<select id="h_border_count" name="h_border_count">
 <option value="0">0</option>
 <option value="1">1</option>
 <option value="2" selected="selected">2</option>
 <option value="3">3</option>
</select>
```

On the canvas, the lines are randomly placed, as well as randomly sized in regard to their thickness. The random value of the line thickness is determined with this line of code:

```
rand_linewidth=(Math.floor(Math.random()*20));
```

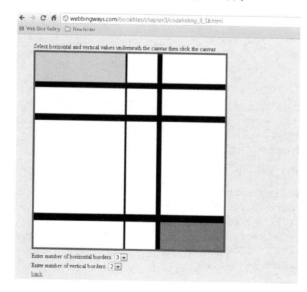

Figure 4-3   Computer-generated art

A number of equations and limits, such as 500 to match the canvas, are used to ensure that the lines appear in a way that is similar to how the painter painted.

Another section of code always fills the top-left box with yellow and the bottom-right box with red. The dimensions of these boxes are dependent on the randomly placed lines, but the code keeps track of the line placement and fills what is effectively a set of correctly sized rectangles.

The final piece to this example is the event. The canvas itself has a click event, which creates a work of art. In other words, you must click on the canvas to create the image. When first rendered in a browser, the canvas is empty. One click on the canvas, and a "painting" appears. Each successive click provides a variation because of the randomness. Selecting different amounts of lines to appear affects the image as well.

Code Listing 4-3 shows the full code for this example.

Code Listing 4-3   Mondrian-inspired art

```
<!doctype html>
<html lang="en">
<head>
<meta charset="utf-8">
<title>Mondrian Style Computer Generated Art</title>
<style>
body { background-color:#eeeeee; }
#canvas1 {background-color:white;
          border: 5px blue solid; }
#outer {margin-left:40px;
        margin-top:20px;
        }
</style>
</head>
<body>
<div id="outer">
Select horizontal and vertical values underneath the canvas
    then click the canvas<br>
<canvas id="canvas1" width="500" height="500" onclick="create_image()">
Your browser doesn't support the canvas! Try another browser.
</canvas>
<form>
Enter number of horizontal borders:
<select id="h_border_count" name="h_border_count">
 <option value="0">0</option>
 <option value="1">1</option>
 <option value="2" selected="selected">2</option>
 <option value="3">3</option>
</select>
<br>
Enter number of vertical borders:
```

```
<select id="v_border_count" name="v_border_count">
 <option value="0">0</option>
 <option value="1">1</option>
 <option value="2" selected="selected">2</option>
 <option value="3">3</option>
</select>
</form>
</div>
<script>
var mycanvas=document.getElementById("canvas1");
var cntx=mycanvas.getContext('2d');
function create_image() {
 mycanvas.width = mycanvas.width; //clears canvas
cntx.strokeStyle='rgb(0,0,0)';
var h=document.getElementById("h_border_count").value;
var v=document.getElementById("v_border_count").value;
cntx.lineWidth="2";
h_line=500;
v_line_1=0;
v_line_2=0;
v_line_3=0;
h_line_1=0;
h_line_2=0;
h_line_3=0;
for (i=1;i<=h;i++) {
 cntx.beginPath();
 rand_linestart=(Math.floor(Math.random()*500));
 rand_linewidth=(Math.floor(Math.random()*20));
 if (rand_linestart<h_line) {
   h_line=rand_linestart-(rand_linewidth/2);
 }
 if (i==1) {
   h_line_1=rand_linestart+(rand_linewidth/2);
 }
 if (i==2) {
   h_line_2=rand_linestart+(rand_linewidth/2);
 }
 if (i==3) {
   h_line_3=rand_linestart+(rand_linewidth/2);
 }
 cntx.lineWidth=rand_linewidth;
 cntx.moveTo(0,rand_linestart);
 cntx.lineTo(500,rand_linestart);
 cntx.closePath();
 cntx.stroke();
}
v_line=500;
for (i=1;i<=v;i++) {
```

```
cntx.beginPath();
rand_linestart=(Math.floor(Math.random()*500));
rand_linewidth=(Math.floor(Math.random()*20));
if (rand_linestart<v_line) {
  v_line=rand_linestart-(rand_linewidth/2);
}
if (i==1) {
  v_line_1=rand_linestart+(rand_linewidth/2);
}
if (i==2) {
  v_line_2=rand_linestart+(rand_linewidth/2);
}
if (i==3) {
 v_line_3=rand_linestart+(rand_linewidth/2);
}
cntx.lineWidth=rand_linewidth;
cntx.moveTo(rand_linestart,0);
cntx.lineTo(rand_linestart,500);
cntx.closePath();
cntx.stroke();
}
//fill in rectangle
cntx.fillStyle='rgb(255,255,0)';
cntx.fillRect(0,0, v_line,h_line);
v_max=Math.max(v_line_1,v_line_2,v_line_3);
h_max=Math.max(h_line_1,h_line_2,h_line_3);
cntx.fillStyle='rgb(255,0,0)';
cntx.fillRect(v_max,h_max,500,500);
} //function
</script>
</body>
</html>
```

A Drawing Tablet

The canvas is an ideal element for creating free-form artwork. After all, it is a "canvas." The example in this section lets you draw free-form lines. Figure 4-4 shows the canvas before any drawing has commenced. Notice the small palette of colors to select from, and a drop-down menu to select the width of the line.

Figure 4-5 shows the selection of line widths, which range from 1 (a thin line) to 20 (on the thick side). Besides the artistic possibilities with the thick lines, another reason I included them is to erase parts of the picture. This example does not offer an eraser or way of clearing the canvas. If you need to erase something, select the color white and an appropriate line width. The canvas is white, so drawing white onto the canvas achieves the same result as using an eraser.

Figure 4-4   The blank drawing tablet

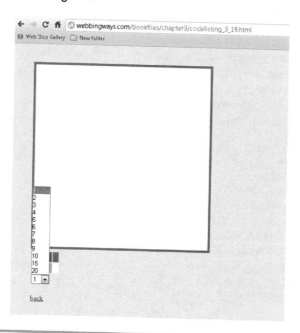

Figure 4-5   Possible line widths

The code for the drawing tablet involves using the three mouse events:

- The mousedown event determines where drawing begins.

- The mousemove event draws as the mouse moves, as long as the mouse button is still held down. This example draws a line wherever you move the mouse. The lines are not limited to being straight.

- The mouseup event stops the drawing; in other words, it ends the line.

These make up the drawing of one line. You can draw many lines; there is no effective limit (perhaps an artistic one, but not a technical one).

The events here are set up using event handlers. This is a technique to tell an element to watch for an event. What occurs when the event fires depends on what is coded. These lines set up the listeners:

```
mycanvas.addEventListener('mousedown', ev_canvas, false);
mycanvas.addEventListener('mousemove', ev_canvas, false);
mycanvas.addEventListener('mouseup',   ev_canvas, false);
```

Overall, the code used in creating the drawing tablet differs from other code in this chapter in that a bit of object-oriented JavaScript comes into play, like this:

```
// instantiate a new brush
brush = new paintbrush();
```

This snippet is called when mousedown is fired. Of note here is the lineTo method. In practice, the lineTo method does not need to be in this event. However, I put it here to serve a particular need. Note how lineTo adds just 1 pixel of color to the spot that mousedown touched. This allows making dots—1-pixel dots, which is as small as a dot can be. With a steady hand, you could create a picture out of dots. Admittedly, this would be tedious, but if you're in a creative mood, you could try it.

```
// This mouse DOWN allows the brush to draw
this.mousedown = function (ev) {
        brush.started = true;
        cntx.beginPath();
        cntx.moveTo(ev._x, ev._y);
        // by moving the line by one pixel a dot is put on the canvas
        cntx.lineTo(ev._x+1, ev._y+1);
        cntx.stroke();
};
```

The following snippet is the mousemove piece:

```
this.mousemove = function (ev) {
        if (brush.started) {
                //which color?
```

```
      var color=document.getElementById('colorchoice').innerHTML;
      var linewidth=document.getElementById('linewidth').value;
      cntx.strokeStyle='rgb(' + color + ')';
      cntx.lineWidth=linewidth;
      cntx.lineTo(ev._x, ev._y);
      cntx.stroke();
   }
};
```

This is where `lineTo` is needed. The selected color and line width are set into variables and used with the `lineTo` to draw the line. It will keep on drawing wherever you move the mouse as long as the mouse button is still pressed.

The following snippet is what fires when the mouse button is released (`mouseup`).

```
this.mouseup = function (ev) {
      // you could put something interesting here
      // like draw a small flower when the mouse is released
      if (brush.started) {
        brush.started = false;
      }
};
```

In this code, the brush is turned off to end drawing the line. This is really just a flag used throughout to indicate whether drawing should occur.

Code Listing 4-4 shows the code used to create and use the drawing tablet.

Code Listing 4-4   The drawing tablet

```
<!doctype html>
<html lang="en">
<head>
<meta charset="utf-8">
<title>canvas example 3-19</title>
<style>
body { background-color:#eeeeee; }
#canvas1 {background-color:white;
        border: 5px red solid;

          }
#outer {margin-left:40px;
        margin-top:40px;
        position: relative;
      }
</style>
</head>
<body>
<div id="outer">
```

```html
<canvas id="canvas1" width="400" height="400">
Your browser doesn't support the canvas! Try another browser.
</canvas>
<br>
<table>
<tr>
<td style="background-color:black;"
onclick="newcolor('00,00,00')">   </td>
<td style="background-color:blue;"
onclick="newcolor('00,00,255')">   </td>
<td style="background-color:green;"
onclick="newcolor('00,64,00')">   </td>
<td style="background-color:gray;"
onclick="newcolor('128,128,128')">   </td>
</tr>
<tr>
<td style="background-color:red;"
onclick="newcolor('255,00,00')">   </td>
<td style="background-color:yellow;"
onclick="newcolor('255,255,00')">   </td>
<td style="background-color:orange;"
onclick="newcolor('255,165,00')">   </td>
<td style="background-color:white;"
onclick="newcolor('255,255,255')">   </td>
</tr>
</table>
<div id="colorchoice"></div>
<select id="linewidth">
<option value="1">1</option>
<option value="2">2</option>
<option value="3">3</option>
<option value="4">4</option>
<option value="5">5</option>
<option value="6">6</option>
<option value="7">7</option>
<option value="8">8</option>
<option value="9">9</option>
<option value="10">10</option>
<option value="15">15</option>
<option value="20">20</option>
</select>
</div>
<script>
//add an event listener
if(window.addEventListener) {
  window.addEventListener('load', function () {
  var mycanvas = document.getElementById('canvas1');
  var  cntx = mycanvas.getContext('2d');
```

```
var brush;
function init () {
  // instantiate a new brush
  brush = new paintbrush();
  // Attach the mousedown, mousemove and mouseup event listeners.
  mycanvas.addEventListener('mousedown', ev_canvas, false);
  mycanvas.addEventListener('mousemove', ev_canvas, false);
  mycanvas.addEventListener('mouseup',   ev_canvas, false);
}
function paintbrush () {
  var brush = this;
  this.started = false;
  //which color?
  var color=document.getElementById('colorchoice').innerHTML;
  cntx.strokeStyle='rgb(' + color + ')';
  // This mouse DOWN allows the brush to draw
  this.mousedown = function (ev) {
        brush.started = true;
      cntx.beginPath();
      cntx.moveTo(ev._x, ev._y);
      // by moving the line by one pixel a dot is put on the canvas
      cntx.lineTo(ev._x+1, ev._y+1);
      cntx.stroke();
  };
  // This mouse MOVE allows the brush to continue to draw
  this.mousemove = function (ev) {
      if (brush.started) {
//which color?
var color=document.getElementById('colorchoice').innerHTML;
var linewidth=document.getElementById('linewidth').value;
cntx.strokeStyle='rgb(' + color + ')';
cntx.lineWidth=linewidth;
      cntx.lineTo(ev._x, ev._y);
      cntx.stroke();
    }
  };
  // This is called when you release the mouse button.
  this.mouseup = function (ev) {
    // you could put something intersting here
    // like draw a small flower when the mouse is released
    if (brush.started) {
      brush.started = false;
    }
  };
}
// Determines the mouse position relative to the canvas
function ev_canvas (ev) {
  if (ev.layerX || ev.layerX == 0) { // Firefox
```

```
  ev._x = ev.layerX;
  ev._y = ev.layerY;
} else if (ev.offsetX || ev.offsetX == 0) { // Opera
  ev._x = ev.offsetX;
  ev._y = ev.offsetY;
}
// Call the event handler
var func = brush[ev.type];
if (func) {
  func(ev);
}
}
}
init();
}, false); }
function newcolor(color) {
document.getElementById('colorchoice').innerHTML=color;
}
</script>
</body>
</html>
```

Figure 4-6 shows a picture drawn on the tablet.

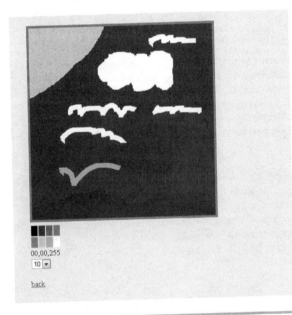

Figure 4-6 A work of art

Summary

The canvas is a powerhouse of technical prowess and creative possibilities. This chapter built on the introduction of the canvas in the previous chapter, showing how to use animation and events. The canvas is capable of much more. A thorough coverage of the canvas would take up an entire book.

I encourage you to find out more about the canvas on the Internet, look at what others have done (some of which is amazing), and also consider ramping up both your JavaScript and math skills. Yes, math—in particular, geometry and trigonometry. I can almost hear the groans from some readers. The reason for this suggestion is that much animation is achieved with the use of sine waves and other items associated with trigonometry, and knowing coordinates, angles, radius, radians, and more of these geometry-based items helps when working with arcs and lines.

Chapter 5

Getting Visual with Video

Movies, web shows, video clips, and more—watching video is ubiquitous Web-wise. With YouTube, Vimeo, Netflix, Hulu, and other video-centric web sites, watching the Web has become as much an activity as exploring the Web or interacting with web sites and applications. There is so much video out there! Video is now a staple of the Web and will be until the day we can just implant the video clips in our brain cells.

However, to watch videos from the popular sites that serve them, there is overhead to manage, such as an account, uploading your own video, making decisions about the audience, and so forth. Also, you need to make a choice between having links back to the videos or embedding the code in your pages, which still means the video is coming from that "other" site. Now the game gets leveled.

HTML5 has a native video element. Since it's a core HTML element, you can treat it with CSS, JavaScript, and whatever tricks you have up your sleeve. Add to this that the video file itself can sit on your web server, which should give a performance boost when the page showing the video is physically in the same place.

In this chapter, you will learn how to use the video element. It's tag-based (`<video>`... `</video>`) like other elements.

Although the video element is a core piece of HTML at this point, that doesn't mean you can avoid browser considerations. This is because of the various formats that video can come in. Here, we focus on Ogg, MPEG-4, and WebM. As of this writing, these are the formats being used, based on the browser. We can hope that one format will be decided on by the browser creators, but for now, we live with incompatibilities. Luckily, though, there is an easy and neat trick to make it not matter, as you'll learn in this chapter.

NOTE

Internet Explorer is not mentioned or demonstrated in this chapter, as it does not support the video element yet. Internet Explorer 9, which is on its way to the marketplace at the time of this writing, will supposedly support the video element, with additional codecs installed.

Of Formats, Codecs, and Other Confusing Matters

A few years ago, if someone said "ogg" to me, I would have thought of eggnog. That's not so anymore. Ogg is a video format that supports video and audio. Theora and Vorbis are codecs that supply the capability for video and audio, respectively, to work in a browser that supports them. You could think of Ogg as a wrapper or container for Theora and/or Vorbis.

Codec (compression/decompression) technology is used to streamline, or stream media for use on the Web (the point mainly to be making files smaller; media files can get quite large). Currently, two codec wrappers have garnered popularity for showing video on the Web: H.264 and the aforementioned Ogg. H.264 is also known as MPEG-4. This format is synonymous with Apple products. For example, the Safari browser will play MPEG-4 videos on a computer, and also on an iPhone or iPad. There is a caveat though. H.264 has patent protection, making it an iffy proposition to have it become a standard across all browsers. So, the other browsers adopted Ogg, since it is open source and free to use without cost.

TIP

Ogg is maintained by the Xiph.Org Foundation (xiph.org). Much can be learned at this site. Of note is the decision for video files (Theora) to have the .ogv file extension and audio files to have the .oga extension.

The videos you create with your videocam, camera, webcam, or other device might not be saved in either of the formats (for example, I have a videocam that creates .mov files). So they need to be converted to MPEG-4 and/or Ogg in order to work in a browser. The support of these formats among browsers is spotty, so yet another format—WebM—is making inroads as the possible standard that the browser companies will agree on. To summarize, the following formats are available at the time of this writing:

- Theora (Ogg)

- MPEG-4 (H.264)

- WebM

If I were to supply a matrix here of which browser supports which technology, it would probably be old news by the time this book reaches your hands. Luckily, there is a way out of this mess. When coding a page to play video through the HTML5 video element, you can place a succession of source files for the video element to use. This is known as *fallback*. If the first format doesn't work, the video element will attempt to play the next one. You'll see how this works in the examples presented in this chapter.

Reformatting Files

The first step on the road to video use is to convert your native video files into the formats that are supported. Many converters are available. I will mention the ones I use. You can follow how these work or find your own.

The Firefox browser has a great plug-in/extension available called Firefogg, used for converting files to Ogg. To get Firefogg, visit www.firefogg.org and follow the instructions for downloading and any required installation steps. Figure 5-1 shows the Firefogg site. Note that when I visit the site, the page recognizes that I already have Firefogg installed. On your first visit, you should see another version of the page that leads to the download. Be sure to visit the Firefogg site from the Firefox browser!

After Firefogg is installed, it is available on the Tools menu in Firefox, at least through version 3.*x*. (Otherwise, navigate to the Firefogg site, and you're ready to go.) Choosing Firefogg brings you back to the Firefogg site, but to a page where you select a file on your computer, as shown in Figure 5-2.

Click the Select File button, and you'll see a file finder dialog, as shown in Figure 5-3. In the figure, a target file has been found. If the print isn't too small, you might be able to see that the file is more than 16MB. By the way, the file being converted is a .mov video from my videocam.

Figure 5-1   Firefogg is downloaded.

Figure 5-2   Preparing to convert a file

After you choose a file, the next step is still on the Firefogg web site, as shown in Figure 5-4. A number of tabs appear, each containing settings to select. The top tab is open, and you make a selection from the drop-down list, which is to make a high-quality Ogg Theora/Vorbis file in this example. Note that selections to make WebM files are available here, too.

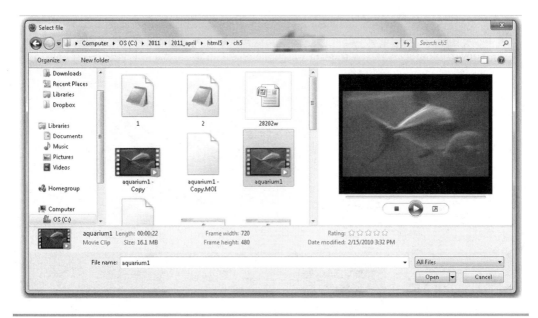

Figure 5-3   Selecting a file to convert

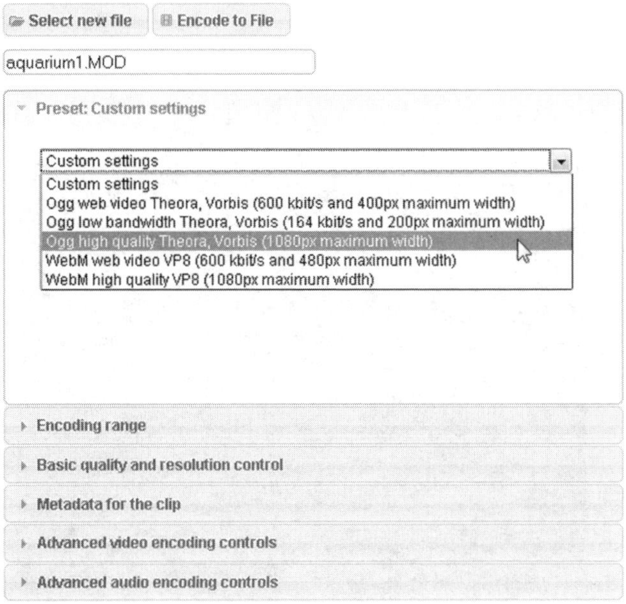

Figure 5-4   Selecting the format for the converted file

After you've made your conversion selection, click the Encode to File button. You'll see a dialog for selecting the location where the converted file will go on your computer. Then the conversion process starts. You can watch the progress, as shown in Figure 5-5. Figure 5-6 shows the completion of the conversion.

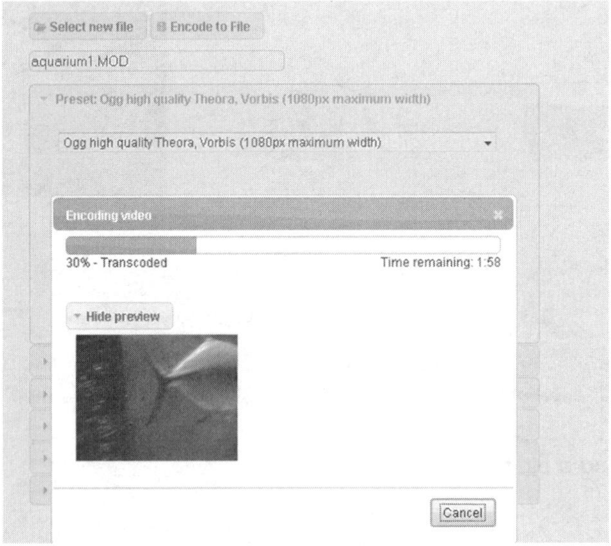

Figure 5-5 The file conversion in progress

Figure 5-6 The file conversion is complete.

The converted file is saved on the local computer, and you can send it via FTP to the web site space when needed. In the example, the conversion reduced the file size to a bit over 3MB. That may still seem substantial, but consider that the file will most likely be in the same location as the web page that displays it. The transmission time from the video file to the video element will effectively be seamless. The transmission to your browser may still be an issue; however, intelligent buffering in modern browsers handles this well.

Firefogg is also used to create a WebM version of the original video file. The steps are the same as those used to create the Ogg format file.

To convert the .mov file to MPEG-4, you need to use a converter other than Firefogg. You can find numerous converters via a search of the Web. Figure 5-7 shows a useful converter called the Total Video Converter, by OJOsoft (www.ojosoft.com).

After all this conversion work, you should now have three versions of the source video, in Ogg, WebM, and MPEG-4. As shown in Figure 5-8, the converted file sizes differ, but all are much smaller than the original 16MB.

TIP

The reduction of converted file sizes also depends on the quality you selected (high, low, or web quality).

A final word on formats, file types, and codecs: You'll find a confusing mess of competing technologies, as well as inconsistencies from browser to browser. An issue that comes into play is specifying the MIME type (for example, `type='video/ogg; codecs="theora, vorbis"'`). This is introduced in the upcoming examples.

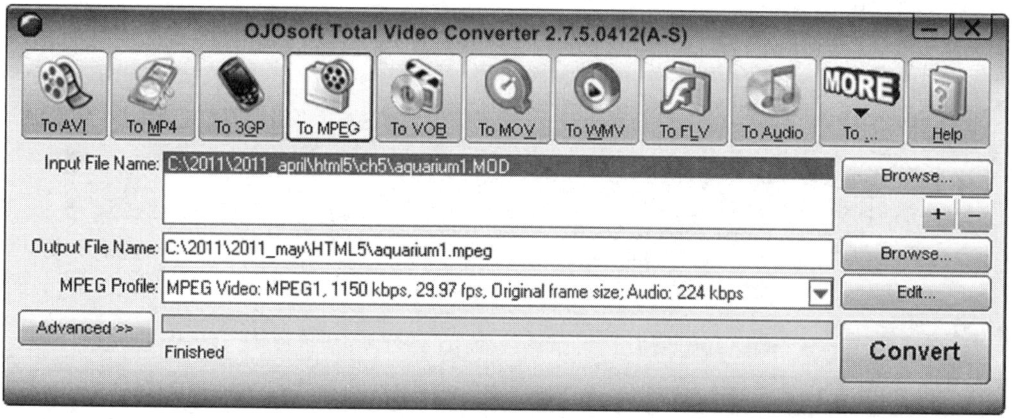

Figure 5-7   A video converter that can convert to MPEG-4

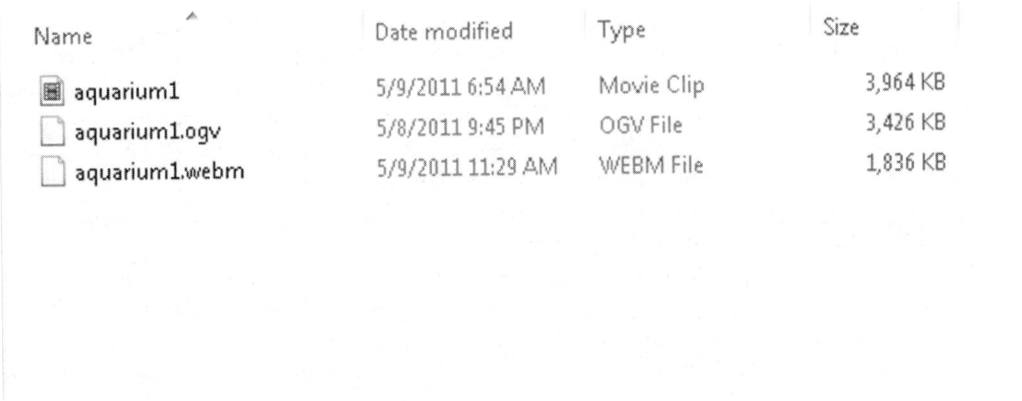

Name	Date modified	Type	Size
aquarium1	5/9/2011 6:54 AM	Movie Clip	3,964 KB
aquarium1.ogv	5/8/2011 9:45 PM	OGV File	3,426 KB
aquarium1.webm	5/9/2011 11:29 AM	WEBM File	1,836 KB

Figure 5-8   Three converted files, all smaller in file size than the original version

Watching Video!

Enough prep and theory—time for a video! Code Listing 5-1 shows the code for a page that contains three video elements. This is to point out the different formats supported, or not, in different browsers. Each of the video elements has the same video file as its source, but in a different format.

Code Listing 5-1   Using the video tag

```
<!doctype html>
<html lang="en">
<head>
<meta charset="utf-8">
<title>Video</title>
<style>
body { background-color:#eeeeee; }
#outer {margin-left:10px;
        margin-top:20px;
        }
</style>
</head>
<body>
<div id="outer">
<video controls width="200" height="150" loop>
    <source src="aquarium1.ogv">
</video>
<video controls width="200" height="150" loop>
    <source src="aquarium1.webm">
</video>
```

```
<video controls width="200" height="150" loop>
    <source src="aquarium1.mpeg">
</video>
</div>
</body>
</html>
```

Here is one of the video tags, a core piece of this code:

```
<video controls width="200" height="150" loop>
    <source src="aquarium1.ogv">
</video>
```

The video tag has an opening and closing pair of tags. Within these tags, you provide a source, which is the path to the video. The video can be located anywhere on the Internet. In this example, it is simply sitting in the same directory with the web page. As the file name indicates, this is the Ogg version (ending in the .ogv extension). In the opening tag are a few attributes. The `width` and `height` define the size of the video. The presence of `controls` indicates the video has a play/pause toggle and a volume control. The presence of `loop` indicates the video will repeat endlessly.

Figure 5-9 shows three browsers displaying the same page with the three video elements. Notice that Firefox displays the Ogg and WebM versions, and puts up a blank gray box where the MPEG-4 version goes. Conclusion: Firefox does not play MPEG-4 files. Google Chrome follows suit in displaying the first two file types. Safari, on the other hand, shows only the

Figure 5-9   Three browsers, three video file types. Top left is Firefox, bottom left is Google Chrome, and on the right is Safari.

MPEG-4 version. The vertical box above the middle video space must be some oddity of the browser giving it a shot to display the video, but not succeeding.

Falling Back

Code Listing 5-2 shows a rearrangement of Code Listing 5-1. In Code Listing 5-2, one video element is present, and within it are three lines indicating the source: one for each type. Now, if a browser cannot use the first format, it will try the second, and then the third, if necessary.

Code Listing 5-2   Arranging fallback in the video tag

```
<!doctype html>
<html lang="en">
<head>
<meta charset="utf-8">
<title>Video</title>
<style>
body { background-color:#eeeeee; }
#outer {margin-left:10px;
        margin-top:20px;
        }
</style>
</head>
<body>
<div id="outer">
<video controls width="300" height="200" loop>
    <source src="aquarium1.webm">
    <source src="aquarium1.mpeg">
    <source src="aquarium1.ogv">
</video>
</div>
</body>
</html>
```

Figure 5-10 shows the three browsers—Firefox, Google Chrome, and Safari, left to right—all displaying the video. Success!

TIP

It is likely necessary to indicate MIME types to get the videos to play from a web server.

MIME types are useful, and perhaps necessary to get the various configurations of videos to run. I use a Linux server running Apache, on which I am able to place an .htaccess file in the directory with the web pages and videos. In the .htaccess file, I have indicated some MIME types:

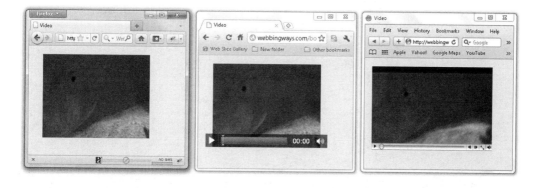

Figure 5-10   Three browsers, all able to play the video

```
AddType video/ogg .ogv
AddType video/webm .web
```

Web-hosting solutions differ, and you may not be able to create .htaccess files. The best advice I can give here is to research what you can do with your hosting company. (If .htaccess files are not something you are familiar with, you can find plenty of information about them on the Internet.)

An alternative is to provide the MIME types directly in the video tag, like this:

```
<source src="aquarium1.webm" type='video/webm; codecs="vp8, vorbis"' />
<source src=" aquarium1.ogv" type='video/ogg; codecs="theora, vorbis"' />
```

In the following examples, these `type` statements are left out, as my hosting solution allows me to create .htaccess files. You will need to figure out the best solution for configuring the MIME types to run video.

Video Controls

In its simplest form, a video tag is placed in the HTML source of a web page. Giving it a width and height is prudent (or perhaps using CSS to provide these properties). That is basically it for showing the video. However, adding the `controls` attribute provides a way for viewers to control the video, which is a good idea. Code Listing 5-3 shows an example. Looping has been removed, so when viewed, the video plays once.

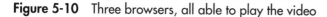

Code Listing 5-3   Controlling a video

```
<!doctype html>
<html lang="en">
<head>
<meta charset="utf-8">
<title>Video</title>
```

```
<style>
body { background-color:#eeeeee; }
#outer {
  margin-left:10px;
  margin-top:20px;
}
#myvideo {
  border-style:ridge;
  border-width:16px;
  border-color:#ffff00;
}
</style>
</head>
<body>
<div id="outer">
<video controls width="400" height="300">
    <source src="redbird.webm">
</video>
</div>
</body>
</html>
```

Figure 5-11 shows the video brought to life from the code in Code Listing 5-3. Styling—in particular a thick, yellow ridge type border—has been set around the video element. The styling is set in the head section of the page's HTML code.

Figure 5-11 Adding controls for watching a video

More Video Attributes

The video tag has a few more attributes that allow flexibility in presenting video. First up is autoplay. When a web page with a video is presented, it doesn't start playing unless specifically told to do so. You could just let the user click the play button, or you can have the autoplay feature start the video. In practical terms, this can be annoying if the people visiting the web page are not in control after the video starts. Common sense dictates including the controls attribute so they can stop the video once it has autostarted. The following shows the autoplay attribute added to the video tag from Code Listing 5-3:

```
<video controls autoplay width="400" height="300">
    <source src="redbird.webm">
</video>
```

As noted earlier in the chapter, loop is the attribute that keeps the video chugging along; that is, the video will repeat, ad infinitum, until stopped (or if you navigate away from the page). This snippet is taken from Code Listing 5-2, with loop at the end of the opening video tag:

```
<video controls width="300" height="200" loop>
```

As pointed out with autoplay, do your viewers a favor and also provide the controls attribute, so they can stop the video.

The poster attribute is used to display a still image until the video starts playing. The poster is not necessary. If it's not used, the first frame of the video is displayed. The catch is that the first frame may not be something desirable to have in view as a still image. For example, the first frame may be just a blur if the camera was in motion when shooting the video. Using a poster allows you to override the first frame and put something useful or desirable in its place. Code Listing 5-4 shows the poster attribute in use. In the video tag, the poster is set to an image—in this case, a .jpg.

Code Listing 5-4   Using the poster attribute

```
<!doctype html>
<html lang="en">
<head>
<meta charset="utf-8">
<title>Video</title>
<style>
body { background-color:#eeeeee; }
#outer {margin-left:10px;
        margin-top:20px;
        }
```

```
</style>
</head>
<body>
<div id="outer">
<video controls poster="greetings.jpg" width="400" height="300">
    <source src="redbird.webm">
</video>
</div>
</body>
</html>
```

Since `autoplay` is not used, the `poster` attribute displays the image (greetings.jpg), as shown in Figure 5-12.

Events and Video

The video element is useful in many ways. As a native HTML element, it can be formatted. It's easily recognizable by JavaScript, and therefore can take advantage of events. Code Listing 5-5 shows how to do this. The video element is given an identifer (`myvideo`), and two events are added to the tag: a click event and a double-click event. The click event starts the video, and the double-click pauses it (or consider that "pausing" stops the video).

Figure 5-12 Using a poster image

Code Listing 5-5   Using events with video

```
<!doctype html>
<html lang="en">
<head>
<meta charset="utf-8">
<title>Video</title>
<style>
body { background-color:#eeeeee; }
#outer {margin-left:10px;
        margin-top:20px;
        }
</style>
</head>
<body>
<p>Click the video to play, double click to pause the video.</p>
<div id="outer">
<video id="myvideo" controls  width="400" height="300" onclick="playme
()"ondblclick="stopme()">
    <source src="redbird.webm">
</video>
</div>
<br><br>
<script>
function playme() {
 var vid=document.getElementById("myvideo");
 vid.play();
}
function stopme() {
 var vid=document.getElementById("myvideo");
 vid.pause();
}
</script>
</body>
</html>
```

Simply, the onclick event calls the playme function, in which the play method is used. The ondblclick event calls the stopme function, in which the pause method is used.

Summary

Video on web sites was once a dream for many, but reality would have it that bandwidth, file sizes, and other problematic issues made having video an iffy proposition. Over time, however, high-speed connectivity became the norm for nearly all. Then sites such as YouTube showed what creativity and impact video can have as a feature offered on your web pages.

Now, with the native HTML5 video element, an extra step is achieved in that not only can you display video, but you can do so without any dependency on a third-party web service or even a third-party video player (such as a Flash player). In addition, since the native HTML5 video element is not Flash-based, it will play anywhere, on any device.

As seen in this chapter, with the use of video controls, CSS styling, and JavaScript interaction, the possibilities are nearly endless. Video display is now fully in the hands of the web site owner/developer and able to blend into any design. In the next chapter, the audio equivalent is explored.

Part III

Advanced HTML5 Features

Chapter 6

Audio the HTML5 Way

Audio on a web page can serve a number of needs: music, lectures, webcasts, and even just sound effects for some spookier or odd web sites (it's all in the ambience).

The audio element in HTML5 is very much like the video tag, except for the obvious difference of no visuals. It is a native element, eliminating the need for a third-party player. Like the video element, the audio element can be styled with CSS (although if it is so altered as to not be recognizable as an audio player, up comes a red flag of bad design).

Another approach you can take is to not show the audio player at all! The audio element can be on a web page, but made invisible, as will be demonstrated in this chapter. Why might you want to do this? Some web site owners desire to have a type of audio, usually background music, play while viewing the page. (This is not necessarily the best choice—some people get annoyed.)

As of this writing, three audio formats are supported: Ogg (Vorbis), MP3, and WAV. Not all browsers play these file types; however, you can use the fallback technique introduced in the previous chapter so at least one version will be played.

Introducing the Audio Element

The audio element is tag-based (`<audio>...</audio>`). Figure 6-1 shows three audio players on one page. Each has a different look (thanks to CSS), and each is set to play a different format of the same piece of music.

Code Listing 6-1 shows the three instances of the audio element used to create the players shown in the figure, with corresponding CSS in the head section of the page.

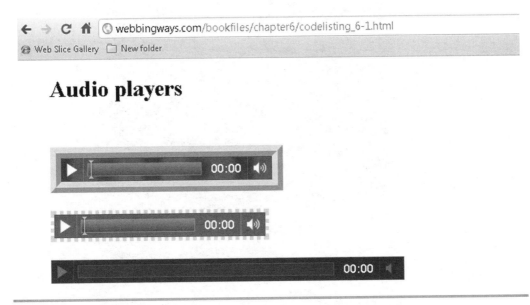

Figure 6-1 Styled audio players

Code Listing 6-1   Using the audio tag

```html
<!doctype html>
<html lang="en">
<head>
<meta charset="utf-8">
<title>Audio</title>
<style>
#audio1 {border-style:ridge;
         border-color:#c3eefd;
         border-width:15px;
         background: url(gradient1.jpg);
  }
#audio2 {border-style:dotted;
         border-color:#00ff00;
         border-width:5px;
         width:300px;
  }
#audio3 {background-color:red;
         width:500px;
}
</style>
</head>
<body>
 <div style="margin-left:40px;">
  <h1>Audio players</h1>
  <br><br>
  <audio controls id="audio1" src="song1.ogg">
    Your browser does not support the audio tag
  </audio>
  <br><br>
  <audio controls id="audio2" src="song1.mp3">
    Your browser does not support the audio tag
  </audio>
  <br><br>
  <audio controls id="audio3" src="song1.wav">
    Your browser does not support the audio tag
  </audio>
 </div>
</body>
</html>
```

Note that the three audio elements in this example contain the same song (song1), but with a different format type. Depending on the browser, a page could display all three audio elements, or just one or two.

As shown in the previous chapter on the video element, the audio element can be structured to provide fallback; that is, the different format types are listed one after the other inside the opening and closing tags. If a browser can't render the first type, it will try the second, and so on. Code Listing 6-2 demonstrates this approach.

Code Listing 6-2   Using fallback in the audio element

```
<!doctype html>
<html lang="en">
<head>
<meta charset="utf-8">
<title>Audio</title>
<style>
#audio1 {border-style:ridge;
         border-color:#c3eefd;
         border-width:15px;
         background: url(gradient1.jpg);
  }
</style>
</head>
<body>
 <div style="margin-left:40px;">
  <h1>Audio players</h1>
  <br><br>
  <audio controls id="audio1">
  <source src="song1.ogg" type="audio/ogg" />
  <source src="song1.oga" type="audio/ogg" />
  <source src="song1.mp3" type="audio/mpeg" />
  <source src="song1.wav" type="audio/wav" />
 Your browser does not support the audio element
  </audio>
  <br><br>
</div>
</body>
</html>
```

You might notice something peculiar in Code Listing 6-2. I have listed the Ogg version of the song twice: once with the .ogg extension and once with the .oga extension. Testing has shown some confusion (for want of a better word) on the part of some browsers on how to interpret the audio part (Vorbis) of the Ogg format. So to be on the safe side, I include both:

```
<source src="song1.ogg" type="audio/ogg" />
<source src="song1.oga" type="audio/ogg" />
```

♪ song1.mp3	587 KB	...	May 10 20:25
song1.oga	280 KB	...	May 10 20:25
⊞ song1.ogg	280 KB	...	May 10 21:03
♪ song1.wav	5,625 KB	...	May 10 20:25

Figure 6-2   Providing two variations of the Ogg audio

This means that two copies—one for each file extension—should be in the directory that the song is sourced from, as shown in Figure 6-2.

NOTE

You can specify multiple file types for the fallback, but be sure all that are referenced are placed in the directory that the web page looks in for the source.

Also notice that both Code Listings 6-1 and 6-2 use the audio tag's `controls` attribute, which displays play/pause and volume controls, as shown in Figure 6-3. Additionally, like the video element, the audio element has the `autoplay` and `loop` attributes.

Look Ma, No Audio Player!

When you don't include the `controls` attribute, the audio player does not appear. The user cannot use the standard controls to start playing the audio. However, there is a way to play audio with no apparent player. All that is needed is a way to get the audio started. In the example in Code Listing 6-3, I have put such a method in place by using the load event.

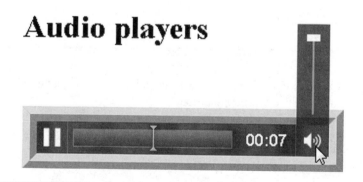

Figure 6-3   Providing controls to stop and start the audio

Code Listing 6-3   An audio player without a controls attribute

```html
<!doctype html>
<html lang="en">
<head>
<meta charset="utf-8">
<title>Audio</title>
<style>
#audio1 {border-style:ridge;
         border-color:#c3eefd;
         border-width:15px;
         background: url(gradient1.jpg);
   }
</style>
<script>
function playmusic() {
 document.getElementById("audio1").play();
}
</script>
</head>
<body onload="playmusic();">
<div style="margin-left:40px;">
  <h1> Music Plays without any Visible Player</h1>
  <br><br>
  <audio id="audio1">
  <source src="song1.ogg" type="audio/ogg" />
  <source src="song1.oga" type="audio/ogg" />
  <source src="song1.mp3" type="audio/mpeg" />
  <source src="song1.wav" type="audio/wav" />
Your browser does not support the audio element
  </audio>
  <br><br>
</div>
</body>
</html>
```

Of note in Code Listing 6-3 are the load event and the function that is called (and, of course, the removal of the `controls` attribute):

```html
<script>
function playmusic() {
 document.getElementById("audio1").play();
}
</script>
</head>
<body onload="playmusic();">
```

Upon the page load, the `playmusic()` function is called, and within the function, the audio element is given the `.play()` method. When you open this page in your browser, the audio plays. It's simple.

Events and Audio

As with the video tag, numerous events can be fired with the audio tag. Many are the standard set, such as click, mouse move, and focus. Some are unique to the audio element, including play, pause, volume change, and ended, to name a few.

Using Audio Events

As an example, Code Listing 6-4 shows the source for a page that uses the play, pause, and ended events. When the page loads, an image (musicstaff.jgp) is given an identifier of `musicstaff`. The image is set to be not visible (`.visibility="hidden"`). Once the player is started, the play event fires, calling a JavaScript function that makes the image visible. If the player is paused, the pause event fires, calling another JavaScript function that toggles the image visibility back to hidden. Finally when the song ends, the ended event fires and displays a "Thanks for listening" message. The message appears from the `innerHTML` property of a div being given the message to display.

Code Listing 6-4   Using audio element events

```
<!doctype html>
<html lang="en">
<head>
<meta charset="utf-8">
<title>Audio</title>
<style>
#audio1 {border-style:ridge;
         border-color:#c3eefd;
         border-width:15px;
         background: url(gradient1.jpg);
    }
</style>
<script>
function showpicture() {
 document.getElementById("musicstaff").style.visibility="visible";
}
function hidepicture() {
 document.getElementById("musicstaff").style.visibility="hidden";
 }
function thanks() {
 document.getElementById("thanks").innerHTML=
    "<h2>Thanks for listening!</h2>";
 }
```

```
</script>
</head>
<body>
 <div style="margin-left:40px;">
  <h1>Music Play with Events</h1>
  <br>
<div id="thanks"></div>
<br>
  <audio controls id="audio1" onplay="showpicture()"
    onpause="hidepicture()" onended="thanks()">
  <source src="song1.ogg" type="audio/ogg" />
  <source src="song1.oga" type="audio/ogg" />
  <source src="song1.mp3" type="audio/mpeg" />
  <source src="song1.wav" type="audio/wav" />
Your browser does not support the audio element
  </audio>
  <br><br>
  <img id="musicstaff" src="musicstaff.jpg" style="visibility:hidden;">
 </div>
</body>
</html>
```

Let's see this in action. Figure 6-4 shows the page when it is first rendered in the browser. The audio element is visible and not yet clicked to start playing. So, all you see is the player.

When the play control is clicked, the music staff appears, as shown in Figure 6-5.

If the song is paused by clicking the pause button, the image reverts to no visibility. When pause is released, and play resumes, the image appears again. This toggling will occur as often as the play and pause controls are toggled. Finally, when the song ends, a message appears, as shown in Figure 6-6.

Music Play with Events

Figure 6-4 The page starts with the idle player.

Figure 6-5   When the play control is clicked, music plays and an image is shown.

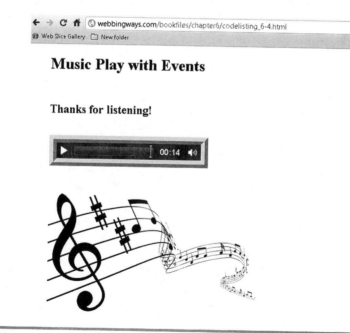

Figure 6-6   The "thank you" message appears when the song is finished playing.

Using Other Events with Audio

The audio element is a key new feature of HTML5, as it makes third-party players unnecessary. A subjective goal in development is to keep code consistent. The third-party solutions typically require embedding some code, referencing something external to the site, or a plug-in of some type, typically Flash Player. This is not bad per se, however, having a native audio player allows bypassing any of the overhead.

A popular aspect of third-party players has been leveraging the visual aspect of the player. This might be enough reason for some web developers to want to wait for broader support of the new core audio element until perhaps it can be styled to the hilt the way a Flash creation can be designed. But there is another alternative.

As you saw in this chapter's example, it's possible to have the player not appear at all by removing the controls attribute. With some planning and creative ingenuity, you could keep the player invisible, and control the audio play and pause using events attached to another item on the screen. Code Listing 6-5 provides such a scenario. The music staff image used in the previous example is now always visible. It has been given JavaScript functions attached to its click and double-click events. Click the music staff, and the song plays. Double-click the music staff, and the song pauses. No audio player appears, and yet audio is fully functional.

Code Listing 6-5   Using the audio element through events attached to other page items

```
<!doctype html>
<html lang="en">
<head>
<meta charset="utf-8">
<title>Audio</title>
<style>
#audio1 {border-style:ridge;
        border-color:#c3eefd;
        border-width:15px;
        background: url(gradient1.jpg);
    }
</style>
<script>
function playmusic() {
  document.getElementById("audio1").play();
}
function pausemusic() {
  document.getElementById("audio1").pause();
  }
</script>
</head>
<body>
 <div style="margin-left:40px;">
  <h1>Music Play with Events</h1>
```

```
<br>
<h2>Click the music staff to start the song playing</h2>
<h2>Double click the music staff to pause playing</h2>
<br>
<audio id="audio1">
<source src="song1.ogg" type="audio/ogg" />
<source src="song1.oga" type="audio/ogg" />
<source src="song1.mp3" type="audio/mpeg" />
<source src="song1.wav" type="audio/wav" />
Your browser does not support the audio element
</audio>
<br><br>
<img id="musicstaff" src="musicstaff.jpg" onclick="playmusic()"
ondblclick="pausemusic()" >
</div>
</body>
</html>
```

With a visual element as a clue (the music staff), a person might click it for no other reason than it's there. Perhaps an image such as a single music note will become known as the way to start playing music on a page. That would be neat!

Summary

Audio has many uses in a web presentation strategy. A lot of information can be given to visitors when all they have to do is listen. We tend to think of music as the main purpose of audio, but the spoken word is just as relevant. Certainly a recording of a company's president talking up a new product, or a specialist in a given field (such as a veterinarian) talking a web site visitor through a sequence of steps (such as diagnosing why your dog is not eating), provides useful and pertinent information.

In this chapter we explored how to make audio happen with the native HTML5 audio element. Some codec and format issues are taken into consideration to handle the various browsers. CSS and the use of events make it possible to greatly control how the audio element appears and acts.

With the knowledge gained in the previous chapter on video and this chapter on audio, you have at your disposal the tools to add much impact on your web pages. Audio and video will continue to gain more and more "real estate" on web sites. Having a strategy to use these tools will bring new traffic and repeat visitors. And isn't that the whole point?

Chapter 7

Be Persistent with Local Storage

I t is rare to have nary a need to store some information. No matter where you look, you might be asked to provide information, such as your name to join some service. Or you may be initiating retrieving some already stored information, such as looking up movies in your neighborhood by providing a ZIP code or city name. These uses involve a server and a database of some sort, which could be a standard SQL-based database such as MySQL or SQL Server, a text file, an XML file, and so forth. The point is that the data is stored in some traditional repository.

Along comes HTML5 and a new way to store information—without a database. In fact, you can even work without being hooked up to the Internet. The examples in this chapter work whether the pages are coming from a web server or just from within your computer.

Local Storage Defined

The term *local storage* needs a definition here, as it could be misleading. Information is stored within the browser. The internal mechanics of how this is done are not relevant to the discussion. The browser handles the storage and retrieval functions through an API. Storage is "local" in the sense that it's essentially within the browser. However, this does not mean you need to work offline, just that you can.

The local storage concept is really one of persistent storage. This means information is maintained even after the browser session ends. You can navigate away from a web page or close the browser. If you saved data using the storage methods you'll learn about in this chapter, then the data is retrievable. The next time you return to the web page, the data is there!

In the past, the methods for maintaining persistent information have been either through cookies or by keeping the information in a database on the server. Cookies have served us well for the most part, but have also been problematic. For example, a browser can be set to reject cookies. Cookies often need to have an expiration date set with them. (Without setting a date, cookies expire when the current browser session ends; they are gone when the browser is closed.) That makes the data they hold persistent, but how long should they last? Cookies are useful for holding small amounts of information, but nothing substantial.

NOTE
In case you're not familiar with cookies, it's not about the chocolate chip or oatmeal types. Cookies are small text files placed on a local computer, in a dedicated place, through the browser. They contain some information, such as a person's name or a value last used. Typically, they hold only a small amount of information.

Saving data on the server is great. There is plenty of memory, and you can fill it up as needed. Server-based databases may easily hold megabytes of data. The catch with using a database on the server is the need for using a server-side language (such as ASP.NET or PHP) for working with the database.

Now, let's look at an example of using the local storage functions. Later, you'll see how to apply this technique to multimedia usage.

Basic Local Storage

Figure 7-1 shows a web page in which users enter a list of to-do tasks. The entry boxes are standard form-based text boxes (although no form is used, since no submitting is done). The user types each task into a box and clicks the Save Task button.

When the user closes the browser and then reopens it to the same page, the boxes are empty. Clicking a Get Task button will fill in the entry box with the original entry. Figure 7-2 shows how the first task has been retrieved.

The storage is handled via a key/value relationship. This is a common configurable approach to storing values. In fact, think of a basic algebra expression: A=5. The value, 5, is assigned to the variable A. So far, just a numeric value is in play. Now consider the variable A equaling something other than a number; for example, A=Wash the dishes. This is how key/value pairs work. In the example, A is the key, and "Wash the dishes" is the value.

Here is a good place to show the code of the to-do task page (see Code Listing 7-1). Following it is an explanation of how the key/value pairing works using local storage.

Code Listing 7-1　　A basic example of local storage

```
<!doctype html>
<html lang="en">
<head>
<meta charset="utf-8">
<title>Local Storage</title>
```

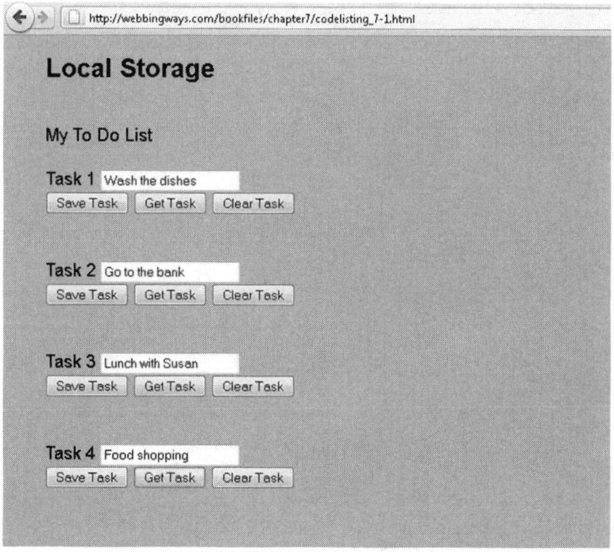

Figure 7-1　Setting up to use local storage

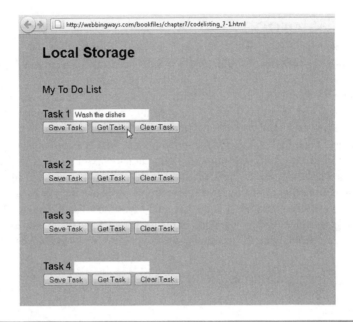

Figure 7-2 Retrieving a stored data value

```
<style>
  body {
    background-color:silver;
    font-family:arial, helvetica; sans-serif;
    font-size:1.2em;
  }
  h1 {
    font-family:arial, helvetica; sans-serif;
    font-size:1.4em;
  }
</style>
<script>
function storetask(task) {
   var taskdetail = document.getElementById(task).value;
     localStorage.setItem(task, taskdetail);
}
function gettask(task) {
   document.getElementById(task).value=localStorage.getItem(task);
}
function cleartask(task) {
       localStorage.removeItem(task);
       document.getElementById(task).value = "";
}
</script>
```

```
</head>
<body>
<div id="outer">
<h1>Local Storage</h1>
<br>
My To Do List
<br><br>
Task 1 <input id="task1" type="text"><br>
    <input type="button" value="Save Task"
      onclick="storetask('task1');">
    <input type="button" value="Get Task"
      onclick="gettask('task1');">
    <input type="button" value="Clear Task"
      onclick="cleartask('task1');">
<br><br><br>
 Task 2 <input id="task2" type="text"><br>
    <input type="button" value="Save Task"
      onclick="storetask('task2');">
    <input type="button" value="Get Task"
      onclick="gettask('task2');">
    <input type="button" value="Clear Task"
      onclick="cleartask('task2');">
<br><br><br>
 Task 3 <input id="task3" type="text"><br>
    <input type="button" value="Save Task"
      onclick="storetask('task3');">
    <input type="button" value="Get Task"
      onclick="gettask('task3');">
    <input type="button" value="Clear Task"
      onclick="cleartask('task3');">
<br><br><br>
 Task 4 <input id="task4" type="text"><br>
    <input type="button" value="Save Task"
      onclick="storetask('task4');">
    <input type="button" value="Get Task"
      onclick="gettask('task4');">
    <input type="button" value="Clear Task"
      onclick="cleartask('task4');"></div>
</body>
</html>
```

Each of the buttons—Store Task, Get Task, and Clear Task—passes an argument to a JavaScript function. The three JavaScript functions `storetask`, `gettask`, and `cleartask` each handles a method of the storage API.

The `storetask` function takes the passed argument, which is the name of the text box (used as the name of the key), and associates it with the entered value (`value`), as shown next.

```
function storetask(task) {
   var taskdetail = document.getElementById(task).value;
      localStorage.setItem(task, taskdetail);
}
```

In the function, the variable `taskdetail` is assigned the entered value. Then the `setItem` method of the `localStorage` object sets the association. This function is reusable and able to work with each of the entries.

The `gettask` function essentially reverses the `storetask` function. It calls back the stored value and places it in the text box:

```
function gettask(task) {
   document.getElementById(task).value=localStorage.getItem(task);
}
```

The code is a single line that targets the text box (using `document.getElementById`) and setting its value to the stored value, by calling the `getItem` method. This method is given the name of the `key`, and the returned value is `value`.

When a web page is reopened, the `gettask` function pulls the value out of the browser. This is an important point. The browser retained the value, even though the browser was closed. Clearly, it stored the value somewhere, and that somewhere is on your local computer. Where on your computer that happens to be is left to how the browser manipulates its storage methods. You can ignore how the browser handles the storage and just depend on the browser to return values using the provided method.

Finally, there is a method to delete a stored value. The `removeItem` method of the `localStorage` object takes the passed argument (the name of a key), and internally deletes it. As this is accomplished, the text box displaying the value is set to be empty as well. This second action is not part of the storage facility, but rather just good programming practice.

```
function cleartask(task) {
        localStorage.removeItem(task);
        document.getElementById(task).value = "";
}
```

Here is a summary of the three methods and their syntax:

- `localStorage.setItem(key name, value)` assigns the value to the key.

- `localStorage.getItem(key name)` returns the value assigned to the key.

- `localStorage.removeItem(key name)` deletes the key, along with the assigned value.

Now that we're reviewed the basics, it's time to focus on media manipulation.

Getting Visual

In a project I worked on, I needed to arrange four images into a single collage. The best arrangement of the four images was trial and error. I used an art program to move the images around, and then uploaded the assembled larger image to the server. This tedious work spurred the inspiration for the next demonstration. Using the local storage methods makes the task of arranging images easier.

The example in this section uses four images: an apple, a banana, a strawberry, and a watermelon. Each image is 75 × 75 pixels. Put together as two rows and two columns, the assemblage is a 150 × 150 pixel graphic. Moving the four components around is easy using absolute-positioned divs and assigning a particular fruit graphic to each div. To be clear, none of this has anything to do with local storage, yet. The key point of local storage is that it allows you to make an arrangement of the fruit images, and come back to that arrangement at a later time to continue working where you left off. In other words, the association of divs with the graphic assigned to each is remembered. Seeing it will make it clear. Figure 7-3 shows the layout of fruit images.

As shown in Figure 7-3, the fruit is arranged by selecting from drop-downs. Each drop-down controls which fruit graphic is placed in one of the divs. No matter how you play around with arranging the graphics, the arrangement is stored and appears the way it was left when the browser was closed (or the page was navigated away from).

Code Listing 7-2 shows the code that makes the page and controls the graphics and storage. A discussion of pertinent points follows the listing.

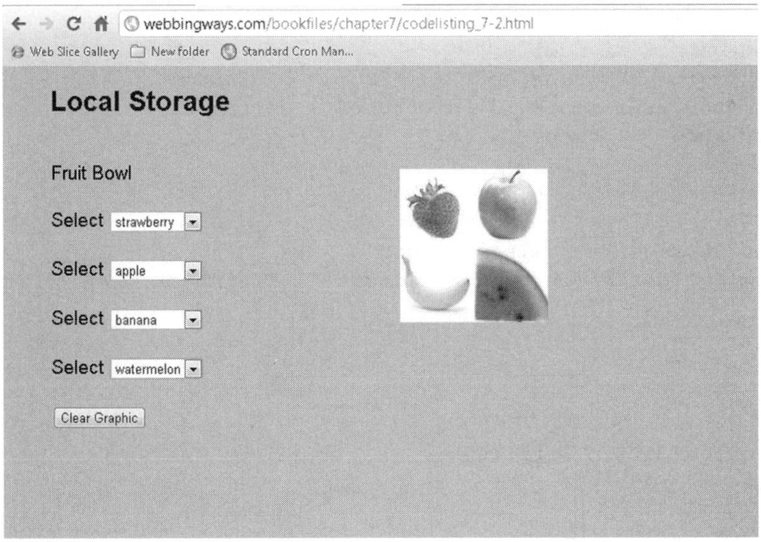

Figure 7-3 Arranged graphics for storage

Code Listing 7-2   Storing and retrieving an arrangement of graphics

```html
<!doctype html>
<html lang="en">
<head>
<meta charset="utf-8">
<title>Local Storage</title>
<style>
 body {
   background-color:silver;
   font-family:arial, helvetica, sans-serif;
   font-size:1.2em;
     }
 h1 { font-family:arial, helvetica, sans-serif;font-size:1.4em;}
 #divfruit1 { position:absolute;left:400px;top:100px; }
 #divfruit2 { position:absolute;left:475px;top:100px; }
 #divfruit3 { position:absolute;left:400px;top:175px; }
 #divfruit4 { position:absolute;left:475px;top:175px; }
</style>
<script>
function storepix(pix,divnum) {
  var pixdetail = document.getElementById(pix).value;
  localStorage.setItem(pix, pixdetail);
  document.getElementById("divfruit" + divnum).innerHTML=
    '<img src="' + pixdetail + '">';
}
function getpix(divnum) {
var thepix=localStorage.getItem("fruit" + divnum);
   document.getElementById("divfruit" + divnum).innerHTML=
    '<img src="' + thepix + '">';
}
function clearpix() {
  for (i=1;1<=4;i++) {
    localStorage.removeItem('fruit' + i);
    document.getElementById('divfruit' + i).innerHTML="";
  }
}
</script>
</head>
<body>
 <div style="margin-left:40px;">
<h1>Local Storage</h1>
<br>
Fruit Bowl
<br><br>
Select <select id="fruit1" onchange="storepix('fruit1',1);">
  <option value="apple.jpg" selected="selected">apple</option>
```

```
  <option value="banana.jpg">banana</option>
  <option value="strawberry.jpg">strawberry</option>
  <option value="watermelon.jpg">watermelon</option>
</select>
<br><br>
Select <select id="fruit2" onchange="storepix('fruit2',2);">
  <option value="apple.jpg">apple</option>
  <option value="banana.jpg" selected="selected">banana</option>
  <option value="strawberry.jpg">strawberry</option>
  <option value="watermelon.jpg">watermelon</option>
</select>
<br><br>
Select <select id="fruit3" onchange="storepix('fruit3',3);">
  <option value="apple.jpg">apple</option>
  <option value="banana.jpg">banana</option>
  <option value="strawberry.jpg" selected="selected">strawberry</option>
  <option value="watermelon.jpg">watermelon</option>
</select>
<br><br>
Select <select id="fruit4" onchange="storepix('fruit4',4);">
  <option value="apple.jpg">apple</option>
  <option value="banana.jpg">banana</option>
  <option value="strawberry.jpg">strawberry</option>
  <option value="watermelon.jpg" selected="selected">watermelon</option>
</select>
<br><br>
<input type="button" value="Clear Graphic" onclick="clearpix();">
<br><br>

div id="divfruit1"></div>
<div id="divfruit2"></div>
<div id="divfruit3"></div>
<div id="divfruit4"></div>
<script>
  //restore the arrangement of fruit graphics when the page opens
  //or display default images
  var fruit1=localStorage.getItem("fruit1");
  var fruit2=localStorage.getItem("fruit2");
  var fruit3=localStorage.getItem("fruit3");
  var fruit4=localStorage.getItem("fruit4");
if (fruit1==null) {
  document.getElementById("divfruit1").innerHTML=
    '<img src="apple.jpg">';
} else {
  document.getElementById("divfruit1").innerHTML=
    '<img src="' + fruit1 + '">';
}
```

```
if (fruit2==null) {
  document.getElementById("divfruit2").innerHTML=
    '<img src="banana.jpg">';
} else {
  document.getElementById("divfruit2").innerHTML=
    '<img src="' + fruit2 + '">';
}
if (fruit3==null) {
  document.getElementById("divfruit3").innerHTML=
    '<img src="strawberry.jpg">';
} else {
  document.getElementById("divfruit3").innerHTML=
    '<img src="' + fruit3 + '">';
}
if (fruit4==null) {
  document.getElementById("divfruit4").innerHTML=
    '<img src="watermelon.jpg">';
} else {
  document.getElementById("divfruit4").innerHTML=
    '<img src="' + fruit4 + '">';
}
</script>
</div>
</body>
</html>
```

The divs are set to absolute positions to ensure that the four graphics appear as one larger graphic. If you look at the `left` and `top` properties of the graphics, you can see how each one covers a quarter of the overall larger square. Each graphic is 75 × 75 pixels, so there is no need to set the width or height of the divs.

```
#divfruit1 { position:absolute;left:400px;top:100px; }
#divfruit2 { position:absolute;left:475px;top:100px; }
#divfruit3 { position:absolute;left:400px;top:175px; }
#divfruit4 { position:absolute;left:475px;top:175px; }
```

Each drop-down has an `onchange` event that calls the `storepix` function, sending it two arguments: the name of the drop-down itself and the div it is meant to alter. Actually, the second argument is just a number (1, 2, 3, or 4) that is concatenated with `divfruit` to match the name of the associated div. Next, `setItem` is used to create the key/value pair. The key name is the same as the drop-down (for convenience, not out of necessity), and the value is the name of the graphic file (such as apple.jpg). Finally, the selected graphic is placed in the div using the `innerHTML` property.

```
function storepix(pix,divnum) {
  var pixdetail = document.getElementById(pix).value;
```

```
localStorage.setItem(pix, pixdetail);
document.getElementById("divfruit" + divnum).innerHTML=
  '<img src="' + pixdetail + '">';
}
```

A default arrangement is used (apple, banana, strawberry, and watermelon) unless the graphics have been rearranged. When the page opens, JavaScript code runs to retrieve the stored values using the getItem method. The code is not in a function, and therefore runs whenever the page is rendered in the browser. This code snippet is placed toward the bottom of the overall page code so the divs are already rendered and in place before a graphic is placed in each.

So, the possibilities are that key/value pairs have been stored from previously using the page, it's the first time the page is being opened, or the Clear Graphic button was used.

If it is the first time the page is displayed, then the variables being assigned the stored values will be null. Each variable is tested to see if a stored value (the name of a file) was found. If one is found, that graphic is displayed. If a variable is null, a default is used; for example, apple.jpg is used if fruit1 is null.

```
  var fruit1=localStorage.getItem("fruit1");
  var fruit2=localStorage.getItem("fruit2");
  var fruit3=localStorage.getItem("fruit3");
  var fruit4=localStorage.getItem("fruit4");
if (fruit1==null) {
  document.getElementById("divfruit1").innerHTML=
    '<img src="apple.jpg">';
} else {
  document.getElementById("divfruit1").innerHTML=
    '<img src="' + fruit1 + '">';
}
```

Finally, the code contains a JavaScript function to delete the saved keys and remove the graphics when the user clicks the Clear Graphic button. The function clearpix uses a for loop to iterate over the four divs, using removeItem of the localStorage object to delete the key/value pair, and setting the innerHTML property of the div to be empty.

```
function clearpix() {
  for (i=1;1<=4;i++) {
    localStorage.removeItem('fruit' + i);
    document.getElementById('divfruit' + i).innerHTML="";
  }
}
```

The clearpix function is provided as a way to clear the combined graphic quickly, most likely to start over. In this case, with just four graphics, it doesn't add much value. However, if this example were expanded to work with a larger number of graphics and divs, this ability would be useful as a time-saver.

Summary

The capability to save information with the browser as the repository streamlines and simplifies the process of storage. It's streamlined in the sense that storage happens with no interaction with the web server and, likely, a remote database. This removes a bit of bandwidth usage—not much in most cases, but a bit here and a bit there adds up. Imagine a web site with hundreds of pages, each needing to store data for some function the site offers.

Stored values are accessible from other pages, as long as the same browser is used, and any other such pages use the getItem method with the same key name(s) used with the setItem method. In other words, values are stored from one page and retrieved from another page to be used for their intended purpose. A likely use of this approach is when form data is entered in more than one page. The values entered on each page are stored, and a final page in the entry process submits all of it to the server. However, between pages, the data is kept local until it is necessary to send it to the server at the last step. Why do this? To cut down on bandwidth. Big web sites need to save bandwidth and keep performance fast.

Subjectively, the best facet of local storage is working offline. When building a sophisticated web application, it is most often necessary to be online, with data going back and forth, to and from the web server (and probably the database). Local storage allows creating an application like this without being on the Internet—all the more reason to bring a laptop wherever you go!

Chapter

Drag-and-Drop: Moving Things Around the Screen

The drag-and-drop technology of HTML5 offers ways to take interesting ideas and make them real. For example, can you really put a square peg in a round hole? Probably so with drag-and-drop.

Drag-and-drop works by identifying two types of items: ones that can be dragged and ones that can accept something being dropped on them. A number of events are in play when dragging and dropping happens. Essentially, you provide an attribute to an item (a div, an image, and so on) that makes it draggable. Other elements are set to accept the drop. In other words, a draggable element is dragged to a drop-enabled element.

Along the way in this process are events for when the dragging starts, when the dragging ends, when the item is dropped, and so forth. All of this is possible with the inclusion of a new object called `dataTransfer`. Similar to the way the canvas and other HTML5 features have an API or set of methods, the `dataTransfer` object is the conduit to making use of the events used in drag-and-drop.

A number of HTML5 sources demonstrate how a box or two or three can be dragged and dropped into another box elsewhere on the screen. Yes, this introduces the technology, but does a demo like that show anything useful? I would like to present a more relevant and useful application of this functionality. In this chapter, I'll show you the basic drop a box into another, just to get your feet wet, and then continue with a couple more useful applications.

A Box in a Box

We'll begin with an example that's like "Hello World" for drag-and-drop. In the example, you click the mouse on the box on the left, drag it over to the box on the right, and then release the mouse button. The box that was on the left is now inside the box on the right. The box on the left has been set as draggable, and the box on the right has been set to accept a dropped object. Figure 8-1 shows

Figure 8-1 The boxes before drag-and-drop

webbingways.com/bookfiles/chapter8/codelisting_8_1.html

Web Slice Gallery   New folder

Drag and Drop Example

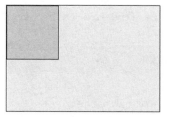

Figure 8-2   The boxes after drag-and-drop

the setup before the dragging has begun, and Figure 8-2 shows the smaller box inside the larger one after it was dropped into the larger box.

Code Listing 8-1 shows how the drag-and-drop is made operational. I phrase it this way since the code does not perform an active action—the user does. In the code, HTML elements are set as being draggable or accepting a drop.

Code Listing 8-1   A basic drag-and-drop example

```
<!doctype html>
<html lang="en">
<head>
<meta charset="utf-8">
<title>HTML5 Drag and Drop</title>
<style>
#dropoff {
position:absolute;
width:300px;
height:200px;
top:200px;
left:400px;
background-color:#ededed;
border-style:solid;
border-width:thin;
}
#box {
width:100px;
```

```
height:100px;
background-color:#00efef;
border-style:solid;
border-width:thin;
}
</style>
</head>
<body>
<h1>Drag and Drop Example</h1>
<div id="dropoff" ondrop="drop(this, event)"
   ondragenter="return false" ondragover="return false">
</div>
<div id="box" draggable="true" ondragstart="drag(this, event)"
   ondragend="return false">
</div>
<script>
function drag(drag_object, e) {
e.dataTransfer.dropEffect='move';
e.dataTransfer.effectAllowed='move';
e.dataTransfer.setData('Text', drag_object.id);
}
function drop(drop_target, e) {
var id = e.dataTransfer.getData('Text');
drop_target.appendChild(document.getElementById(id));
e.preventDefault();
}
</script>
</body>
</html>
```

The two boxes are div elements, positioned and styled with color and borders. Appropriately, one is named `dropoff` and the other is named `box`. Here is the CSS that positions and styles them:

```
<style>
#dropoff {
position:absolute;
width:300px;
height:200px;
top:200px;
left:400px;
background-color:#ededed;
border-style:solid;
border-width:thin;
}
#box {
width:100px;
```

```
height:100px;
background-color:#00efef;
border-style:solid;
border-width:thin;
}
</style>
```

The divs are given the appropriate attribute and events:

```
<div id="dropoff" ondrop="drop(this, event)"
   ondragenter="return false" ondragover="return false">
</div>
<div id="box" draggable="true" ondragstart="drag(this, event)"
   ondragend="return false">
</div>
```

The `dropoff` div has a drop event (`ondrop`), an event for when the dragged element enters the div (`ondragenter`), and an event that fires while the dragged element is over the div but not yet released (the mouse button is still being held down). Once the mouse is released, the drag-over event ends. In Code Listing 8-1, the drag-enter and drag-over events are simply set to `false`, as they are not used in the example.

The box div has the attribute `draggable` set to `true`. This attribute can be set to many other HTML elements, not just divs. The box div also has the drag-start and drag-end events. The drag-end event is also just set to `false` in this example.

So, the example uses just two events: the drop event and the drag-start event. Each of these calls a JavaScript function (`ondrop` calls `drop`, and `ondragstart` calls `drag`). The real action is in these functions. Well, not quite—as I pointed out, the actual action is (shudder) performed by one of us humans. Here are the two functions:

```
<script>
function drag(drag_object, e) {
e.dataTransfer.dropEffect='move';
e.dataTransfer.effectAllowed='move';
e.dataTransfer.setData('Text', drag_object.id);
}
function drop(drop_target, e) {
var id = e.dataTransfer.getData('Text');
drop_target.appendChild(document.getElementById(id));
e.preventDefault();
}
</script>
```

In the divs, the events send the functions two arguments: the element itself and the event itself. Both function calls are structured in the format *function-name*(this, event). These two arguments are necessary, and others can be included as well, as you'll see in an example later in this chapter.

The box div has the drag event, so let's look at that first. The event (e) connects to the dataTransfer element, which in turn sets a property. The first line in the drag function sets the effect (dropEffect) to be move. Other possible values are copy, link, and none. In practice (or until the browsers catch up), it seems move is the reliable usable action.

The second line is similar to the first. It defines the allowed effect (effectAllowed), which is also set as move. I must stop here a moment and point out how this is a confusing matter. What if the allowed effect is move, but the drop effect is copy? This is where the standardization and implementation in the browsers lose meaning for these properties. It seems at this point that these properties just move items around the screen. In fact, these first two lines can be left out!

```
function drag(drag_object, e) {
e.dataTransfer.dropEffect='move';
e.dataTransfer.effectAllowed='move';
e.dataTransfer.setData('Text', drag_object.id);
}
```

On the other hand, the setData property is needed. The first argument of setData is the format of the second argument. In this example, the second argument returns the identifier of the div, and the first argument indicates for it to be treated as text. In other words, the id of the div is text. Although it seems rather obvious, you must still include this.

NOTE
For other setData formats, there does not yet seem to be consistency in what they are or how they are implemented. However, 'Text' does work. A specification of the setData property simply states "Adds the specified data" (see http://dev .w3.org/html5/spec-author-view/dnd.html#datatransfer).

The drop function, called from the drop event, of the dropoff div, is easier to follow. A variable (id) is set to the identifer of the div of the box (the draggable object), and then the following line appends it as a Document Object Model (DOM) child element, which places it inside the bigger dropoff box.

```
function drop(drop_target, e) {
var id = e.dataTransfer.getData('Text');
drop_target.appendChild(document.getElementById(id));
e.preventDefault();
}
```

The e.preventDefault() statement effectively stops further JavaScript activity. Whether you need to have this statement in the code is questionable, since it is at the end of a function; the thought being that activity will end anyway. However, testing has shown that it is needed in at least FireFox (FireFox 7) to prevent the browser from trying to navigate to another web page named box. This is clearly buggy behavior and should not happen, but from another view, it does no harm to include the statement.

Adding Actions to Drag-and-Drop Events

The example presented in this section expands on the previous simple box-drop example. Here, two other divs—`secretdiv1` and `secretdiv2`—start as hidden, and then become visible when a given event is fired. When the drag-enter (`dragenter`) event is fired, `secretdiv1` is set to `visible`, and when the drop (`drop`) event is fired, `secretdiv2` is set to `visible`.

The web page initially looks the same as shown earlier in Figure 8-1. When the box is dragged to the point of entering the space of the bigger `dropoff` box, the drag-enter event fires, and `secretdiv1` appears. Figure 8-3 shows how this occurs at the point of the smaller box entering the bigger one.

The second hidden div remains unseen for as long as the mouse button is held down. Once the button is released, the drop event fires, and `secretdiv2` becomes visible, as shown in Figure 8-4.

Code Listing 8-2 shows how these events are used.

Code Listing 8-2   An enhanced drop-the-box example

```
<!doctype html>
<html lang="en">
<head>
<meta charset="utf-8">
<title>HTML5 Drag and Drop</title>
<style>
#dropoff {
position:absolute;
width:300px;
```

Figure 8-3 The drag-enter event is fired.

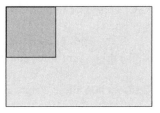

Drag and Drop Example

I appear when the small box enters the big box.

I appear when the small box is dropped.

Figure 8-4 The drop event is fired.

```
height:200px;
top:200px;
left:400px;
background-color:#ededed;
border-style:solid;
border-width:thin;
}
#box {
width:100px;
height:100px;
background-color:#00efef;
border-style:solid;
border-width:thin;
}
#secretdiv1 {
position:absolute;
width:600px;
height:100px;
top:100px;
left:200px;
font-size:1.6em;
visibility:hidden;
}
#secretdiv2 {
position:absolute;
width:600px;
height:100px;
top:150px;
```

```
left:200px;
font-size:1.6em;
visibility:hidden;
}
</style>
</head>
<body>
<h1>Drag and Drop Example</h1>
<div id="dropoff" ondrop="drop(this, event)"
   ondragenter="enter(event)" ondragover="return false">
</div>
<div id="box" draggable="true" ondragstart="drag(this, event)"
   ondragend="return false">
</div>
<div id="secretdiv1">I appear when the small box enters the big box.
</div>
<div id="secretdiv2">I appear when the small box is dropped.</div>
<script>
function drag(drag_object, e) {
e.dataTransfer.setData('Text', drag_object.id);
}
function drop(drop_target, e) {
var id = e.dataTransfer.getData('Text');
drop_target.appendChild(document.getElementById(id));
document.getElementById("secretdiv2").style.visibility="visible";
e.preventDefault();
}
function enter(e) {
document.getElementById("secretdiv1").style.visibility="visible";
return true;
}
</script>
</body>
</html>
```

The two new divs are found in the body of the web page:

```
<div id="secretdiv1">I appear when the small box enters the big box.
</div>
<div id="secretdiv2">I appear when the small box is dropped.</div>
```

Each of the divs is styled, including having visibility set to hidden. Therefore, when the page opens, they are not seen.

```
#secretdiv1 {
position:absolute;
width:600px;
```

```
height:100px;
top:100px;
left:200px;
font-size:1.6em;
visibility:hidden;
}
#secretdiv2 {
position:absolute;
width:600px;
height:100px;
top:150px;
left:200px;
font-size:1.6em;
visibility:hidden;
}
```

The dropoff div (the bigger box) now makes use of the enter event by calling a function named enter. The function is passed a single argument: the event.

```
<div id="dropoff" ondrop="drop(this, event)"
    ondragenter="enter(event)" ondragover="return false">
```

In the enter function, secretdiv1 is set to visible. Note that this style change is in JavaScript syntax, not CSS, but the result is the same.

```
function enter(e) {
document.getElementById("secretdiv1").style.visibility="visible";
return true;
}
```

Finally, the drop event has an extra line that sets secretdiv2 to visible.

```
function drop(drop_target, e) {
var id = e.dataTransfer.getData('Text');
drop_target.appendChild(document.getElementById(id));
document.getElementById("secretdiv2").style.visibility="visible";
e.preventDefault();
}
```

This example showed how events specific to drag-and-drop can do more than just handle the dragging and dropping. Making the two divs become visible serves as a demonstration of how the events can be used to make other actions occur. The rest of the chapter shows two real-life uses of drag-and-drop: a shopping cart application and a familiar game.

Online Shopping Made Easy

Typically, you make online purchases by adding items to a cart, and then checking out to pay. You fill the cart by clicking a button that has a caption like "Add to Cart" or something similar. The point is that you need to click a button to get the item into the cart. Granted, not all online shopping experiences follow this structure, but the majority do; it's the tried-and-true approach.

In such purchasing activities, if you decide to remove an item from the cart, it's typically done on a different web page, and the purchase amount is recalculated. The example in this section does not reinvent the wheel, but it does show an easier way of adding and removing items from a shopping cart. Perhaps when drag-and-drop technology is fully stable, this will be the acceptable way of using a cart.

Figure 8-5 shows several pieces of fruit: apples, bananas, and strawberries. In this visually simple example, the fruit is effectively on a shelf, although it's just a div styled with color. Below is a shopping cart. The page also includes a purchase price, which starts at 0.00.

Each piece of fruit has been made draggable, and the shopping cart is the drop area. The drop area is not quite the shopping cart itself, but rather an area within the cart, about the size of the basket part. So, when moving fruit into the cart, you cannot drop it onto the wheels or handle, for example.

As each fruit is dragged into the cart, the price is updated. Apples are 20 cents each, bananas are 25 cents, and strawberries are 45 cents. These are some extraordinary strawberries to be priced so high! It's all in the interest of showing how the example works. Figure 8-6 shows the cart filled with two apples, one banana, and one strawberry. The total price is $1.10.

The interior of the shopping cart is a drop-enabled area, and so is the shelf where the fruit is kept. Therefore, you can drag fruit out of the cart and drop it back onto the shelf. This action is the same as the typical "Remove from Cart" function in many e-commerce web sites. Common sense dictates that the price should be lowered by the cost of the items being dragged

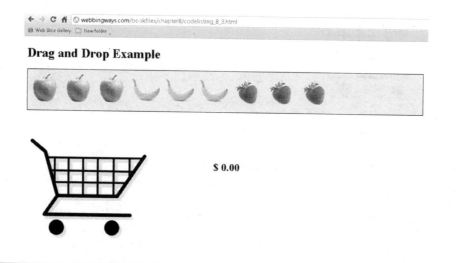

Figure 8-5 Preparing to shop

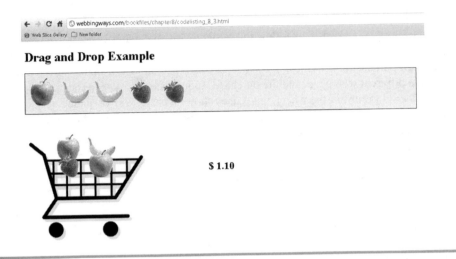

Figure 8-6 Placing some fruit in the cart

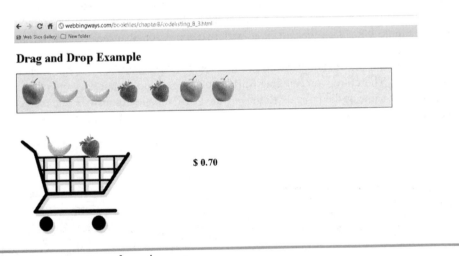

Figure 8-7 Removing items from the cart

out of the cart. This is precisely what happens here. Figure 8-7 shows that the two apples have been returned to the shelf. The banana and the strawberry remain in the cart, and the price has adjusted to 70 cents.

Incidentally, the fruit images are within their respective divs, not just the plain divs, as shown earlier in the chapter. This confirms that drag-and-drop can be applied to various elements. Essentially, a div is being dragged, but effectively, a fruit image is what appears to be dragged! The shelf and the interior of the cart accept items being dropped. Code Listing 8-3 shows how all of this works.

Code Listing 8-3   A drag-and-drop shopping cart application

```
<!doctype html>
<html lang="en">
<head>
<meta charset="utf-8">
<title>HTML5 Drag and Drop</title>
<style>
#shelf {
width:1000px;
height:100px;
background-color:#eeeeee;
border-style:solid;
border-width:thin;
}
#shoppingcartcenter {
position:absolute;
width:180px;
height:180px;
top:220px;
left:75px;
}
.fruit {
width:75px;
height:30px;
float:left;
margin-left:10px;
margin-top:10px;
}
#dollarsign {
position:absolute;
top:300px;
left:480px;
font-size:1.6em;
font-weight:bold;
}
#cost {
position:absolute;
top:300px;
left:500px;
font-size:1.6em;
font-weight:bold;
}
.container {
width:250px;
height:250px;
float:left;
margin-left:10px;
```

```
margin-top:10px;
}
</style>
</head>
<body>
<h1>Drag and Drop Example</h1>
<div id="shelf" ondrop="drop(this, event, 'shelf')"
ondragenter="return false" ondragover="return false">
  <div draggable="true" id="apple1" class="fruit"
ondragstart="drag(this, event)"><img src="apple.gif"
alt="apple" /></div>
  <div draggable="true" id="apple2" class="fruit"
ondragstart="drag(this, event)"><img src="apple.gif"
alt="apple" /></div>
  <div draggable="true" id="apple3" class="fruit"
ondragstart="drag(this, event)"><img src="apple.gif"
alt="apple" /></div>
  <div draggable="true" id="banana1" class="fruit"
ondragstart="drag(this, event)"><img src="banana.gif"
alt="banana" /></div>
  <div draggable="true" id="banana2" class="fruit"
ondragstart="drag(this, event)"><img src="banana.gif"
alt="banana" /></div>
  <div draggable="true" id="banana3" class="fruit"
ondragstart="drag(this, event)"><img src="banana.gif"
alt="banana" /></div>
  <div draggable="true" id="strawberry1" class="fruit"
ondragstart="drag(this, event)">
<img src="strawberry.gif" alt="strawberry" />
</div>
  <div draggable="true" id="strawberry2" class="fruit"
ondragstart="drag(this, event)">
<img src="strawberry.gif" alt="strawberry" />
</div>
  <div draggable="true" id="strawberry3" class="fruit"
ondragstart="drag(this, event)">
<img src="strawberry.gif" alt="strawberry" />
</div>
</div>
<br><br><br>
<div id="shoppingcart" class="container">
 <div id="shoppingcartcenter"
   ondrop="drop(this, event, 'shoppingcart')"
   ondragenter="return false" ondragover="return false">
</div>
 <img src="shoppingcart.png" alt="shopping cart" /></div>
<div id="dollarsign">$</div>
<div id="cost">0.00</div>
```

```
<script>
function drag(drag_object, e) {
e.dataTransfer.setData('Text', drag_object.id);
}
function drop(drop_target, e, elementname) {
var id = e.dataTransfer.getData('Text');
drop_target.appendChild(document.getElementById(id));
e.preventDefault();
currentcost=parseFloat(document.getElementById("cost").innerHTML);
//get type of fruit to determine price
if (id.indexOf("apple")>-1) { price=.2 }
if (id.indexOf("banana")>-1) { price=.25 }
if (id.indexOf("strawberry")>-1) { price=.45 }
switch (elementname) {
case "shoppingcart":
 newcost=(currentcost + price).toFixed(2);
 break;
case "shelf":
 newcost=(currentcost - price).toFixed(2);
 break;
}
document.getElementById("cost").innerHTML=newcost;
}
</script>
</body>
</html>
```

The style tag in the head contains the styling for many elements of the page. A few are of particular note. First is a class named `container`, which is applied to the shopping cart. The class specifies the size of the cart:

```
.container {
width:250px;
height:250px;
float:left;
margin-left:10px;
margin-top:10px;
}
```

Next is the styling for the interior of the cart. This div, named `shoppingcartcenter`, is positioned `absolute` to be within the overall cart image. Notice how the cart image occupies a 250 × 250-pixel area, and the shopping cart center is sized at 180 × 180 pixels. The `shoppingcartcenter` div is smaller than the cart itself. Using `top` and `left` settings, this div is placed in the middle of the cart (previously referred to as the basket area). The `shoppingcartcenter` div is enabled to accept dropped items.

```
#shoppingcartcenter {
position:absolute;
width:180px;
height:180px;
top:220px;
left:75px;
}
```

A class named `fruit` is used to style each piece of fruit. Each fruit image is sized to the same dimensions, and the margins keep them a bit separated from each other and vertically centered on the shelf.

```
.fruit {
width:75px;
height:30px;
float:left;
margin-left:10px;
margin-top:10px;
}
```

Each fruit is a div of its own, and these nine divs are inside the `shelf` div. This places the fruit on the shelf. The `shelf` div has the drop event, and each fruit is draggable. The drop event sends three arguments to the `drop` function: the element itself, the event, and a name used in the function, which is `shelf` in this example. Note that each fruit type—apple, banana, and strawberry—is a .gif image. There are just three images: one for each fruit. However, each image is used three times, showing a total of nine pieces of fruit. Each fruit is a separate div, and therefore has a unique `id`. For example, the three apples are `apple1`, `apple2`, and `apple3`.

```
<div id="shelf" ondrop="drop(this, event, 'shelf')"
   ondragenter="return false" ondragover="return false">
  <div draggable="true" id="apple1" class="fruit"
ondragstart="drag(this, event)"><img src="apple.gif"
alt="apple" /></div>
  <div draggable="true" id="apple2" class="fruit"
ondragstart="drag(this, event)"><img src="apple.gif"
alt="apple" /></div>
  <div draggable="true" id="apple3" class="fruit"
ondragstart="drag(this, event)"><img src="apple.gif"
alt="apple" /></div>
  <div draggable="true" id="banana1" class="fruit"
ondragstart="drag(this, event)"><img src="banana.gif"
alt="banana" /></div>
  <div draggable="true" id="banana2" class="fruit"
ondragstart="drag(this, event)"><img src="banana.gif"
alt="banana" /></div>
  <div draggable="true" id="banana3" class="fruit"
```

```
ondragstart="drag(this, event)"><img src="banana.gif"
alt="banana" /></div>
   <div draggable="true" id="strawberry1" class="fruit"
ondragstart="drag(this, event)">
<img src="strawberry.gif" alt="strawberry" />
</div>
   <div draggable="true" id="strawberry2" class="fruit"
ondragstart="drag(this, event)">
<img src="strawberry.gif" alt="strawberry" />
</div>
   <div draggable="true" id="strawberry3" class="fruit"
ondragstart="drag(this, event)">
<img src="strawberry.gif" alt="strawberry" />
</div>
</div>
```

The shoppingcartcenter div is inside the shoppingcart div. The shoppingcart div uses the image shoppingcart.png, which is what appears on the page. The shoppingcart div does not have any drag-and-drop properties or events. However, the inner shoppingcartcenter div uses the drop event. As with the shelf div, the call to the drop function uses a third argument, which is set to the name shoppingcart here:

```
<div id="shoppingcart" class="container">
 <div id="shoppingcartcenter" ondrop="drop(this, event, 'shoppingcart')"
 ondragenter="return false" ondragover="return false"></div>
 <img src="shoppingcart.png" alt="shopping cart" /></div>
```

The drag function is used in the same manner as with the earlier box examples. The real action here is in the drop function. Recall that a third argument—a name indicating which element is calling the function—is sent to the function. The purpose is to differentiate whether to add to the price or subtract from it. When shoppingcart is the third argument, the price is increased as a piece of fruit is being dragged into the shopping cart. When shelf is the third argument, the price is decreased as a piece of fruit is being put back on the shelf.

These price changes depend on the cost of a piece of fruit and what the current total price is, so a few lines of code manage what happens. The current total price is stored in a variable named currentcost (by taking the innerHTML of the cost div, which displays the price). The id variable has been given the identifier of the dropped item. If it's an apple, the variable price is set to .2 (20 cents). The same procedure applies to bananas and strawberries. The price variable is set to the price of the particular type of fruit. A new total price is calculated by adding or subtracting the price of the fruit (the add or subtract operation is determined by that third argument, used in a switch statement). Finally, the new total price is assigned to the innerHTML property of the cost div, which displays the new total price.

```
function drop(drop_target, e, elementname) {
var id = e.dataTransfer.getData('Text');
drop_target.appendChild(document.getElementById(id));
```

```
e.preventDefault();
currentcost=parseFloat(document.getElementById("cost").innerHTML);
//get type of fruit to determine price
if (id.indexOf("apple")>-1) { price=.2 }
if (id.indexOf("banana")>-1) { price=.25 }
if (id.indexOf("strawberry")>-1) { price=.45 }
switch (elementname) {
case "shoppingcart":
 newcost=(currentcost + price).toFixed(2);
 break;
case "shelf":
 newcost=(currentcost - price).toFixed(2);
 break;
}
document.getElementById("cost").innerHTML=newcost;
}
```

That wraps up the functionality of this shopping cart example. Much more functionality could be added to suit the requirements of the application (or your imagination). For example, you could have two carts, each designated with a different ship-to address. The entire page could be rendered as part of a past purchase (appearing upon opening with items already in the shopping cart), and then you could drag items out of the cart, as the initiation of processing a refund. Overall, the fact that you can have multiple draggable elements *and* multiple drop areas provides ample opportunity for many varieties of applications.

Playing Tic-Tac-Toe

It's a game we all know. It's easy. Sometimes you win, sometimes you lose, and sometimes no one wins. Most of the time, we play it on paper. That's old hat! Let's drag-and-drop our way to tic-tac-toe fun!

NOTE
Tic-tac-toe is a game in which two players try to get three of their pieces in a line (horizontal, vertical, or diagonal), on a three-row-by-three-column grid (nine squares in all). The players take turns placing a piece (usually drawing an *O* or an *X*) onto the grid. For example, if the player using *X*s can get three in a row, then *X* wins. The difficulty is that the other player places *O* pieces to block you.

The application of tic-tac-toe in this example uses drag-and-drop functionality. The grid of nine squares is a drop-enabled area. To be more precise, the grid is nine drop-enabled areas placed so that they resemble a grid (an HTML table is used). Two areas to the side each hold pieces: one with four *X*s, and the other with four *O*s. The pieces are set to be draggable. They are images. In turn, a piece is dragged over and dropped onto one of the grid's squares. Figure 8-8 shows how this looks at the start.

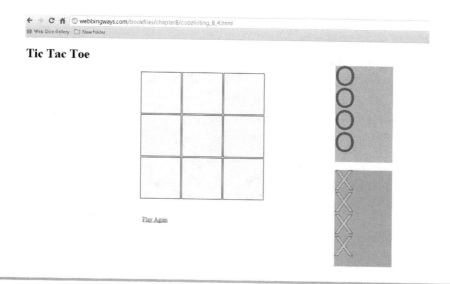

Figure 8-8   Preparing to play tic-tac-toe

The game as described here is dependent on the players keeping tabs on if someone wins. You can find an enhanced version online that incorporates having the code determine a winner. The JavaScript is extensive, so the simpler version is demonstrated here. You can review the enhanced version at www.webbingways.com/bookfiles/chapter8.

TIP

Two versions of the tic-tac-toe game are available online for review. Visit www
.webbingways.com/bookfiles/chapter8 to see them both.

Figure 8-9 shows the game board after all moves have been made. Neither side won; there are not any three consecutive *O*s or *X*s.

Figure 8-10 shows that *X* won a round, since there are three *X*s in a diagonal line. Player *O* missed seeing that coming!

Code Listing 8-4 shows all the code involved in the game.

Code Listing 8-4   The code behind tic-tac-toe

```
<!doctype html>
<html lang="en">
<head>
<meta charset="utf-8">
<title>HTML5 Drag and Drop</title>
<style>
td {
border-style:solid;
```

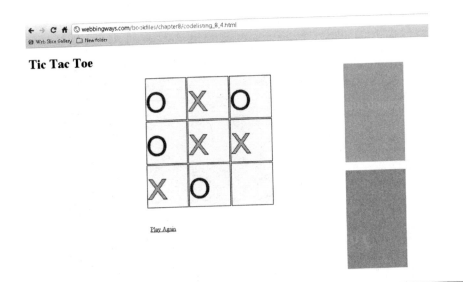

Figure 8-9 No one wins this game.

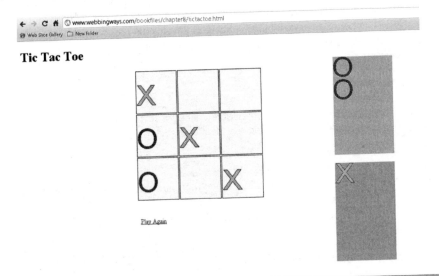

Figure 8-10 X wins!

```
border-width:thin;
width:100px;
height:100px;
background-color:yellow;
}
```

```
#O {
position:absolute;
width:150px;
height:240px;
top:60px;
left:800px;
background-color:silver;
}
#X {
position:absolute;
width:150px;
height:240px;
top:320px;
left:800px;
background-color:goldenrod;
}
#tictactoetable {
position:absolute;
top:80px;
left:300px;
}
</style>
</head>
<body>
<h1>Tic Tac Toe</h1>
<div id="O"
    ondrop="drop(this, event)"
    ondragenter="return false"
    ondragover="return false">
<div draggable="true" id="o1"  ondragstart="drag(this, event)">
    <img src="o.gif" alt="O" />
</div>
<div draggable="true" id="o2"  ondragstart="drag(this, event)">
    <img src="o.gif" alt="O" />
</div>
<div draggable="true" id="o3"  ondragstart="drag(this, event)">
    <img src="o.gif" alt="O" />
</div>
<div draggable="true" id="o4"  ondragstart="drag(this, event)">
    <img src="o.gif" alt="O" />
</div>
</div>
<div id="X"
    ondrop="drop(this, event)"
    ondragenter="return false"
    ondragover="return false">
<div draggable="true" id="x1"  ondragstart="drag(this, event)">
    <img src="x.gif" alt="X" />
```

```
</div>
<div draggable="true" id="x2"  ondragstart="drag(this, event)">
   <img src="x.gif" alt="X" />
</div>
<div draggable="true" id="x3"  ondragstart="drag(this, event)">
   <img src="x.gif" alt="X" />
</div>
<div draggable="true" id="x4"  ondragstart="drag(this, event)">
   <img src="x.gif" alt="X" />
</div>
</div>
<div id="tictactoetable">
<table>
<tr>
<td id="box1"  ondrop="drop(this, event)"
ondragenter="return false" ondragover="return false"> </td>
<td id="box2"  ondrop="drop(this, event)"
ondragenter="return false" ondragover="return false"> </td>
<td id="box3"  ondrop="drop(this, event)"
ondragenter="return false" ondragover="return false"> </td>
</tr>
<tr>
<td id="box4"  ondrop="drop(this, event)"
ondragenter="return false" ondragover="return false"> </td>
<td id="box5"  ondrop="drop(this, event)"
ondragenter="return false" ondragover="return false"> </td>
<td id="box6"  ondrop="drop(this, event)"
ondragenter="return false" ondragover="return false"> </td>
</tr>
<tr>
<td id="box7"  ondrop="drop(this, event)"
ondragenter="return false" ondragover="return false"> </td>
<td id="box8"  ondrop="drop(this, event)"
ondragenter="return false" ondragover="return false"> </td>
<td id="box9"  ondrop="drop(this, event)"
ondragenter="return false" ondragover="return false"> </td>
</tr>
</table>
<br><br>
  
<a ref="http://www.webbingways.com/bookfiles/chapter8/tictactoe.html">
Play Again</a>
<script>
function drag(drag_object, e) {
e.dataTransfer.setData('Text', drag_object.id);
}
function drop(drop_target, e, elementname) {
var id = e.dataTransfer.getData('Text');
```

```
drop_target.appendChild(document.getElementById(id));
e.preventDefault();
}
</script>
</body>
</html>
```

The grid is a table. The table is absolute positioned.

```
#tictactoetable {
position:absolute;
top:80px;
left:300px;
}
```

Within the table, the cells (the td tag) are given a size, a border, and a color. The width and height are the same (100 pixels), thereby making them appear as squares.

```
td {
border-style:solid;
border-width:thin;
width:100px;
height:100px;
background-color:yellow;
}
```

The areas that hold the pieces are divs with absolute positions and fixed dimensions. The divs are appropriately named O and X.

```
#O {
position:absolute;
width:150px;
height:240px;
top:60px;
left:800px;
background-color:silver;
}
#X {
position:absolute;
width:150px;
height:240px;
top:320px;
left:800px;
background-color:goldenrod;
}
```

Each table cell is drop-enabled. The following is the first row of the table. Each cell uses the drop event.

```
<table>
<tr>
<td id="box1"  ondrop="drop(this, event)" ondragenter="return false"
ondragover="return false"> </td>
<td id="box2"  ondrop="drop(this, event)" ondragenter="return false"
ondragover="return false"> </td>
<td id="box3"  ondrop="drop(this, event)" ondragenter="return false"
ondragover="return false"> </td>
</tr>
```

The divs that hold the pieces (O and X) are drop-enabled. This allows returning a piece to its holding area in case a mistake was made. These divs are containers for the inner divs that hold the actual pieces. These inner divs are set to draggable, and are shown as images (such as o.gif). Here is the O div with the four inner divs:

```
<div id="O"
   ondrop="drop(this, event)"
   ondragenter="return false"
   ondragover="return false">
<div draggable="true" id="o1"  ondragstart="drag(this, event)">
   <img src="o.gif" alt="O" />
</div>
<div draggable="true" id="o2"  ondragstart="drag(this, event)">
   <img src="o.gif" alt="O" />
</div>
<div draggable="true" id="o3"  ondragstart="drag(this, event)">
   <img src="o.gif" alt="O" />
</div>
<div draggable="true" id="o4"  ondragstart="drag(this, event)">
   <img src="o.gif" alt="O" />
</div>
</div>
```

The drag-and-drop functions are basic in this version. Simply, the players drag pieces to the grid and keep an eye on who wins.

```
<script>
function drag(drag_object, e) {
e.dataTransfer.setData('Text', drag_object.id);
}
function drop(drop_target, e, elementname) {
var id = e.dataTransfer.getData('Text');
drop_target.appendChild(document.getElementById(id));
e.preventDefault();
}
</script>
```

The enhanced version (available online, as mentioned earlier) uses a programmable approach to find the winner. It tests for a winner by examining the position of the pieces after each move. This requires gathering the top and left positions of the eight pieces and seeing if any three Os or Xs have the following:

- The same top position (three are in a row going across)

- The same left position (three are in a column going down)

- A series of three pieces with consecutive increasing tops and increasing lefts (a diagonal from upper left to lower right)

- A series of three pieces with consecutive increasing tops and decreasing lefts (a diagonal from upper right to lower left)

Summary

Drag-and-drop might at first seem fun but of not much use. This is simply not so. This chapter has shown how this technology can be applied to business needs and entertainment enjoyment. No doubt, you will find many ways that drag-and-drop can be put to use.

The technology involved here contains enough specialized events to present variety in developing applications. With events capturing everything from the start to the end of a drag-and-drop, putting intelligent programming in the event functions offers many possibilities for sophisticated web page offerings. As more developers adapt to this new technology, we should see many new ways of interacting with web sites.

Chapter 9

Geolocation

When I was a child, my parents took me to Manhattan. While walking around, we came across a big map of the city. On the map was a big circle saying "You are here." I clearly remember asking my parents how the map knew where we were. Many years later, I relived the moment when I realized that web sites were sending ads targeted to my location. Again, I asked how they knew where I was.

The answer to my first question is pretty obvious. The person who made the map knew where it would be placed. The answer to the second is the subject of this chapter: geolocation.

Geolocation is the process of determining where in the world a device or user is. Geolocation is useful for advertisers, developers, and the average consumer. In short, it is a very important addition to your HTML5 toolbox.

Geolocation Methods

Today, web sites can use three methods to determine your location. The original method of determining your location is through your IP address. The IP addresses of all public-facing networks and their latitude/longitude positions are stored in a database. Once a site obtains your IP address, a simple query can determine roughly where in the world you are. Depending on the quality of your device, this method can discern your location in the world within a few-meter radius.

You can try the IP method for yourself. Visit the web site www.ip2location.com to determine your location. You should see that the service likely determined your city, but not your actual location. This method is useful for advertisers to deliver ads for your area, but is of no use for developers trying to deliver turn-by-turn directions.

Another method of determining your location is through the Global Positioning System (GPS). GPS is a system of 24 satellites in earth orbit. A GPS device will send a message to these satellites. Using the time it takes to send and receive messages, your exact latitude and longitude can be determined within a few-meter radius. GPS is the ideal solution for developers who need an exact location. Most mobile devices are capable of delivering GPS information. Some systems include a built-in GPS device. However, very few desktop computers can deliver this information.

A third technique for location discovery is to triangulate based on cell tower locations. Used by most cell phones, this method returns a quick, if sometimes imprecise, location.

Luckily, HTML5 will work with whichever location method is available. The HTML5 geolocation functions can determine your latitude, longitude, and altitude. Depending on your device, it may also calculate other values, as discussed in the chapter.

TIP

Latitude is the angular distance north or south of the equator. On the globe, latitude is represented by horizontal lines. Positive values are north of the equator. *Longitude* is the angular distance east or west of the meridian at Greenwich, England. On a globe, longitude is represented by vertical lines. Positive values are west of Greenwich, England. HTML5 works with decimal degree values.

Privacy Concerns

Geolocation is an incredible technology; however, not everyone wants to share their location. The W3C takes your privacy very seriously. The W3C Geolocation API Specification, located at http://dev.w3.org/geo/api/spec-source.html, contains strong language protecting the consumer. Specifically, a site will not gather the location information for a device until the user approves.

The W3C specification requires the permission request to include the name of the site requesting the permission and clear responses. Figure 9-1 shows the Google Chrome permission popup. Not shown in the figure is a link to more information regarding the service.

The API provides a method for the developer to track the current location of an object. However, to protect the user, the method must be in an active browser session. Since the session must be active, the user cannot unknowingly be tracked using HTML5.

Depending on the browser you choose, you can change your mind regarding sharing your location. Google Chrome places an icon in the address bar that allows you to change the share settings, as shown in Figure 9-2. In Firefox, you need to select Tools | Page Info | Permissions to bring up the dialog shown in Figure 9-3.

As a developer, you need to respect your users' rights to privacy. If they deny your request, no matter how benign it seems to you, the session is over. Later in the chapter, you will see how to graciously respond to errors in acquiring location information.

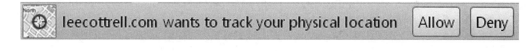

Figure 9-1   Chrome asking for permission to share your location

Figure 9-2   Setting Chrome location-sharing options

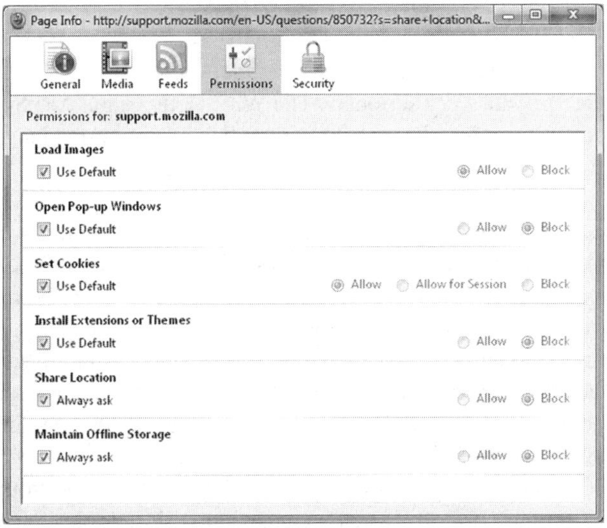

Figure 9-3 Setting Firefox location-sharing permissions

Finding Your Location

Tracking your user's location is handled through a new property of the JavaScript `navigator` object. JavaScript's `navigator` is the perfect choice, as this is the object on the device that is requesting the location. The new `navigator` property is `geolocation`.

TIP

The examples in this chapter work better from a web site rather than locally. I suggest running them from www.webbingways.com or a server that you control.

The `geolocation` property contains very few methods. Currently, only the following three methods are supported (each function is named well):

- The `getCurrentPosition` method attempts to retrieve the current position of the object.

- The `watchPosition` method updates the page as the device moves, effectively tracking the device's movements.

- The `clearWatch` method stops `watchPosition` from tracking the device.

To start the process of getting a user's location, you need to begin with `getCurrentPosition` or `watchPosition`. Both will request the location from the device but will not do anything with the information.

Code Listing 9-1 shows the beginning of a program that will display your latitude and longitude. The function `findYou` calls `navigator.geolocation.getCurrentPosition()`. This initiates the request for location information.

Code Listing 9-1   The request for your location

```
<!doctype html>
<html lang="en">
<head>
<meta charset="utf-8">
<title>HTML5Geolocation</title>
</head>
<body>
<h1>Your Location</h1>
<script>
navigator.geolocation.getCurrentPosition();
</script>
</body>
</html>
```

This code does not do anything exciting. It merely requests the location from the device. The browser will ask if you wish to share the location. Once you respond, nothing else happens. We are going to expand on this code, to display your latitude and longitude.

NOTE

Your computer will respond to this code immediately. Your smart phone will need to have location sharing enabled. On my Android phone, this was done via the menu option Settings | Location and Security | Use Wireless Networks.

The `getCurrentPosition` function takes zero to three parameters, as follows:

- Calling `getCurrentPosition` without any parameters is used to validate that the browser and device support geolocation.

- The first parameter is the name of an asynchronous callback function that will handle the location information. This function must accept a parameter of type `Position`.

- The second parameter is a name of a callback function that should handle errors.

- The third parameter lists the position options, which change how the device gathers the location. Table 9-1 lists the position options.

The position options are passed into the `getCurrentPosition` function set inside a set of curly braces ({ }). The value is set as *variableName* : *value*. The syntax is shown here:

```
navigator.geolocation.getCurrentPosition([successCallbackFunction],
    [errorCallbackFunction],[{[enableHighAccuracy],[maximumAge],
[timeout:]}]);
```

Option	Description
enableHighAccuracy	Accepts `true` or `false`. Defaults to `false`. When set to `true`, the device will return the best positioning information if it can.
timeout	Accepts whole numbers from 0 to over 2 billion. Defaults to 0. It represents the number of milliseconds the program will wait until the device returns the location information. This time starts *after* the user grants permission.
maximumAge	The maximum age for a cached position. This can speed up your requests. The default is 0. Values range from 0 to infinite.

Table 9-1   Position Options for getCurrentPosition

Code Listing 9-2 shows a complete call to `getCurrentPosition`. Sample output is shown in Figure 9-4. The function `showPosition` will display the detected latitude and longitude in paragraphs. Function `noLocation` is the error function. Finally, `maximumAge` is set to 20 minutes, and `timeout` is set to 30 seconds.

Code Listing 9-2   A working location-aware web page

```
<!doctype html>
<html lang="en">
<head>
<meta charset="utf-8">
<title>HTML5 Geolocation</title>
<script>
    function findYou(){
        navigator.geolocation.getCurrentPosition(showPosition,
            noLocation, {maximumAge : 1200000, timeout : 30000});
    }
    function showPosition(location){
        var latitude = location.coords.latitude;
        var longitude = location.coords.longitude;
        var accuracy = location.coords.accuracy;
        document.getElementById("lat").innerHTML=
          "Your latitude is " + latitude;
        document.getElementById("lon").innerHTML=
          "Your longitude is " + longitude;
        document.getElementById("acc").innerHTML=
          "Accurate within " + accuracy + " meters";
    }
    function noLocation(locationError){
        document.write("Request failed");
    }
```

```
</script>
</head>
<body>
<h1>Your Location</h1>
<script>
findYou();
</script>
<p id="lat"> </p>
<p id="lon"> </p>
<p id="acc"> </p>
</body>
</html>
```

The function `showLocation` has all of the action in this page. It accepts the parameter location of type `Position`, which has several properties, as listed in Table 9-2. Of these properties, only `latitude`, `longitude`, `accuracy`, and `timestamp` are guaranteed to be present. The others are device-dependent. The `latitude`, `longitude`, and `accuracy` properties are written into the paragraphs with identifiers (`ids`) in the body.

The accuracy of this page will vary greatly, depending on several factors. In testing, my home Internet connection responded with less than 200 meters of accuracy. The latitude and longitude were actually in my neighbor's swimming pool! At work, the accuracy was more than 42,000 meters. The latitude and longitude were in a different neighborhood of the city. Mobile devices responded differently, depending on the brand and location options set.

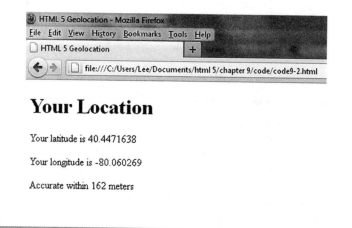

Figure 9-4 Location information displayed in Firefox

Property	Description
coords.latitude	Latitude of the device
coords.longitude	Longitude of the device
coords.accuracy	Accuracy of the latitude and longitude measurement, in meters
coords.altitude	Approximate height off the ground of the device
coords.altitudeaccuracy	Accuracy of the altitude measurement, in meters; null if altitude unavailable
coords.heading	Direction of travel, in degrees; 0 degrees is north, and other directions measured clockwise
coords.speed	Speed in meters per second of the device
timestamp	Date and time the location was acquired, calculated as the milliseconds from the JavaScript epoch (used to determine the "freshness" of a location)

Table 9-2   Properties of Type Position

Handling Rejection and Errors

Retrieving a user's location is not guaranteed. Several errors can occur:

- Recall that sending a location is optional. The user can decide to not share.

- The position may be currently unavailable.

- The device may take too long to respond.

Your code should gracefully respond to these conditions.

NOTE
Demonstrating location-retrieval errors is easiest in Google Chrome.

As noted earlier, the second parameter to getCurrentPosition is the error callback function. This function accepts a parameter of type PositionError. PositionError contains one property code, which is a number that describes the error type. Each of the possible errors is defined as a constant in the PositionError class. The possible errors are PERMISSION_DENIED, POSITION_UNAVAILABLE, and TIMEOUT.

Code Listing 9-3 improves on the noLocation function with a switch statement that prints an error message to the user.

Code Listing 9-3   A useful error response

```html
<!doctype html>
<html lang="en">
<head>
<meta charset="utf-8">
<title>HTML5 Geolocation</title>
<script>
     function findYou(){
          navigator.geolocation.getCurrentPosition(showPosition,
noLocation, {maximumAge : 1200000, timeout : 30000});
     }
     function showPosition(location){
          var latitude = location.coords.latitude;
          var longitude = location.coords.longitude;
          var accuracy = location.coords.accuracy;
          document.getElementById("lat").innerHTML=
          "Your latitude is " + latitude;
          document.getElementById("lon").innerHTML=
          "Your longitude is " + longitude;
          document.getElementById("acc").innerHTML=
          "Accurate within " + accuracy + " meters";
     }
     function noLocation(locationError){
          varerrorMessage = document.getElementById("lat");
          switch(locationError.code)
          {
          case locationError.PERMISSION_DENIED:
             errorMessage.innerHTML=
                "You have denied my request for your location.";
                break;
          case locationError.POSITION_UNAVAILABLE:
             errorMessage.innerHTML=
                "Your position is not available at this time.";
                break;
        case locationError.TIMEOUT:
             errorMessage.innerHTML=
                "My request for your location took too long.";
                break;
          default:
             errorMessage.innerHTML=
                "An unexpected error occurred.";
          }
     }
</script>
</head>
<body>
<h1>Your Location</h1>
```

```
<script>
findYou();
</script>
<p id="lat"> </p>
<p id="lon"> </p>
<p id="acc"> </p>
</body>
</html>
```

Code Listing 9-3 does respond to a user's error; however, it is up to the user to refresh the page. An improvement on this code would be to default to a location or recall the `getCurrentPosition`.

Figure 9-5 shows the output from a denied request. Notice two things:

- The message is displayed on the screen.
- The location icon in the toolbar has a red *x*, indicating that the user chose not to share.

Detecting Browser Support

The code in the previous section assumed that your browser handles HTML5 geolocation. As of this writing, the most recent versions of Chrome, Firefox, and Internet Explorer 9 support geolocation. Additionally, every Android and iPhone I tried supported my pages. However, you should prepare for users still using outdated browsers.

TIP
Google offers a service called Gears (http://gears.google.com). This JavaScript API allows you to use HTML5 geolocation on browsers that do not support the technology.

As justification, consider W3Schools.com. This site delivers tutorials and training on web technologies. Its visitors tend to be on the geeky side. Their own stats report that about 26% of the visitors use Internet Explorer. Only 3.6% used Internet Explorer 9. Users visited with versions of Internet Explorer dating back to version 6! If you were to look at the browser usage for sites such as Google or Yahoo, you would find that the percentage of Internet Explorer usage nearly doubles.

Figure 9-5 Denied response to a location request

TIP

To see current browser usage stats, visit www.w3schools.com/browsers/browsers_stats.asp.

So, if browsers are free, why are people still using outdated browsers? The reasons range from ignorance to serious business needs. For example, a pharmaceutical company in my hometown is still using Internet Explorer 6 on all of its Windows computers. The reason is that many of their internal databases are powered using web pages written with technologies that work only on that version. Rewriting these web sites is a huge undertaking. Thus, Internet Explorer 6 is required for the company to stay in business.

Detecting if a browser supports geolocation is simple. If support exists, `navigator.geolocation` returns a value that JavaScript converts to a Boolean value:true if the browser supports geolocation or false if it does not. Simply place an `if` statement around the call to `navigation.geolocation`. Use the `else` clause to display an error message. Code Listing 9-4 shows the modification needed to detect browser support.

NOTE

The detection trick for geolocation in Code Listing 9-4 really does not return a Boolean value. Instead, we are depending on JavaScript's weak typing.

Code Listing 9-4   Detecting browser support

```
<!doctype html>
<html lang="en">
<head>
<meta charset="utf-8">
<title>HTML5 Geolocation</title>
<script>
    function findYou(){
        if(!navigator.geolocation.getCurrentPosition(showPosition,
noLocation, {maximumAge : 1200000, timeout : 30000})) {
        document.getElementById("lat").innerHTML=
        "This browser does not support geolocation.";
        }
    }
    function showPosition(location){
            var latitude = location.coords.latitude;
        var longitude = location.coords.longitude;
        var accuracy = location.coords.accuracy;
        document.getElementById("lat").innerHTML=
        "Your latitude is " + latitude;
        document.getElementById("lon").innerHTML=
        "Your longitude is " + longitude;
        document.getElementById("acc").innerHTML=
        "Accurate within " + accuracy + " meters";
    }
```

```
        function noLocation(locationError){
        var errorMessage = document.getElementById("lat");
            switch(locationError.code)
        {
        case locationError.PERMISSION_DENIED:
            errorMessage.innerHTML=
                "You have denied my request for your location.";
                break;
        case locationError.POSITION_UNAVAILABLE:
            errorMessage.innerHTML=
                "Your position is not available at this time.";
                break;
      case locationError.TIMEOUT:
            errorMessage.innerHTML=
                "My request for your location took too long.";
                break;
        default:
            errorMessage.innerHTML=
                "An unexpected error occurred.";
        }
    }
</script>
</head>
<body>
<h1>Your Location</h1>
<script>
findYou();
</script>
<p id="lat"> </p>
<p id="lon"> </p>
<p id="acc"> </p>
</body>
</html>
```

Mapping Your Place in the World

Geolocation as presented so far in the chapter is not very exciting. The example in this section demonstrates the use of the Google Maps API. This service, which is free to individuals and sites that do not charge for their services, allows you to easily add a map to your site.

TIP

Google, as usual, provides excellent documentation and tutorials. For details, visit http://code.google.com/apis/maps/index.html.

Figure 9-6 The result of a Google Map call

Figure 9-6 shows the results of a Google Map call. To create a simple map like this on your web page, you will need to peform several steps.

The first step is to create a div section on your page named map and style it appropriately.

Next, add the Google Maps API to your project. The Google Maps API loads the Map code for use on the web page. It also tells Google whether you have a device with a GPS sensor. The following snippet shows the loading for a device without a GPS sensor. If you have a sensor, change the false to true.

```
<script
src="http://maps.googleapis.com/maps/api/js?sensor=false">
</script>
```

Once the API is loaded, you can begin to create your map. In your showPosition function, create a variable called position that instantiates a variable of type google. maps.LatLng. Pass into the constructor your latitude and longitude values. The following snippet shows map creation.

```
var position = new google.maps.LatLng(latitude, longitude);
```

Map Style	Description
google.maps.MapTypeId.SATELLITE	Shows the map using satellite photos
google.maps.MapTypeId.ROAD	Displays a road map
google.maps.MapTypeId.HYBRID	Displays the satellite images with the road map overlaid
google.maps.MapTypeId.TERRAIN	Shows roadnames and elevations

Table 9-3 Basic Google Map Styles

Now you need to set the options for this map. You have many choices, including these three basic options:

- The zoom level, which ranges from 0 to 20. A 0 value is basically the view from space; 20 is as close as you can get.

- The center position, which is the LatLng variable that sits in the center of the map.

- The map style, which changes the map. Table 9-3 details the choices. I encourage you to experiment with the styles.

The following code snippet shows the setting of map options.

```
varmyOptions = {
        zoom: 18,
        center: position,
        mapTypeId: google.maps.MapTypeId.HYBRID
};
```

The last step is to actually draw the map. As with the latitude and longitude information, you draw the map into an object referenced by the getElementById function. Code Listing 9-5 shows the code for drawing a map, with the error code removed for brevity. The complete code is available on www.webbingways.com.

Code Listing 9-5   Drawing a map

```
<!doctype html>
<html lang="en">
<head>
<meta charset="utf-8">
<title>HTML5 Geolocation</title>
<style>
#map{
    width:500px;
    height:500px;
}
</style>
```

```
<!--set the api -->
<script type="text/javascript"
    src="http://maps.googleapis.com/maps/api/js?sensor=false">
</script>

<script>
    function findYou(){
        if(!navigator.geolocation.getCurrentPosition(showPosition,
    noLocation, {maximumAge : 1200000, timeout : 30000})){
    document.getElementById("lat").innerHTML=
    "This browser does not support geolocation.";
}
    }
    function showPosition(location){
        var latitude = location.coords.latitude;
        var longitude = location.coords.longitude;
        var accuracy = location.coords.accuracy;
        //build the map
        var position = new google.maps.LatLng(latitude, longitude);
        //build the options
        var myOptions = {
          zoom: 18,
          center: position,
          mapTypeId: google.maps.MapTypeId.HYBRID
          };
    //display the map
    var map = new google.maps.Map(document.getElementById("map"),
        myOptions);
        document.getElementById("lat").innerHTML=
        "Your latitude is " + latitude;
        document.getElementById("lon").innerHTML=
        "Your longitude is " + longitude;
        document.getElementById("acc").innerHTML=
        "Accurate within " + accuracy + " meters";
    }
    function noLocation(locationError)
    {
        var errorMessage = document.getElementById("lat");
        switch(locationError.code)
        {
        case locationError.PERMISSION_DENIED:
            errorMessage.innerHTML=
                "You have denied my request for your location.";
                break;
        case locationError.POSITION_UNAVAILABLE:
            errorMessage.innerHTML=
                "Your position is not available at this time.";
                break;
```

```
    case locationError.TIMEOUT:
        errorMessage.innerHTML=
            "My request for your location took too long.";
            break;
    default:
        errorMessage.innerHTML=
            "An unexpected error occurred.";
    }
}
</script>
</head>
<body>
<h1>Your Location</h1>
<script>
findYou();
</script>
<p id="lat"> </p>
<p id="lon"> </p>
<p id="acc"> </p>
<div id="map">
</div>
</body>
</html>
```

Getting on the Map

The sample map is pretty plain. It needs markers showing important places. This is defined as *geocoding*. To geocode, you need to instantiate `LatLng` objects with the coordinates of your objects. Figure 9-7 shows locations of earth's natural wonders placed on a Google map. Notice that most of the icons are the familiar Google-placed teardrop. However, I changed the icon over my house.

The google.maps.Marker API provides the functionality to place icons on the map at specified latitude and longitude locations. You are able to provide additional metadata, such as a custom icon and a title. The title is available when you hover over the icon. For details on additional properties, consult with the Google documentation.

TIP

Thanks to openstreetmap.org for providing an easy-to-use interface that gives very close latitude and longitude values.

Geocoding a location requires two items: the latitude and longitude of a location you wish to plot, and a map object. In your code, after the creation of the `map` object, you will instantiate an object of type `google.maps.Marker`. The metadata is passed in as options, similarly to how you built the map.

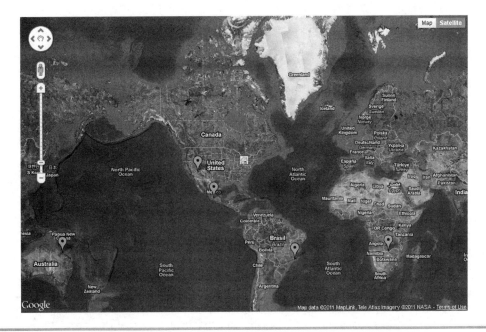

Figure 9-7   Locations placed on the map

Code Listing 9-6 shows a specific example for my house and the Grand Canyon. The complete code is available on www.webbingways.com, in the Chapter 9 link.

Code Listing 9-6   Geocoding locations

```
varhouseIcon = 'house.png';
var point = new google.maps.Marker({
icon: houseIcon,
position: position,
map: map,
title:"Your place"});

var canyon= new google.maps.Marker({
position: new google.maps.LatLng(35.9766,-113.7717),
map: map,
title:"Grand Canyon, USA"});
```

Continuously Tracking Movement

The function getCurrentPosition allows developers to acquire a device's location on demand. However, HTML5 offers the ability to update your location as it changes,

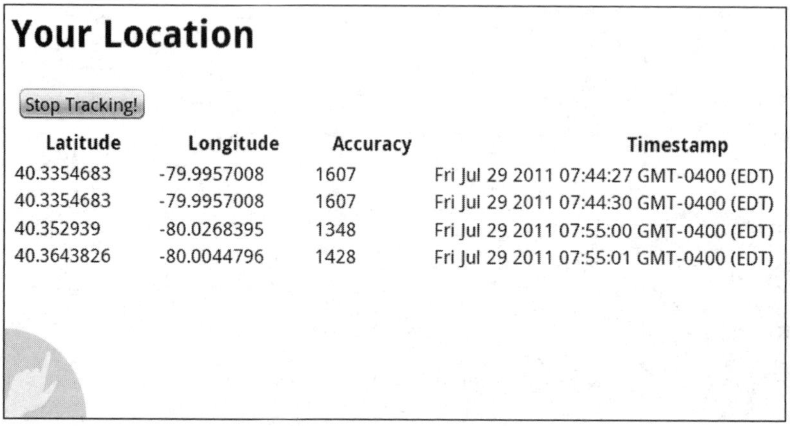

Your Location

[Stop Tracking!]

Latitude	Longitude	Accuracy	Timestamp
40.3354683	-79.9957008	1607	Fri Jul 29 2011 07:44:27 GMT-0400 (EDT)
40.3354683	-79.9957008	1607	Fri Jul 29 2011 07:44:30 GMT-0400 (EDT)
40.352939	-80.0268395	1348	Fri Jul 29 2011 07:55:00 GMT-0400 (EDT)
40.3643826	-80.0044796	1428	Fri Jul 29 2011 07:55:01 GMT-0400 (EDT)

Figure 9-8 Tracking a user's location

in real time. For this feature, instead of using getCurrentPosition, you use watchPosition.

The watchPosition method takes the same parameters as getCurrentPosition. However, whenever the device detects a change in location, the showLocation function will be called. Your job as the developer is to handle what to do with this information.

The call to watchPosition returns a unique identifier for the watch operation. This identifier can be used to cancel the track later with the clearWatch function.

Code Listing 9-7 shows watchPosition in action. This code will create a new table row whenever the device's position updates. I added the timestamp for proof that the page is updating. Figure 9-8 shows an example of the results. This code will probably not work well on your computer, but it works great on a smartphone. The complete code is at www .webbingways.com.

Code Listing 9-7   Tracking your locations

```
<!doctype html>
<html lang="en">
<head>
<meta charset="utf-8">
<title>HTML5Geolocation</title>
<script>
    varwatchOperation;
    function stopTracking(){
      navigator.geolocation.clearWatch(watchOperation);
    }
    function findYou(){
        watchOperation = navigator.geolocation.
watchPosition(showPosition,
noLocation, {maximumAge : 60000, timeout : 30000});
```

```
    }
    function addRow(lat, lon, acc, tim){
    vartbody = document.getElementById("posTable");
    var row = document.createElement("TR");
    vartdlat = document.createElement("TD");
    tdlat.appendChild(document.createTextNode(lat));
    vartdlon = document.createElement("TD");
    tdlon.appendChild(document.createTextNode(lon));
    vartdacc = document.createElement("TD");
    tdacc.appendChild(document.createTextNode(acc));
    vartdtim = document.createElement("TD");
    tdtim.appendChild(document.createTextNode(tim.toString()));
    row.appendChild(tdlat);
    row.appendChild(tdlon);
    row.appendChild(tdacc);
    row.appendChild(tdtim);
    tbody.appendChild(row);
}
    function showPosition(location)
    {
        var latitude = location.coords.latitude;
        var longitude = location.coords.longitude;
        var accuracy = location.coords.accuracy;
        var timestamp = location.timestamp;
        addRow(latitude, longitude, accuracy, timestamp);
    }
    function noLocation(locationError)
    {
        var errorMessage = document.getElementById("lat");
        switch(locationError.code)
        {
        case locationError.PERMISSION_DENIED:
            errorMessage.innerHTML=
                "You have denied my request for your location.";
                break;
        case locationError.POSITION_UNAVAILABLE:
            errorMessage.innerHTML=
                "Your position is not available at this time.";
                break;
      case locationError.TIMEOUT:
          errorMessage.innerHTML=
                "My request for your location took too long.";
                break;
        default:
          errorMessage.innerHTML=
                "An unexpected error occurred.";
        }
    }
```

```
</script>
</head>
<body>
<h1>Your Location</h1>
<script>
findYou();
</script>
<form>
<button onclick="stopTracking();">Stop Tracking!</button>
</form>
<table style="width:100%"id="posTable">
<tr><th>Latitude</th>
<th>Longitude</th>
<th>Accuracy</th>
<th>Timestamp</th>
</tr>
</table>
<p id="err"></p>
</body>
</html>
```

Summary

HTML5 allows you to build a location-aware web page. Using the new features of `navigator.geolocation`, you can quickly determine user location. For example, the `getCurrentPosition` method allows you to retrieve the latitude and longitude of your end user.

Of course, tracking offline locations brings up some privacy worries, and thus geolocation technology is completely dependent on user acceptance. HTML5 will not track users without their express permission.

While HTML5 Geolocation APIs are useful to determine location, adding the Google Maps API to the mix brings the technology to life. With a very few lines of code, you can render a fully interactive Google map in a div on the screen and also place icons at desired locations.

In the final section of this chapter, you learned how to track the movements of a device with the `navigator.geolocation.watchPosition` method.

The use of this geolocation technology will grow in the coming years as advertisers and developers dream up new ways of using your location data.

Chapter 10

HTML5 Document Structure

Web designers have been struggling with layout since the first version of HTML. Originally, layout was accomplished using tables. This practice, while still appropriate in some cases, lost favor to CSS and the div element, which is HTML4's method of placing elements on the page. The div element allows developers to chop the page into as many logical sections as they want. CSS classes can then set custom formats for each div. However, the div element presents a couple of problems. In this chapter, we'll first look at those problems and then describe how HTML5's new layout tags help to solve them.

The Problems with Div

There are two big problems with the div element. The first problem that new developers encounter is the arbitrary use of divs. They seem to appear everywhere in HTML markup. Developers use them for headings, columns, footers, and random callouts. The only way to track their use is to create clever class names for them.

The second problem with divs lies in how they interact with screen readers. Screen readers—such as Microsoft Narrator, Fire Vox, and Apple's VoiceOver—can be confused by divs. The screen reader often identifies a div element has been entered, but its relationship on the page can be hard to describe.

The div element is still supported in HTML5. However, it has been augmented by several new semantic layout tags. Seasoned web veterans probably remember when the `<strong>` and `<em>` tags entered the HTML tag lexicon. The `<strong>` tag was to replace the `<b>` tag, and `<em>` to replace the `<i>`. The argument was that the `<i>` tag was used for both a title of a book and to emphasize a point. For sighted readers of the web page, the distinction was quite clear. *The Lord of the Rings* is clearly a book title, while *holy cow* is an emotional statement. *Holy cow* should be screamed, while *The Lord of the Rings* should be spoken in normal voice. A screen reader, encountering the `<i>` tag surrounding these entries, would speak both louder.

Sighted web users often have a hard time understanding why the semantic tags are so important. To demonstrate, I have my students perform an activity. They pair up at a computer. One places a blindfold over his eyes and grabs the mouse. The other reads the page as it is written. The blindfolded person attempts to navigate the page to a desired point. This is always a fun and instructive lesson that helps the students understand the need for semantic tags.

For those developers who have not had such a good lesson, the United States and other countries have enacted laws protecting differently abled people. The American laws are stated within Section 508 of the US Rehabilitation Act. Basically, these laws guarantee that all Americans, regardless of physical ability, should have equal access to technology. Professional web designers should understand how these laws apply to their work.

TIP
Visit www.section508.gov/ for information about Section 508 of the US Rehabilitation Act.

HTML5's new layout tags help to solve both of div's problems. The tags are named by their function. For example, `<header>` and `<footer>` obviously refer to their location on the page. Both designers and screen readers can identify that the footer is at the bottom of a section. The W3C did a very good job with the new tags. For the most part, they follow the naming convention that most web developers use on modern web pages.

HTML5 Layout Tags

The new HTML5 layout tags were developed with both the designer and the programmer in mind. As mentioned, the tag names match with the current div names used by most modern web developers. In addition, the tag names correspond with divisions created within content management systems like Joomla and WordPress. Content managers allow a developer to create a site and let regular users submit articles. The system will place the posted article within <div class="article">.

TIP

For an up-to-date description of browser support, visit http://caniuse.com/. Select the index, and click the tag in question.

Layout Tag Overview

Table 10-1 lists and defines the new layout tags. Most of the names indicate their usage.

Table 10-1 shows quite an extensive list. Unfortunately, at the time of this writing, not all of the tags are fully supported by browsers. Eventually, the HTML5 tags should be supported in some fashion by all browsers.

Each new HTML5 tag supports the standard attributes, as listed in Table 10-2.

Using the New Layout Tags

Now let's look at when to use each tag. These tags are so new that there are no best practices associated with them yet, so I have spent a lot of time looking at how other developers are using the tags.

<div>

I know what you are thinking. The <div> tag is older than dirt. Why is it listed as a new tag in an HTML5 book? The <div> tag is here because W3C more clearly defined when *not* to use it.

You use a <div> tag to create sections for styling or grouping main content, or for use when scripting. Use the <div> tag if *a more appropriate semantic tag is not available*.

Other than being more clearly defined, the <div> tag acts the same as it always has.

TIP

While the <div> tag is for generic styling, you are allowed to apply styles to the semantic tags.

Tag	Description
`<article>`	Used for information that can stand alone, without the web page structure
`<aside>`	Used for content that is related to the surrounding items
`<command>`	Implementation of this one is not quite clear; eventually, may provide some manner of interacting with the site
`<details>`	Used to contain information about a section on the page
`<div>`	Used to format large portions of a web page
`<figcaption>`	Used for a figure's caption
`<figure>`	Used for any visual graphical element on the page
`<footer>`	Used for the footer of an element on the page
`<header>`	Used for an introduction of a document or section; could include navigation
`<hgroup>`	Used to group headings together (for example, a main heading and a subheading) to avoid multiple entries in the document's outline as generated by the HTML5 outlining process
`<mark>`	Used to identify parts of the text, such as to replace `<span>` for individual words
`<menu>`	Used for a menu on the web page
`<nav>`	Used for a navigation section on the page
`<section>`	Used for any section in a document that does not fit any of these other types
`<summary>`	Used for a summary of an element, like an abstract (contained within the `<details>` element)
`<time>`	Used for defining a time, date, or both

Table 10-1   The HTML5 Structure Tags

<header>

You use the `<header>` tag to provide a header for a document or another section of a page. Traditionally, web developers have created a masthead section using a div. This is fine on pages with only one main piece of content, but starts to break down on sites controlled by a content management system. Quite often, content-managed sites have several pieces of content per page. Each large piece of content can have its own header. Thus, the `<header>` tag is used to identify the header for each content piece.

The header element typically has the title of the content and perhaps the author and date of creation. It is always placed at the top of a layout element. Code Listing 10-1 in the next section shows an example of its use.

As with `<div>` tags, it is suggested that you use the `id` attribute to name each header element. This will help both screen readers and yourself track the header.

<footer>

The `<footer>` tag usually falls at the end of the document or large piece of content. Footers often contain copyright information, links to contact the author and web designer, the last

Attribute	Value	Description
accesskey	character	Identifies the keyboard shortcut to access a page element
class	classname	Applies a CSS class name for formatting
contenteditable	true false	Allows you to unlock objects to allow user editing
contextmenu	menu_id	Creates a context menu for an element
dir	ltr rtl	Indicates the text direction
draggable	true false auto	Sets whether an object is draggable (see Chapter 8 for details on the drag-and-drop features)
dropzone	copy move link	Sets the reaction to a dropped item
hidden	hidden	Hides the object on the page
id	id	Creates a unique name for an element (useful for scripting, linking, and formatting purposes)
lang	language_code	Sets the language code for an element
spellcheck	true false	Sets the spellcheck flag
style	style_definition	Allows you to apply an in-line style to an element
tabindex	number	Specifies the tab order of an element
title	text	Adds information about an item (for compatibility with older browsers, make the same as the alt attribute)

Table 10-2 Standard Attributes for All HTML5 Elements

modification date, and perhaps badges the page has earned. You will typically have one footer per page, and perhaps one per content item.

Code Listing 10-1 shows a good use of the `<header>`, `<footer>`, and `<div>` tags on a web page. The page could be formatted using whatever style elements you feel are appropriate. I formatted the header and footer as an example.

Code Listing 10-1   A simple page layout

```
<!doctype html>
<html lang="en">
<head>
<meta charset="utf-8">
```

```
<title>Chapter 10 Layouts</title>
<style>
body
{
      font-family:Verdana, Geneva, sans-serif;
}
#pageFooter{
      text-align:center;
      font-size: .65em;
      font-variant:small-caps;
      border-top:thin solid gray;
}
#masthead{
      font-size:1.5em;
      font-family:Impact, Charcoal, sans-serif;
}
</style>
</head>
<body>
<header id="masthead">
<h1>Page Title Here</h1>
</header>
<div id="mainContent">
<p>Your page contents here.</p>
</div>
<footer id="pageFooter">
<p>Copyright 2011 webbingways.com </p>
</footer>
</body>
</html>
```

Code Listing 10-1 creates a simple page layout. The traditional header, content, and footer areas are represented. In CSS, I named the classes #mastHead and #footer, allowing me to use the id attribute of each tag to apply formatting. Alternatively, you could name the classes .mastHead and .footer, and use the class attribute instead.

The complete code for this and the other listings in this chapter is available on www .webbingways.com.

<article>

The <article> tag is used to enclose a portion of your page that could stand by itself. It is closely related to the article that content managers like Joomla and WordPress place onto web pages. Use the <article> tag when styling Joomla's user-generated content.

The W3C specification gives <article> broad uses. The list of suggestions includes forum posts, magazine articles, blog entries, user-submitted comments, and interactive objects or any other independent content. Your article elements can be independent content. They have meaning outside your site.

Your articles will typically be major components of your page. As such, the article may have several additional layouts, such as a header, a footer, details, a summary, and figures. Code Listing 10-2, in the next section, demonstrates the use of the `<article>` tag.

TIP

Remember the acid test for `<article>`: The content should be able to stand on its own.

`<section>`

The `<section>` tag is probably the most confusing layout tag. W3C describes it as a generic section of a document, usually with a heading. These tags often enclose items that cannot stand on their own.

The section makes sense only within some larger context. Examples include chapters of a book, tabs for a tabbed interface, portions of a really large table, and small portions of your web site (such as your greeting, personal quote, or joke of the day). You should not use `<section>` to separate pieces of content or styling. In these cases, use the `<div>` tag.

There is much debate over how to best use the section element, if at all. In general, use what makes the most sense for your page. And make sure your sections have heading elements and content that needs additional structure for readability.

Code Listing 10-2 adds a section and an article to the web page started in Code Listing 10-1. The only change is the addition of the `<section>` and `<article>` tags inside the body.

Code Listing 10-2   Using sections and articles

```
<!doctype html>
<html lang="en">
<head>
<meta charset="utf-8">
<title>Chapter 10 Layouts</title>
<style>
body{
    font-family:Verdana, Geneva, sans-serif;
}
#pageFooter{
    text-align:center;
    font-size:.65em;
    font-variant:small-caps;
    border-top:thin solid gray;
}
#masthead{
    font-size:1.5pt;
    font-family:Impact, Charcoal, sans-serif;
}
```

```
#articleFooter{
     border-bottom:thin dotted gray;
}
</style>
</head>
<body>
<header id="masthead">
<h1>Page Title Here</h1>
</header>
<div id="mainContent">
<section id="greeting">
<header id="greetingHeader">
<h1>Welcome to our web page</h1>
</header>
<p>This page is devoted to showing how to lay out pages using HTML5.</p>
<footer id="articleFooter">
</footer>
</section>
<article id="mainArticle">
<header id="mainArticleHeader"><h1>HTML5 Layout Techniques</h1></header>
<section id="layoutTags">
<p>List of tags</p>
<ul>
<li>&lt;header&gt;</li>
<li>&lt;footer&gt;</li>
<li>&lt;article&gt;</li>
<li>&lt;section&gt;</li>
</ul></section>
<footer id="articleFooter">
Content added by Webbingways.com</footer>
</article>
</div>
<footer id="pageFooter">
<p>Copyright webbingways.com
<script>
var lastMod = new Date(document.lastModified);
document.write((lastMod.getMonth() + 1) + "-" + lastMod.getFullYear());
</script>
<noscript>
7-25-2011
</noscript>
</p>
</footer>
</body>
</html>
```

Code Listing 10-2 provides a complete article. The article has a header, content section, and footer. The article header and footer are separate from the page headers and footers. Reusing the header here allows you to include more `<h1>` tags in your document. Without these sections, multiple `<h1>` tags would be considered inappropriate because they would lead to confusion regarding the title of the content. With the sections, both sighted and vision-impaired readers will clearly see the relationship of the headers to their content.

<aside>

The `<aside>` tag has many uses. W3C suggests the tag should hold information that is somehow related to the main content, such as sidebars, tips, related information, and pull quotes. (*Pull quotes* are the primary knowledge that you want readers to absorb.) Generally, you can use the `<aside>` tag to discuss information that adds or clarifies the main content. Code Listing 10-3, in the next section, demonstrates the use of the `<aside>` tag.

<nav>

The `<nav>` container will hold navigation elements for the web page. It can contain links for site navigation, page navigation, or navigation within a section. Common uses for the `<nav>` tag are menu bars in the header or sidebar of a page.

Most pages currently use a `<div id="menu">` tag to build a navigation menu. Replacing this with `<nav id="menu">` will retain the same formatting and functionality in your site but add the semantic information necessary to help screen readers.

Code Listing 10-3 shows a `<nav>` tag and an `<aside>` tag used properly. The `<nav>` tag creates a menu bar within the header of the page, and the `<aside>` tag adds a pull quote. In this code, I removed the placeholder text.

Code Listing 10-3   Using an aside and a nav container

```
<!doctype html>
<html lang="en">
<head>
<meta charset="utf-8">
<title>Chapter 10 Layouts</title>
<style>
body{
     font-family:Verdana, Geneva, sans-serif;
}

#pageFooter{
     text-align:center;
     font-size:.65em;
     font-variant:small-caps;
     border-top:1pt solid gray;
}
#masthead{
     font-size:1.5em;
```

```
        font-family:Impact, Charcoal, sans-serif;
        padding:0;
margin-top:-.4em;
}
#menu ul{
padding:0em;
font-size:.75em;
margin:0em;
}
#menu ul li{
display: inline;
font-weight: bold;
font-family:Verdana, Geneva, sans-serif;
}
#menu ul li a:hover, .menu ul li a.selected{
border-bottom-color: black;
}
#menu ul li a{
color: #494949;
padding: .5em .25em .33em .25em;
margin-right: 1.5em; /*spacing between each menu link*/
text-decoration: none;
border-bottom: .25em solid gray;
}
#masthead h1{
        font-size:2em;
        padding:0em;
        margin:0em;
}
#pullQuote
{
        border:thin solid;
        background-color:gray;
        width:15%;
        float:right;
        margin:2em 0em 0em 0em;
}
</style>
</head>
<body>
<header id="masthead">
<h1>Page Title Here</h1>
<nav id="menu">
<ul>
<li><a href="#">Home</a></li>
<li><a href="#">Features</a></li>
<li><a href="#">Contact Us</a></li>
```

```
<li><a href="#">Other Stuff</a></li>
</ul>
</nav>
</header>

<div id="mainContent">
<section id="greeting">
<header id="greetingHeader">
<h1>Welcome to our web page</h1>
</header>
<p>This page is devoted to showing how to lay out pages using HTML5.</p>
</section>

<article id="mainArticle">
<header id="mainArticleHeader"><h1>HTML5 Layout Techniques</h1></header>
<section id="layoutTags">
<p>List of tags</p>
<ul>
<li>&lt;header&gt;</li>
<li>&lt;footer&gt;</li>
<li>&lt;article&gt;</li>
<li>&lt;section&gt;</li>
<li>&lt;aside&gt;</li>
<li>&lt;nav&gt;</li>
</ul></section>
<section id="mainArticleContent">
<p> First paragraph here.
</p>
<aside id="pullQuote">
<h1>This is my callout</h1>
</aside>
<p> Second paragraph here.
</p>
</section>
<footer id="mainArticleFooter">
Content added by Webbingways.com</footer>
</article>
</div>
<footer id="pageFooter">
<p>Copyright webbingways.com
<script>
var lastMod = new Date(document.lastModified);
document.write((lastMod.getMonth() + 1) + "-" + lastMod.getFullYear());
</script>
<noscript>
7-25-2011
</noscript>
```

```
</p>
</footer>
</body>
</html>
```

Figure 10-1 shows the output from Code Listing 10-3. I added more formatting in this example than earlier. The `#pullQuote` right-aligns and shades the pull quote. I placed the pull quote between paragraphs simply because it looked better. For the menu, I changed the `<li>` tags to be on the same line, using `display:inline;` inside the `#menu ul li` entry. I then applied some common link-formatting tricks. I removed the normal underline and replaced it with a thick border. For rollover, I changed the color of the border to black. Finally, the `#masthead h1` formats the `<h1>` tag in the header to have no padding or margins. This places the `<h1>` very close to the top left of the page, and places the menu bar close to the bottom of the `<h1>` tag.

<figure> and <figcaption>

At first glance, the `<figure>` tag seems the easiest to understand. Obviously, figures are the intended content. However, what constitutes a figure is debatable. Pictures and videos are obvious entries. W3C also recommends using figures for illustrations and code blocks. The geolocation maps presented in Chapter 9 could also be figures.

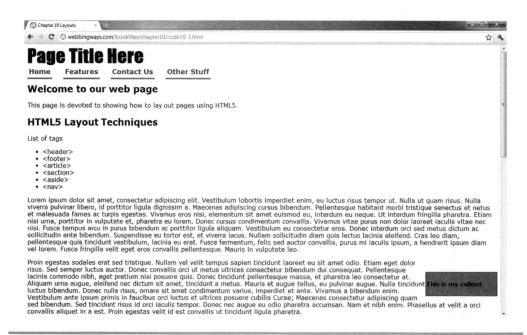

Figure 10-1 A pull quote and menu bar added to a web page

Recall that the `<article>` tag can hold interactive widgets. Thus, videos, audio controls, and the maps from Chapter 9 could be enclosed in either an `<article>` or a `<figure>` tag. My suggestion for resolving this problem lies in the definition of the article element. The `<article>` tag is used for content that can stand on its own. So, if your video could stand alone without the site describing it, use an `<article>` tag. If your video needs the surrounding text to be meaningful, use the `<figure>` tag.

The optional `<figcaption>` tag places a title with the figure. To use the `<figcaption>` tag, place it within the `<figure>` tag, either above or below the content. The placement of the `<figcaption>` tag controls where the caption appears. Putting it below the image will result in the caption appearing under the image on the browser.

Code Listing 10-4 shows the `<figure>` and `<figcaption>` tags in action. Figure 10-2 shows the result.

Code Listing 10-4   Using the <figure> and <figcaption> tags

```
<!doctype html>
<html lang="en">
<head>
<meta charset="utf-8">
```

Figure 10-2   The figure and figcaption tags on a web page

```
<title>HTML5 Figures</title>
<style>
figcaption{
        font-style:italic;
}
img{
padding:.5em;
border:.5em dashed grey;
}
</style>
</head>
<body>
<figure>
<img src="images/kids.jpg" width="409" height="512" />
<figcaption>All Star Athletes</figcaption>
</figure>
</body>
</html>
```

<details> and <summary>

The `<details>` tag holds metadata about the content. The author, creation date, abstract, and other important facts could be stored here. W3C intended this tag to be an expandable box that shows the details on command. Even though this functionality is easily replicated in JavaScript, the developers of HTML5 introduced this tag to simplify a developer's job.

NOTE

Currently, only Google Chrome supports the `<details>` tag.

The details section can hold other tags. The `<time>` tag is exceptionally useful to display the content-creation date of the article. Any tag, except for `<summary>`, will be hidden by default. If you include a `<summary>` tag, this will be visible at all times, and the rest of the details section will be hidden.

Code Listing 10-5 adds details to the image shown in Code Listing 10-4. In the details section, I added the descriptive paragraph as a summary. As Figures 10-3 and 10-4 show, the summary is visible on page load, while the details are shown on demand.

Figure 10-3 The details are hidden when the page loads.

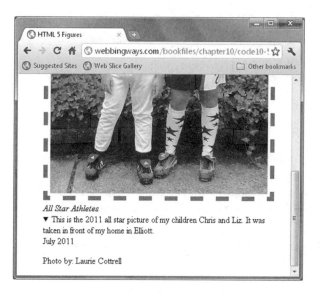

Figure 10-4 The details are shown on demand.

Code Listing 10-5   Using the <details> tag

```
<!doctype html>
<html lang="en">
<head>
<meta charset="utf-8">
<title>HTML5 Figures</title>
<style>
figcaption{
     font-style:italic;
}
img{
padding:.5em;
border:.5em dashed grey;
}
</style>
</head>
<body>
<figure>
<img src="images/kids.jpg" alt="Picture of my kids"
     width="409" height="512" />
<figcaption>All Star Athletes</figcaption>
<details>
<summary>
This is the 2011 all star picture of my children Chris and Liz.
It was taken in front of my home in Elliott.
</summary>
<time>July 2011</time>
<p>Photo by: Laurie Cottrell</p>
</details>
</figure>
</body>
</html>
```

As of the time of this writing, only Google Chrome fully supports the <details> tag. For other browsers, you still need to code the JavaScript to create an expanding box. Code Listing 10-6 includes an example of the JavaScript needed to show and hide the details. The functionality is not perfect, but its results are similar to the previous example.

Code Listing 10-6   Simulating the details functionality in other browsers

```
<!doctype html>
<html lang="en">
<head>
<meta charset="utf-8">
```

```html
<title>HTML5 Figures</title>
<style>
figcaption{
      font-style:italic;
}
img{
padding:.5em;
border:.5em dashed grey;
}img.triangle{
padding:0em;
      border:none;
      display:inline;
}
</style>
<script>
function isChrome(){
var chrome = navigator.userAgent.toLowerCase().indexOf('chrome') > -1;
return chrome;
}function expand() {
      if(!isChrome(){ ){
            var details = document.getElementById("displayDetails");
            var triImage = document.getElementById("triImage");
            if(details.style.display == "block") {
                    details.style.display = "none";
                    triImage.src= "images/triangle.png";
            }
            else {
                  details.style.display = "block";
                  triImage.src= "images/triangleDown.png";
            }
      }
}
function hideDetails() {
      if(!isChrome(){) {
       document.getElementById("displayDetails").style.display="none";
      }
}

</script>
 </head>
<body>
<figure>
<img src="images/kids.jpg" width="409" height="512"></img>
<figcaption>All Star Athletes</figcaption>
<script>
if (!isChrome(){){
      document.write('<img class="triangle" id="triImage"
```

```
           src="images/triangle.png" width="8" height="8"
            onclick="expand();">');
}
window.onload = function () { hideDetails(); };

</script>
<details>
<summary>
This is the 2011 all star picture of my children Chris and Liz.
It was taken in front of my home in Elliott.</summary>
<div id="displayDetails">
<time>July 2011</time>
<p>Photo by: Laurie Cottrell</p>
</div>
</details>
</figure>
</body>
</html>
```

Code Listing 10-6 adds a `<div>` tag around the portion of the details section I wish to hide. Recall that `<div>` tags are to be used for styling or scripting. Loading the page calls the `hideDetails` function, which determines the browser in use. If the browser is Chrome, the JavaScript functionality across the entire page is ignored. For other browsers, `hideDetails` will set the div display style to `none`, effectively hiding the details.

Inside the `<figure>` tag, a JavaScript function displays a triangle image in browsers other than Chrome. This image is clickable. When clicked, the image calls `expand()`, which shows or hides the div.

`<hgroup>`

The `<hgroup>` tag is designed to allow you to create a series of headings, which are not intended for page structuring. Typically, a heading on a page signifies a change in content, or at least subcontent.

A good use of the `<hgroup>` tag is to create a section listing all of the sections in a chapter. This can either be at the top of a section as a preview of coming attractions or at the end of the code as a summary.

Summary

HTML5 has added several new sectioning tags to the designer's toolbox. These new tags complement the trusty `<div>` tag. In addition to helping with layout, the new tags provide semantic meaning to your divisions. These semantic tags help you organize your markup more logically to reflect the meaning of content, provide hints for search engines, and help the vision-impaired to better navigate your site. The `<div>` tag still hangs around, as an object for styling and scripting, or to use if none of the new tags suits your needs.

Chapter 11

New HTML Form
Elements and Usage

Collecting data with HTML has always been an important facet of web design. Forms have evolved to support the current data needs. HTML5 continues this trend by introducing new methods of collecting data that are more secure, more user-friendly, and easier for the developer to use than with previous versions. They are also very browser-dependent.

The new items in HTML5 are not necessarily new tags, but modifications on how the existing tags can be used. For example, the < input > tag has many new types to use, well beyond the text boxes and menus offered by HTML4. Trying a new input type is completely safe, as browsers that do not support the new tag will convert them to a standard text box. Since the new types will revert to an HTML4 text box, you can safely experiment. (Of course, this has been a feature of HTML for quite some time; any mistaken input type becomes a text box.) Once browser support improves, your experiments will become more functional.

NOTE

At the time of this writing, Opera supported more form features than any other browser. Given the importance of forms, this is likely to change in the near future.

HTML5 Input Types

The most common form element in HTML4 is the < input > tag, a polymorphic tag that changes based on the type parameter supplied, such as text, password, hidden, radio, and checkbox.

HTML5 adds many new types for the < input > tag. The new types provide many benefits for the developer and user, including the following:

- They provide better functionality on mobile devices. The email type, for example, makes the @ symbol easy to find on Android and iOS on-screen keyboards.

- They add more semantic meaning to the tags. For example, < input type="URL" > is clearly asking for a web page. Screen readers and mobile devices can present the correct prompts or helpers to the user for URL input.

Table 11-1 lists the new types, which we will explore in this chapter.

In addition to new types, HTML5 introduces attributes that better support form-based input. These new attributes help validate the page and provide information for the types. Table 11-2 lists the new attributes.

Creating a Form

Creating a form in HTML5 is little different than building one in HTML4. You still need to use a name and an ID, and select a method and an action. The name and ID are used for scripting purposes; either can be used. The method can be either GET or POST. Use GET for an action that is repeatable, such as for a search form. Use POST for a nonrepeatable action, such as for

New Input Type	Description
color	A text box holding an RGB value. Depending on the browser, it can render as a color picker dialog.
date	A date entry control storing only a date. Depending on the browser, this can display a calendar.
datetime	A date and time entry control storing the UTC date and a time value. Depending on the browser, this can display a calendar.
datetime-local	A date and time entry control storing the local date and a time value. Depending on the browser, this can display a calendar.
email	A text box that provides an input for an e-mail address.
month	A date control holding the month and year.
number	A numeric input box that holds a number. Depending on the browser, it can render as a spinner or a text box.
range	A numeric input box that holds a number. Depending on the browser, it can render as a slider or a text box.
search	A text box that is intended to provide an interface to a query.
tel	A text box for a numeric phone number entry.
time	A time control that allows the user to pick hours, minutes, and seconds.
url	A text field that provides an entry for an absolute URL to a web page.
week	A control that selects a week from the year.

Table 11-1   The New Values for Input Types

an order form or a contact update. The action is the URL to a script that responds to the form data.

Contained within the form are one or more fieldsets, a legend, and all of your form controls. The *fieldset* is a container for holding fields. It is primarily a styling tag. The legend provides a title for the fieldset. After the legend, your field objects are listed.

Code Listing 11-1 shows an HTML5 form that we will build on in this chapter.

Code Listing 11-1   A basic HTML5 form

```
<!doctype html>
<html lang="en">
<head>
<meta charset="utf-8">
<title>Chapter 11 Forms</title>
<style>
</style>
</head>
```

```
<body>
<form name="form111" id="form111" method="post" action="#" >
<fieldset>
<legend>Your field objects</legend>
</fieldset>
</form>
</body>
</html>
```

Attribute	Description	Value
autocomplete	Toggles whether a field can autocomplete	on, off
autofocus	Places the cursor into the specified control	autofocus
form	Indicates to which form the input control belongs	Form element ID
formaction	Overrides the form action	Valid URL
formenctype	Describes how the form should be encoded before sending it to a server	application/x-www-form-urlencoded, multipart/form-data, text/plain
formmethod	Changes the form HTTP submission method	get, post
formnovalidate	Indicates if a field should be validated before submission	No value needed
formtarget	Lists the target window for the form result	_blank, _self, _parent, _top, window name
height	Sets the height of an image control	Pixels or percentage value
list	Adds a data list control for a drop-down field	Data list ID
max	Sets the largest value for a numeric or date input field	Number, date
min	Sets the smallest value for a numeric or date input field	Number, date
pattern	Holds a regular expression pattern used for validation	Regular expression
placeholder	Shows a hint within the control describing the desired values	Text
required	Indicates that the value must be entered before the form can be submitted	No value needed
step	Specifies the interval for numeric input boxes	Number
width	Sets the width of an image control	Pixels or percentage value

Table 11-2 The New Input Attributes

Adding a Color Picker

The `color` type, when implemented, will present a color dialog to the user, from which the user can visually select a desired color. The proper RGB value will be stored. This value can be used for DOM scripting, product choices, or whatever the programmer desires. Figure 11-1 shows the Opera browser rendering the color object.

NOTE

As of this writing, only Opera properly supports the `color` type. To reproduce the color picker in other browsers, you will need to write JavaScript code.

Code Listing 11-2 shows a form with a color object that changes the background color of the form when you select a new color.

Code Listing 11-2   Responding to the color object

```
<!doctype html>
<html lang="en">
<head>
<meta charset="utf-8">
<title>Chapter 11 Forms</title>
<script>
window.onload = function () {
 document.getElementById("colorPick").onchange = function () {
      document.bgColor=this.value;
 }
}
```

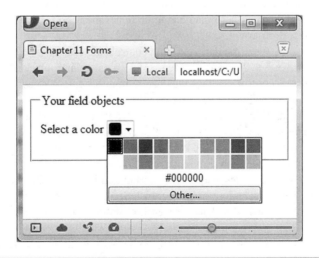

Figure 11-1   The color object running in Opera

```
</script>
</head>
<body>
<form name="form112" id="form112" method="post" action="#" >
<fieldset>
<legend>Your field objects</legend>
<p><label for="colorPick">Select a color</label>
<input type="color" id="colorPick" name="colorPick">
</p>
</fieldset>
</form>
</body>
</html>
```

Code Listing 11-2 shows a typical call to an HTML5 `<input>` element. Notice that it uses both the `id` and `name` attributes: the `id` attribute for scripting purposes, and the `name` attribute to post to the action. Changing a color fires the JavaScript change event that you can handle. The `colorPick` value holds the selected RGB value. In other browsers, if you type a valid HTML color, the page does react properly.

Adding Date and Time Controls

The `date`, `datetime`, `datetime-local`, `month`, `time`, and `week` types are related to date and time values. Depending on the browser, all except the time element will display a calendar control. The time control will display a time spinner. The calendar control provides an integrated method of selecting a date and time.

Date and time entry functionality has been available through JavaScript libraries for some time. W3C believed that including this functionality in the language made complete sense. It allows a unified method of gathering a date and reduces the need for using complex JavaScript to build the calendar drop-down.

As with the `color` type, the date and time controls are created by a value handed to the type attribute of `<input>`. The `date` type displays a calendar control allowing the selection of a date. Clicking this control displays the current month's calendar, as shown in Figure 11-2. Simple navigation controls allow changing months and years.

The `datetime` and `datetime-local` types are very similar in functionality. Both return a value in *mm-dd-yyyy HH:SS* format. The primary difference is where in the world the time applies. The `datetime-local` type returns the time in your time zone, in UTC time, or Zulu time, based in Greenwich, England.

The `month` and `week` types also display a calendar. However, the user can select only a month or a week, depending on the control. Selecting a month control will return data in a form similar to 2012-09. The week control will return data in a form similar to 2012-W42.

The time control is simply a spinner. The spinner will count up in minutes from 0:00 to 24:00. Every 60 minutes results in a new hour. The time returned is independent of a time

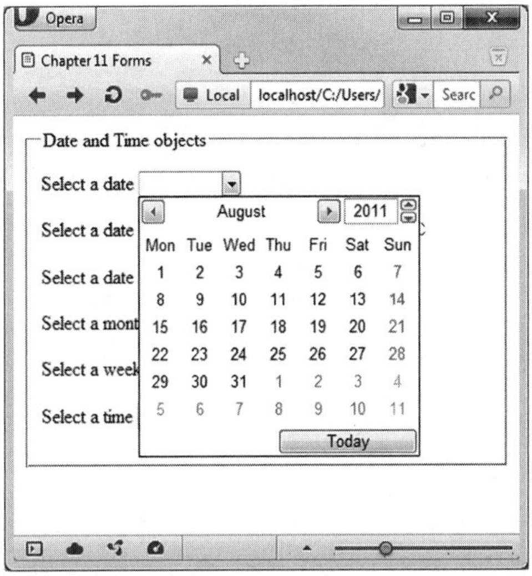

Figure 11-2 The date object displayed in Opera

zone. You can manually enter the time values, but depending on the browser, the control will accept only valid time entries.

Code Listing 11-3 shows a form displaying all of these date and time elements. The change event fires whenever you select a new date or time. The change event calls the display() function, which will display the value returned by the control in a paragraph tag.

Code Listing 11-3   The HTML5 date and time form objects

```
<!doctype html>
<html lang="en">
<head>
<meta charset="utf-8">
<title>Chapter 11 Forms</title>
<script>
function display(dateVal){
     document.getElementById("yourDate").innerHTML = dateVal;
}
</script>
</head>
<body>

<form id="form113" name="form113" method="post" action="#">
<fieldset>
<legend>Date and Time objects</legend>
<p><label for="justDate">Select a date</label>
```

```
<input type="date" id="justDate" name="justDate"
onchange="display(justDate.value);">
</p>

<p><label for="dateTimeUTC">Select a date and a time</label>
<input type="datetime" id="dateTimeUTC" name="dateTimeUTC"
onchange="display(dateTimeUTC.value);">
</p>

<p><label for="dateTimeLocal">Select a date and a time</label>
<input type="datetime-local" id="dateTimeLocal"
name="dateTimeLocal" onchange="display(dateTimeLocal.value);">
</p>

<p><label for="month">Select a month</label>
<input type="month" id="month" name="month"
onchange="display(month.value);">
</p>

<p><label for="week">Select a week</label>
<input type="week" id="week" name="week"
onchange="display(week.value);">
</p>

<p><label for="time">Select a time</label>
<input type="time" id="time" name="time"
onchange="display(time.value);">
</p>

</fieldset>
</form>
<p id="yourDate"></p>
</body>
</html>
```

Using the E-mail and URL Fields

The e-mail and URL fields render as text boxes. Semantically, they are special-purpose text boxes.

On a computer browser, there is little to no difference in functionality between the standard text box and the e-mail and URL fields. Current browsers will simply render them as text boxes. However, regardless of your browser's support for these fields, you should use them. As browser support matures, your form will be future-proofed.

On a mobile browser, the e-mail and URL fields can trigger special on-screen keyboards. For example, on my Android, an e-mail box makes the @ symbol prominent, without needing to hit the Alt lock. For the URL boxes, my Android displays the / (slash) and .com buttons.

The .com button is very useful, as it adds .com to the end of the address. Depending on the Android version, this button can change to a variety of different domains.

CAUTION
Since the e-mail and URL boxes work just like text boxes, you still need to protect your web site. You should use the `maxlength` attribute on all of these fields, and check the data both server-side and client-side for unwanted characters.

Where the e-mail and URL boxes really shine is in validation, which is the process of ensuring that the data entered in your form is correct. The new HTML5 validation tools make validating an e-mail or URL address a snap. Validation is covered later in this chapter.

Adding Number and Range Controls

The number and range controls continue HTML5 semantic and validation improvements over the standard text box. When implemented, both controls allow you to enter only a number. The `range` type provides a slider control, and the `number` type provides a spinner. Figure 11-3 shows the two controls in Opera.

These controls have a number of useful attributes. Each is supposed to take a floating-point value, but currently, only integers seem to be supported. The `min` attribute sets the lowest value the box will accept, and `max` sets the largest value. The `step` property allows you to set an increment, which is used by both controls to determine the next numeric value as you scroll up or down. The default for `step` is 1. Later in the chapter, I will demonstrate how HTML5 can validate these values.

Code Listing 11-4 is the code snippet from the form that created the controls shown in Figure 11-3. The range control allows values from 0 to 100, stepping 5 at a time. The number control allows values from –50 to 50, in steps of 2. In both cases, I included the `maxlength` attribute. Finally, I set a value for the boxes, which acts as a starting point.

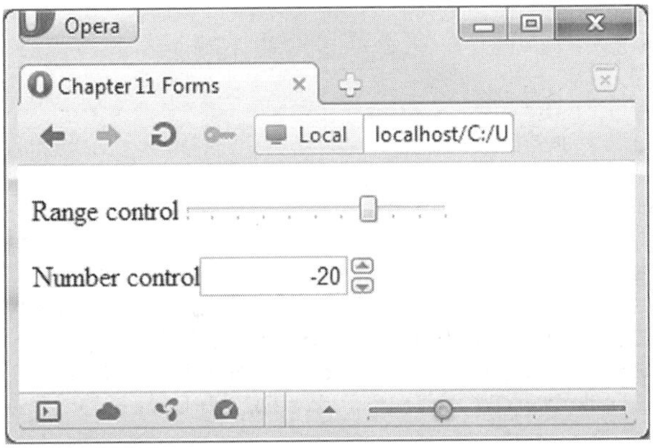

Figure 11-3 The range and number controls displayed in Opera

NOTE

Browsers that do not support range or number boxes will revert to standard text boxes. The `maxlength` attribute limits the number of digits that can be input into the box.

Code Listing 11-4   The range and number controls

```
<p><label for="numRange">Range control</label>
<input name="numRange" id="numRange" type="range"
min="0" max="100" step="5" maxlength="3" value="50"></p>

<p><label for=" numSpinner" id="numSpinner">Number control</label>
<input name="numSpinner" id="numSpinner" type="number"
min="-50" max="50" step="2" maxlength="3" value="0"></p>
```

The form objects are typically used to gather information from the user. However, with a little programming skill, they can be used for a complete user interface. Microsoft has announced that HTML5 tools will be available for developing Windows 8 interfaces. In a similar vein, Apple has long blocked Flash from its iOS devices. Clearly, Apple wants developers to move from Flash to HTML5.

To demonstrate HTML5's abilities for creating a user interface, Code Listing 11-5 revisits the audio player from Code Listing 6-3. In that code, the web site played a song without the player being visible. The version in Code Listing 11-5 adds a form with a range control to change the volume.

Code Listing 11-5   A user interface to the audio object

```
<!doctype html>
<html lang="en">
<head>
<meta charset="utf-8">
<title>Chapter 11 Forms</title>
<script>
function playmusic() {

  document.getElementById("audio1").play();
  document.getElementById("play").innerHTML = "Resume";
  document.getElementById("pause").disabled=false;
  document.getElementById("startover").disabled=false;
  document.getElementById("play").disabled=true;
}
function changeVolume(player, level){
      player.volume = (level / 100);
```

```
            document.getElementById("volumeLevel").innerHTML = level + "%";
}
function pausePlay(player){
        player.pause();
        document.getElementById("play").disabled=false;
        document.getElementById("pause").disabled=true;
}

function setStartPoint(player, seconds){
        player.currentTime = seconds;
        player.pause();
        document.getElementById("pause").disabled=true;
        document.getElementById("startover").disabled=true;
        document.getElementById("play").disabled=false;
        document.getElementById("play").innerHTML = "Play";
}
</script>
</head>
<body onload="document.getElementById('audio1').volume = .5;">
 <div style="margin-left:40px;">
  <h1>Music with volume control</h1>
  <p>Use the buttons to control the player.
 Set the volume level using the slider. If it is not present,
 then type the desired volume level (0-100), and press tab. </p>
  <br><br>
  <audio id="audio1">
  <source src="music/song1.ogg" type="audio/ogg" />
  <source src="music/song1.oga" type="audio/ogg" />
  <source src="music/song1.mp3" type="audio/mpeg" />
  <source src="music/song1.wav" type="audio/wav" />
Your browser does not support the audio element
  </audio>
  <br><br>
</div>
<form name="formvolume" id="formvolume" >
<p><input name="volume" id="volume" type="range"
min="0" max="100" step="5" maxlength="3" value="50"
onChange="changeVolume(audio1, volume.value);" />
<label for="volume" id="volumeLevel">50%</label></p>
</form>
<button id="play" onclick="playmusic();">Play</button>
<button id="pause" disabled onclick="pausePlay(audio1);">Pause</button>
<button id="startover" disabled
onclick="setStartPoint(audio1, 0);">Start Over</button>
</body>
</html>
```

This range control fires the function `changeVolume` whenever the user changes the volume. This function does two things for the program. First, it sets the volume level for the player. This `volume` property takes a value from 0 to 1. Since the range control generates only whole numbers, `changeVolume` divides the value from the slider by 100. The second task performed by `changeVolume` is to address a weakness with the slider. Sliders do not show you what values are associated with the control. I used the label to display the chosen value.

Buttons are present to start, stop, resume, and start the song over. The buttons are clearly labeled. The program disables those buttons that are not valid at any given time. When the song is played, the pause and start over buttons become enabled. The play button changes to a resume button and is disabled. Once the user hits pause, the pause button becomes disabled, and the resume button is enabled. The start over button will pause the song, reset the play button, disable all other buttons, and start the song at position 0.

Using Search

The `search` input type is intended to allow you to create a text box for entering search terms. On computers, all major browsers render this as a standard text box. On Mac OS X and Ubuntu, this will render as a text box with rounded corners.

To add insult to injury, the search box will resist normal attempts at CSS formatting. You can trick CSS to format the search box as a text box, but this seems like a lot of work. Until browser support becomes available, avoid using the `search` input type.

Adding Telephone Number Boxes

The `tel` input type is intended to allow the user to enter numeric telephone numbers. In all browsers, it renders as a simple text box. On the Android and iOS devices, the box triggers a special keyboard that provides easy access to the () and – symbols.

Telephone numbers come in many formats. Without additional attributes, the difference between a standard text box and a telephone number box is only semantic. However, as with the `email` and `url` types, `tel` can be validated using the `pattern` attribute. Validation is discussed in the next section.

Creating Safe Forms

Creating a form to gather user input is easy. Creating a form that users can understand and fill in as desired is much harder. And creating a form that users understand and that guarantees that the user input is correct is very difficult. I often spend more time idiotproofing my forms than actually designing them.

My first professional programming job involved working with a law firm specializing in collections. The collectors had the unenviable job of phoning people who had not paid their jewelry credit card in more than 6 months. Part of the process was to create a payment plan to pay off the loan within 12 months. I wrote a program that asked the collector for the amount of the debt, the interest rate charged by the store, and the number of months to pay off the loan.

I verified that all of the values were within certain limits. For example, the months had to be between 1 and 12. Additionally, local rules required that we audit all entries by saving them to disk.

One collector—let's call her Brenda—used my program and entered 1200 for the amount of the debt, 18 for the percentage rate, and the word *twelve* for the months. Unfortunately, I did not expect string input into my integer variable. The C program then went into an infinite loop. To add insult to injury, the program wrote Brenda's input into the log file. Within a few minutes, the log file filled the disk, dropping the Unix server that controlled the entire law firm. Ultimately, the blame for the server crash was laid on my shoulders.

The moral of this story is to assume that your users will do the most amazingly stupid things to your program. You need to do the absolute best you can to protect your input. In the case of a web form, the challenge is even greater because the form is available 24 hours a day to users that you cannot see. A poorly designed form can lead to server crashes or data breaches.

CAUTION
You need to also validate the data on the server script that receives the data from your form.

Laying Out Forms
The first step is to create a form that is easy to understand. Easy-to-use forms include clear labels and directions for filling out the form. Writing clear instructions is difficult. What is crystal clear to you might be murky to some of your users.

One way to achieve clarity is to provide two prompts that say the same thing in two different ways. Pulling this off is easy in HTML5. You create one prompt using the HTML4 `<label>` tag, and the second prompt using the new HTML5 `placeholder` attribute.

The `<label>` tag attaches a text prompt to a form object. Using CSS formatting, you can easily obtain a nice layout. Screen-reading browsers can determine that the label is associated with the control and provide the proper audio prompts.

The `placeholder` attribute displays text within the input object. In HTML4, this was achieved by creating a value for the object and selecting the text whenever the control gained the focus. The placeholder is background text for the object. Once the object gains the focus, the placeholder text will vanish. If the object loses focus and is still blank, the placeholder text reappears. Placeholders can hold either a direction or sample formatting.

TIP
The currently selected control on a form has the focus.

Figure 11-4 shows an example of a nicely designed form that uses labels and placeholders. Code Listing 11-6 creates the form shown in Figure 11-4, including the placeholder text. The placeholders for the name and company contain instructions. Placeholders for the `tel` and `email` types contain the desired format.

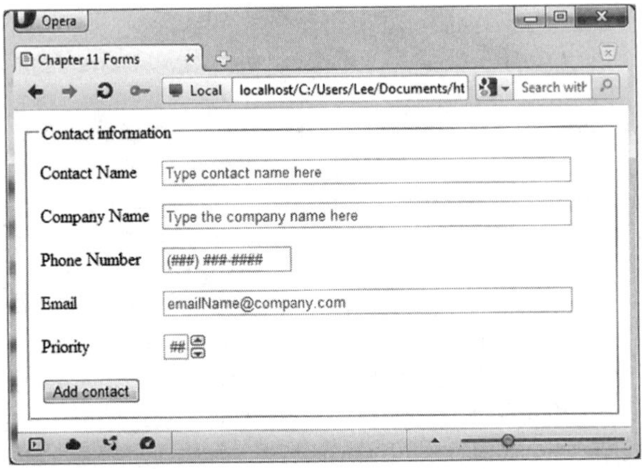

Figure 11-4 Example of labels and placeholders on a form

Code Listing 11-6 A nicely laid out form

```
<!doctype html>
<html lang="en">
<head>
<meta charset="utf-8">
<title>Chapter 11 Forms</title>
<style>
label{
      display:inline-block;
      float:left;
      width:7em;
}
</style>
</head>
<body>
<form method="post" action="#" name="contact">
<fieldset id="contactFields">
<legend>Contact information</legend>
<p><label for="contactName">Contact Name</label>
<input type="text" name="contactName"
id="contactName" autofocus maxlength="50" size="50"
placeholder="Type contact name here"></p>
<p><label for="contactCompany">Company Name</label>
<input type="text" name="contactCompany"
id="contactCompany"  maxlength="50" size="50"
placeholder="Type the company name here"></p>
<p><label for="contactPhone">Phone Number</label>
<input type="tel" name="contactPhone" id="contactPhone"
```

```
maxlength="14" size="14" placeholder="(###) ###-####"></p>
<p><label for="contactEmail">Email</label>
<input type="email" name="contactEmail" id="contactEmail"
maxlength="100" size="50" placeholder="emailName@company.com"></p>
<p><label for="contactPriority">Priority</label>
<input type="number" name="contactPriority" id="contactPriority"
maxlength="2" size="3" min="1" max="10" placeholder="##"></p>
<input type="submit" value="Add contact">
</fieldset>
</form>
</body>
</html>
```

The form in Code Listing 11-6 implements many features of a well-designed form. First, it has a fieldset. This object surrounds your form objects. It is used to logically group form objects. You can have as many fieldsets as you have logical groups. The legend identifies the group for the user. In this case, "Contact Information" appears in the fieldset box. Inside the fieldset are the labels and fields. Each grouping is enclosed within a `<p>` tag for nice formatting. I included the `for` attribute. The value of this attribute matches the `id` of the field it is identifying. The width of the label was set to 7em to ensure the form looks good in all font sizes and screen sizes.

NOTE
The `<label>` tag can also enclose text and form elements. This method is valid but reduces search engine optimization and is slightly harder to format.

Performing Validation
Validation is the act of checking your form data for correctness. Correctness means many things. In general, it means that the data in your form logically makes sense, matches your desired format, and has all of the items you require. The code presented here will validate your form on the client side. The results will alert users to mistakes they made in the form data.

Code Listing 11-6 used two elements that help with validation:

● The `contactName` field uses the `autofocus` attribute. This forces the cursor to rest in this field as soon as the page loads. This feature ensures that your user starts in the first field. You appreciate it because your users have a harder time missing the first field. The users appreciate it, as they do not need to click in the first field.

● The `maxlength` attribute, which has been in the HTML specification as long as I can remember, limits the number of characters you can enter into the box. By limiting your field sizes, you can hinder attackers from flooding your web server by sending thousands of copies of War and Peace from your text boxes.

CAUTION
The `maxlength` attribute is not foolproof. You still need to verify your data in your server-side scripts.

Prior to HTML5, you needed to validate your forms using JavaScript. On this simple form, I would need to verify that every box had a value. I would then need to ensure that the contact name and company name were all alphanumeric characters, with limited punctuation. For the telephone, e-mail, and URL fields, I would need to ensure that the data matched the desired format. This was quite a difficult task. Just in the United States, there are several valid phone number formats. Likewise, the e-mail and URL fields would need validation. The validation for a simple form could easily reach 100 lines of code. Only if everything was valid would I let the data post to my server.

NOTE
Opera and Chrome both automatically added http:// in front of the URL entered in to the URL box. Both validated any e-mail address in the form of a@a.

Validation in HTML5 is much simpler. Many new attributes support automatic validation. The attributes `max`, `min`, and `pattern` work with the browser to validate your data. If any object in your form does not contain valid data, then a global validation flag is set to `false`. This alone can be used to prevent your browser from posting invalid data. In addition to the global validation flag, each object has a validation flag. This allows you to set individual messages and format invalid boxes.

Figure 11-5 shows the sample contact form validated. Valid entries have a thumbs-up icon. Invalid entries have the thumbs-down entry.

CAUTION
Do not rely on just color changes to signify incorrect entries.

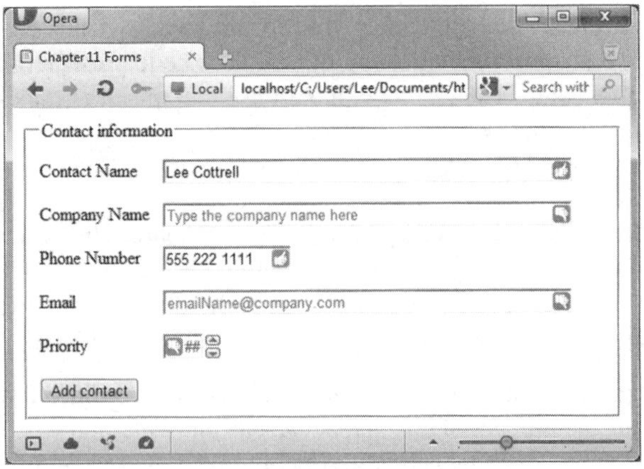

Figure 11-5 Data validated in the contact form

Formatting invalid boxes is handled through new HTML5/CSS3 pseudo classes. The classes `valid`, `invalid`, and `out-of-range` allow custom formatting whenever a box does not meet your constraints. You can validate the existence of an item, if it matches a pattern, or if the value is within a certain range.

Code Listing 11-7 shows complete validation on the contact form from Code Listing 11-6.

Code Listing 11-7	Validation of form data

```html
<!doctype html>
<html lang="en">
<head>
<meta charset="utf-8">
<title>Chapter 11 Forms</title>
<style>
label{
display:inline-block;
      float:left;
      width:7em;
}
input:invalid {
 background-position:right center;
 background-repeat:no-repeat;
 background-image:url("images/ThumbDown.png");
}
input:required:valid{
 background-position:right center;
 background-repeat:no-repeat;
 background-image:url("images/ThumbUp.png");
}
input[type=number]{
      text-align:right;
}
input[type=number]:invalid:out-of-range, input[type=number]:invalid {
 background-position:left center;
 background-repeat:no-repeat;
 background-image:url("images/ThumbDown.png");
}
input[type=number]:valid:in-range{
 background-position:left center;
 background-repeat:no-repeat;
 background-image:url("images/ThumbUp.png");
}
</style>
</head>
<body>
<form method="post" action="#" name="contact">
<fieldset id="contactFields">
```

```
<legend>Contact information</legend>
<p><label for="contactName">Contact Name</label>
<input type="text" id="contactName" required autofocus
maxlength="50" size="50" placeholder="Type contact name here"></p>
<p><label for="contactCompany">Company Name</label>
<input type="text" id="contactCompany" required
maxlength="50" size="50" placeholder="Type the company name here"></p>
<p><label for="contactPhone">Phone Number</label>
<input type="tel" id="contactPhone" required
maxlength="14" size="14" placeholder="(###) ###-####"
pattern="^\D?(\d{3})\D?\D?(\d{3})\D?(\d{4})$"></p>
<p><label for="contactEmail">Email</label>
<input type="email" id="contactEmail" required
maxlength="100" size="50" placeholder="emailName@company.com"
pattern="^\w+[\w-\.]*\@\w+((-\w+)|(\w*))\.[a-z]{2,3}$"/></p>
<p><label for="contactPriority">Priority</label>
<input type="number" id="contactWebsite" required
maxlength="2" size="5" min="1" max="10" placeholder="##"></p>
<input type="submit" value="Add contact">
</fieldset>
</form>
</body>
</html>
```

Wow, this is not a lot of code! The form will validate the data in each object. If the data is invalid, a thumbs-down icon will appear in the box. Valid data receives a thumbs-up icon. The `required` attribute is all that you need to add to verify the existence of data in the box. The pseudo classes of `input:required:valid` and `input:required:invalid` apply the formatting to improperly formatted objects.

For the telephone and e-mail objects, the `pattern` attribute is added to the object. Patterns hold regular expressions. Regular expressions are designed to allow you to write equations that match patterns. If the data typed in the box matches the pattern, HTML5 considers it valid. The regular expressions in this page come from the web site www.regexlib.com.

TIP

Regular expressions are not easy to write. RegExLib.com is the best resource online for working with regular expressions.

Unfortunately, validation through HTML5 and JavaScript alone is not sufficient. You still need to ensure that your server-side scripts validate everything that you check in your forms. It is all too easy to modify an existing web page and remove the validations. Your server is then vulnerable to attack. If you are developing the client side of a form, be sure to talk to your server programmers about the validations they need to include in their sanitizing scripts.

Submitting Data

The contact form presented in Code Listings 11-6 and 11-7 is designed to retrieve information about a business contact. This information needs to be stored somewhere. Typically, a web form such as this one will post to a script that will save the data. Before posting the data, the web developer should validate all data. Additionally, the server-side programmer should revalidate the data.

HTML5 adds another layer of validation when you attempt to submit. If a field does not pass validation, the browser will display a very obvious error message. If multiple fields do not validate, the browser will display one error at a time. If any field fails validation, the form will not send it to the action. Figure 11-6 shows an error on the telephone field.

NOTE

Through the `setCustomValidation` function, you will be able to customize the error message. However, this functionality is not quite ready yet.

The contact form is now validated with HTML5. However, you will still need to validate your forms completely using JavaScript. You cannot predict that all users will access your forms using an up-to-date browser, which means that you cannot depend on HTML5 validation. Additionally, HTML5 cannot handle some validations. An example is validating a credit card number. Many regular expressions exist that can verify that a 16-digit number is present in the box. However, not all 16-digit numbers are credit card numbers. For this trick, you can use the Luhn algorithm.

TIP

The Luhn algorithm mathematically verifies that a sequence of 16 digits is indeed a valid credit card number. It is the algorithm used by the credit card industry to generate account numbers.

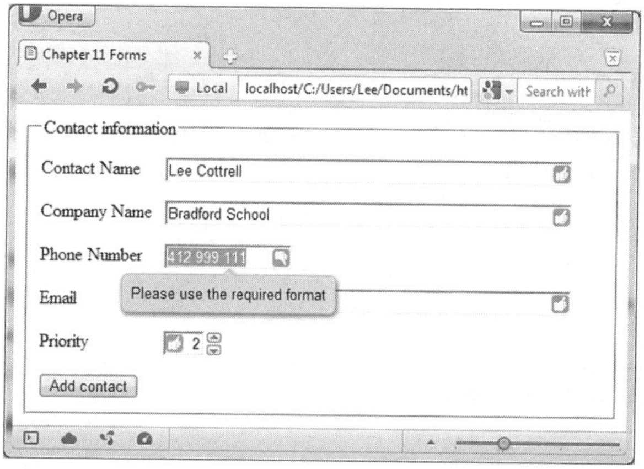

Figure 11-6   HTML5 validation message

In addition to validating, you can provide additional information to users. For those objects that do not pass validation, your script can add on-screen guidance to the user.

Code Listing 11-8 adds JavaScript validation to the contact form.

Code Listing 11-8   The JavaScript validation for the contact form

```
<script>
function checkForm(){
if(typeof contact.checkValidity == "undefined"){
        //check validity in non HTML5 compliant browsers
validForm = true;
if(!contact.contactName.value){
        alert("Please enter a name");
        contact.contactName.focus();
        return;
}
if(!contact.contactCompany.value){
        alert("Please enter a name");
        contact.contactName.focus();
        return;
}
if(!contact.contactCompany.value){
        alert("Please enter a company name");
        contact.contactCompany.focus();
        return;
}
var phoneRegEx = /^\D?(\d{3})\D?\D?(\d{3})\D?(\d{4})$/;
        if(!contact.contactPhone.value.match(phoneRegEx)){
        alert("Please enter a phone number");
        contact.contactPhone.focus();
        return;
}
var emailRegEx = /^\w+[\w-\.]*\@\w+((-\w+)|(\w*))\.[a-z]{2,3}$/;
if(!contact.contactEmail.value.match(emailRegEx)){
        alert("Please enter an email address");
        contact.contactEmail.focus();
        return;
}
if(isNaN(contact.contactPriority.value) ||
        !contact.contactPriority.value)
{
        alert("Please enter a priority between 1 and 10");
        contact.contactPriority.focus();
        return;
}
var priority = parseInt(contact.contactPriority.value);
if(priority < 1 || priority > 10)
```

```
{
     alert("Please enter a priority between 1 and 10");
     contact.contactPriority.focus();
     return;
}
contact.submit();
}
else{
//for HTML5 browsers
validForm = contact.checkValidity();
if(contact.checkValidity()==true){
     contact.submit();
}
}
}
</script>
```

Code Listing 11-8 validates the form in both HTML5 and older browsers. I called this code by modifying the button in the form from `type="submit"` to `type="button"` and added a click event handler. Code Listing 11-9 shows the correct button.

Code Listing 11-9	The new button for our contact form

```
<input type="button" onClick="checkForm();" value="Add contact">
```

The script starts by determining if `contact.checkValidity` is defined. If it is defined, then the browser supports HTML5. If it is not defined, then you need to resort to traditional JavaScript page validation. In the body of the `if` statement, I check each object on the form. For the name and company, I check for the existence of a value. If anything is present, then the box validates. Unfortunately, this technique will validate a space. For the phone and e-mail fields, I validate using the match and the same regular expressions from the form. For the number, I need to check for existence, nonnumeric expressions, and a valid range.

Compare the two versions. For HTML5 browsers, the code is embedded within the form itself. For older browsers, approximately 60 lines of code need to be written to validate the page. Clearly, the HTML5 technique is more efficient. Unfortunately, you will still need the older method until more browsers support HTML5.

Summary

The new HTML5 form objects have added new functionality to web forms. You are able to create semantically correct forms. While these new objects do not yet work on all forms, you should start using them now, as browsers will simply render them as text objects.

Validation is handled by the browser within the form. When this feature becomes commonplace, one huge coding burden will be lifted from developers' hands.

Chapter 12

CSS3: New Styling Techniques

Every chapter up to this point has been about HTML5. However, each chapter has included pieces of CSS code along with the HTML. You cannot learn HTML without touching CSS.

In this chapter, we will explore some of the new properties and functionality that CSS3 provides to web developers. CSS3 offers nearly 200 new properties and enhancements to CSS2. In many cases, the improvements solve problems developers have encountered in the past. Some of the additions make your CSS code easier to read. Other enhancements are purely visual candy. The difficult part of writing this chapter was determining what to leave out.

CSS3 is divided into many different modules. Each module is tasked with one portion of web design. The modules include backgrounds, font, transformations, animation, and user interface improvements. I think that even the most experienced CSS developer will believe that CSS3 is awesome.

CSS3 Modules

Like the new tags in HTML5, not everything in CSS3 works in all browsers. However, the majority of the new properties will work in both current and older browsers. Support in older browsers requires the use of a browser prefix. Table 12-1 lists the prefixes and versions for each browser.

The prefixes arose from browser developers implementing their own competing CSS standards prior to the acceptance of CSS3. However, some of the accepted properties still require the prefixes. Table 12-1 gives a guide as to when the prefix is necessary. As a rule, I include all prefixes in my CSS, just to make sure. I know that it is overkill, but I want to ensure that my CSS works in as many browsers as possible. Unlike HTML5, most of these new properties will work in both modern and older Internet Explorer windows.

Web Fonts

Property	Value
@font-face	Name and location of font files

One of the things that my design students hate about designing web pages is the limited choice of fonts available. I am forever discussing the use of web-safe fonts with the students.

Browser	Version	Prefix
Chrome	7.0 and previous	-webkit
Firefox	3.5 and previous	-moz
Opera	11.0 and previous	-o
Safari	3.1 and previous	-webkit
Internet Explorer	9.0	-ms

Table 12-1   Browsers and Associated Vendor Prefixes

Students always say, "The page font worked at home, but not here at school." Thankfully, W3C has solved this problem for web developers. Designers can now use any font they legally own. CSS3 has included a new rule called `@font-face`.

The `@font-face` property will instruct your browser to download the specified font. Thus, there is no more need to discuss web-safe fonts. With just a little work, all fonts are web-safe.

CAUTION

Using fonts on a web page is tricky from a legal standpoint. Font licenses often allow you to install them on a computer or network and print any document with them. Adding them to a web page will require downloading the font to the client computer. This may be a violation of the user license. For now, stick with fonts that are freeware or have an end-user license agreement (EULA) that supports web use.

CSS3 Rules for Fonts

CSS3 rules are a departure from traditional CSS thinking, which is that CSS properties are used to format a single element. In contrast, the rules apply to other CSS values. You can think of them as programmed defined constants. Once you create and name the `@font-face` rule, you can use it wherever you want in the CSS document.

CAUTION

Downloading large font files can take time. Be sure you truly need the font before uploading a large font file.

You need to set up the rule before you can use it. For `@font-face`, you need to create a new `@font-face` section within your CSS document. Within this section are the properties of your desired font. You need a `src` entry to describe the location of the font. The `src` property can take many parameters. Typically, you list one URL per version of the font you have. The font files should reside on the same web site as the CSS document. If you are using a common font, such as those included with an operating system, the `local()` function can also be added to the `src` entry. In the event that your user already has the font, then the browser does not need to download another copy.

Your `@font-face` section will also need a font family name. This is the name used within your CSS document to apply your font.

In addition to the source and font family, you can specify a font weight and a font style. These optional parameters have been available in CSS for quite some time. The `font-weight` property sets bold or normal font. The `font-style` property applies italics, underline, or strike-through. You'll see an example of a `@font-face` section in Code Listing 12-1, coming up soon.

Font Formats

Unfortunately, there are many different formats for fonts. The old standby in the publishing world is TrueType Fonts (TTF). All browsers, except Internet Explorer, support TTF fonts.

Browser	TTF	EOT	WOFF	SVG
Internet Explorer	9	5+	9	
Firefox	3.5		3.6	3.5
Chrome	4		5	3
Safari	3.1			3.1
Opera	10			9
IOS				1
Android	2.2			

Table 12-2 Font and Browser Support Matrix

Internet Explorer 9 and earlier versions support the proprietary Embedded OpenType (EOT) fonts. Thus, to support all browsers, you need to upload *at least* two font files to your site: a TTF file and an EOT file.

To add confusion to the mix, many other forms of fonts exist. Table 12-2 shows the matrix of fonts and browser support. To be safe, you should upload all versions of the font to your web site. If you want to use italics or other special versions of the font, you will need to upload those files as well.

TIP

To generate your font files, visit www.fontsquirrel.com/fontface/generator. This site will convert your files for free and provide the valid CSS to use the fonts.

Using Fonts on a Web Site

Code Listing 12-1 shows the CSS code needed to use the Nashville and Baskerville Old Face Regular fonts on a web site. Nashville is a freeware font acquired from www.fontspace.com. Baskerville is a Microsoft Office font, which is likely to be on a user's machine. The CSS code was generated by FontSquirrel.com and modified for my web structure. The complete code for this and the other examples in this chapter is available on www.webbingways.com.

Code Listing 12-1   The CSS to declare and use a web font

```
@font-face {
    font-family: 'NashvilleRegular';
    src: url('fonts/nashvill-webfont.eot');
    src: url('fonts/nashvill-webfont.eot?#iefix')
        format('embedded-opentype'),
      url('fonts/nashvill-webfont.ttf') format('ttf'),
      url('fonts/nashvill-webfont.woff') format('woff'),
      url('fonts/nashvill-webfont.svg#NashvilleRegular')
```

```
                format('svg');
        font-weight: bold;
}
@font-face {
        font-family: 'BaskervilleOldFaceRegular';
        src: url('fonts/baskvill-webfont.eot');
        src: local('Baskerville Old Face Regular'),
                url('fonts/baskvill-webfont.eot?#iefix')
                    format('embedded-opentype'),
                url('fonts/baskvill-webfont.woff') format('woff'),
                url('fonts/baskvill-webfont.ttf') format('truetype'),
                url('fonts/baskvill-webfont.svg#BaskervilleOldFaceRegular')
                    format('svg');
}
h1, h2, h3{
        font-family:NashvilleRegular, sans-serif;
        font-weight:bold;
        font-variant:small-caps;
}
body{
        font-family:BaskervilleOldFaceRegular, serif;
}
```

Code Listing 12-1 shows the creation of the @font-face section and the usage within the code. Notice that I list a default font, even though I am downloading the font to the user. In Internet Explorer, this resulted in a temporary rendering of my font while the Nashville font downloaded. On machines that do not support downloading, you still have some control over the visual effect. Figure 12-1 shows the fonts working in Internet Explorer 9.

Fonts embedded within CSS are not entirely new. Internet Explorer supported embedded fonts as far back as version 4. It was not widely implemented for a number of reasons. Many of the problems that plagued Internet Explorer's embedded fonts still exist today:

- The legal issue is very important. Be entirely sure that you have permission to use the font on the web site.

- The user's computer may refuse your font. You need to include a default font.

- Really large files can take a long time to download, especially on mobile devices. Include a font only if it is essential to your page, and then limit its use to logos, headers, or other small amounts of text.

- Embedded fonts may not scale well. They will probably look fine at 12 points, but once you start adjusting the size, pixelation will occur. In many cases, it might be better to simply build images of what you wanted rendered in a different font.

- Embedded fonts often do not respond to other CSS formatting. For example, setting color or transforms on embedded fonts may not work.

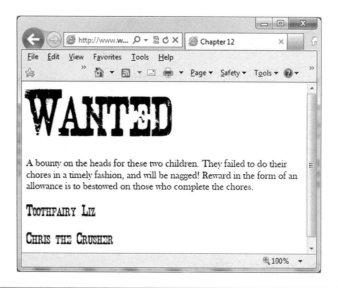

Figure 12-1   Web fonts in Internet Explorer 9

TIP

Microsoft provides a free utility titled Microsoft Web Embedded Font Tool (WEFT). This tool will convert local font files into web-embedded fonts and upload them directly to your web server. Despite being built for Windows 98, the tool still runs well on modern operating systems.

Backgrounds

Property	Values
background-clip	padding-box, content-box, border-box
background	URL to background image

Backgrounds have been around since HTML version 2. CSS3 gives you a little better control over where the background image appears on the page, and even how many different images are in the background.

Multiple Backgrounds

The use of multiple backgrounds is easy to implement, but it is hard to implement well. Using the traditional `background-image:` property, you simply need to list two (or more) `url` functions to background images.

Code Listing 12-2 shows the use of two backgrounds: one a black-marbled tiled pattern as a top border, and the rest of the page light marble. Prior to CSS3, you would need to z-index stack a div on top of the background to achieve this effect. CSS3 will automatically set the z-index for each background you list. The first listed background is on the top, the next is below the previous one. The `background-repeat` property creates a top border without requiring you use divs for the background.

Code Listing 12-2	Multiple backgrounds in CSS

```
body{
     background-image: url("images/blkmarb.jpg"),
          url("images/grymarb.gif") ;
     background-repeat:repeat-x,repeat;
}
```

Background Placement

In addition to stacking backgrounds, CSS3 allows you to decide where in the CSS box model the background starts. Recall that the box model has three components: the border box, the padding box, and the content box. CSS3 backgrounds now allow you to specify which of the three boxes will have the background. The new property that controls which part of the box model has the background is `background-clip`.

The `background-clip` property takes one of three values:

- The `content-clip` value places the background behind the content box only, and not behind the padding box.

- The `padding-clip` value renders the background behind the padding area, completely enclosed within the border. This setting is useful only if you specify a padding value for the cell.

- The `border-box` value will extend the background to behind the border. This effect is visible only if you have a border with transparent portions.

Code Listing 12-3 shows the CSS to view the `background-clip` effect. Notice that I included `-moz-background-clip`. This provides compatibility with Firefox browsers 3.6 and earlier.

Code Listing 12-3	Using background-clip

```
.border{
     -moz-background-clip:border-box;
     background-clip:border-box;
     background-color:#ffff00;
     border:5px dotted #000000;
     padding:10px;
}
```

```
.padding{
      -moz-background-clip:padding-box;
      background-clip:padding-box;
      background-color:#ffff00;
      border:5px dotted #000000;
      padding:10px;
}
.content{
      -moz-background-clip:content-box;
      background-clip:content-box;
      background-color:#ffff00;
      border:5px dotted #000000;
      padding:10px;
}
```

Code Listing 12-3 creates three classes, named `border`, `padding`, and `content`. Each is the same except for the `background-clip` property. The first div shows `background-clip`, which renders the background color between the dots. Using `padding-clip` does not place the background color between the dots. Finally, `content-clip` does not fill the entire box, as the padding does not have the background. I applied each class in an HTML document with three div tags. Figure 12-2 shows the page when viewed in Internet Explorer.

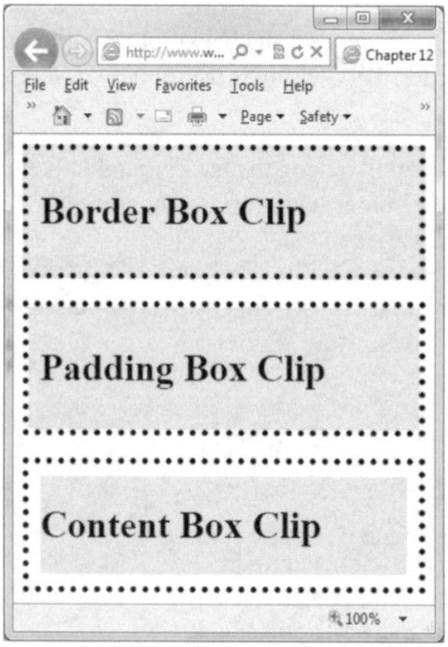

Figure 12-2 The border-clip property applied

Borders

Property	Value
border-image	<image URL> [slice] [width] [repeat | round | stretch]
border-radius	Pixel size describing the radius creating the border circle; sets all corners equally
box-shadow	[inset] <offset-x> <offset-y> [blur-radius] [spread-radius] [color]
border-bottom-left-radius	Pixel size describing the radius creating the border circle on the bottom left
border-top-left-radius	Pixel size describing the radius creating the border circle on the top left
border-bottom-right-radius	Pixel size describing the radius creating the border circle on the bottom right
border-top-right-radius	Pixel size describing the radius creating the border circle on the top right

Borders in CSS have received several improvements, primarily designed to simplify a task that is difficult in CSS. Here, we'll look at how to create borders with rounded corners, shadows, and images.

Borders with Rounded Corners and Shadows

The new border-radius property creates a rounded corner on a border. Prior to the introduction of this property, creating a rounded border required many CSS classes. The border-radius property requires one parameter: the radius of the corner, in pixels. When setting border-radius, remember that the larger the radius, the bigger the circles on the corners. For older Firefox browsers, attach the prefix -moz. If desired, you can set a different radius for each corner.

TIP

border-radius is a shortcut property. If desired, you can set each corner border individually with the border-bottom-right-radius, border-top-right-radius, border-bottom-left-radius, and border-top-left-radius properties.

Another improvement is the box-shadow property, which creates a shadow behind a border box. Creating shadows in CSS2 took a number of properties.

The box-shadow property accepts several parameters:

- The x-offset and y-offset values are required. These pixel measurements are the distances from the box to the shadow. By default, the shadow appears below and to the right of the box. Using negative values can place the shadow above and to the left.

Figure 12-3 Rounded corners and shadows

- The color value of the shadow must be specified.

- The optional blur-radius parameter converts the shadow from having a clearly defined edge to an edge that dissolves into the background.

- The spread-radius parameter can make the shadow a different size than the object.

- The optional inset parameter will convert the shadow to be inside the box. By default, the inset will be on the top left of the box. Using negative numbers will move to the opposite side.

The following is the full syntax for box-shadow:

```
box-shadow: [inset] offset-x offset-y [blur-radius] [spread-radius]
[color];
```

For complete compatibility with older browsers, you need to include three properties: box-shadow, -moz-box-shadow, and –webkit-box-shadow.

Code Listing 12-4 contains the CSS code to create borders with rounded corners, a box shadow, and an inset shadow. Figure 12-3 displays the results in Internet Explorer.

Code Listing 12-4   CSS to create borders and box shadows

```
.round{
     border-radius:1.5em;
     border:.2em solid #000000;
```

```
        padding-left:.75em;
        width:19em;
}
.shadow{
        box-shadow: .75em .75em #cccccc;
        border:.2em solid #000000;
        padding-left:.75em;
        width:19em;
}
.inset{
        box-shadow: inset .75em .75em #cccccc;
        border:.2em solid #000000;
        padding-left:.75em;
        width:19em;
}
```

Images as Borders

The `border-image` property allows you to select an image for the border of a section. Using a border image is not necessarily easy. It takes a little work.

NOTE

Unfortunately, at the time of this writing, the incredible `border-image` property is not yet supported in Internet Explorer.

First, you need to obtain your border image. The best images are those that have a clearly defined corner element and a repeatable element between the corners. For example, I saw a page with flowers on the corner and ivy vines between the corners. For my example, I created a 30-pixel-wide purple diamond for the corners, and 30-pixel-wide gray diamonds for the repeated image. My image was 90 × 90 pixels. Figure 12-4 shows the border as well as the image I used to generate it.

TIP

The size of the elements is crucial. These will become the parameters to your `border-image` property.

Once the image is created, you need to build your CSS. Start by creating a standard CSS border. In particular, be sure that you set the width of the border. Your browser will scale your image to this size. Once this border works, enter the `border-image` property. Your code will be similar to the following:

```
border-image:url(picture.png) elementSize elementWidth round
```

The element size and width are the size of the elements in your image. Remember that the example uses a 30 × 30 diamond, generating a 90 × 90 image. Since I used 30-pixel diamonds,

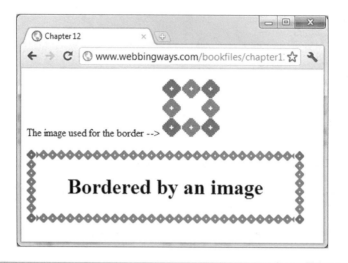

Figure 12-4 The border-image property applied

I tell CSS to slice the top 30 × 90 pixels from the image. The first 30 × 30 image becomes the top-left corner. The last 30 × 30 image in the slice becomes the top-right corner. The middle 30 × 30 image is repeated across the div. This process is repeated for the bottom line, except the bottom 30 × 90 slice is repeated across the bottom. To generate the sides, the middle 30 × 90 image is repeated down until the entire area is bordered.

TIP
One of the uses for the border-image property is to create a dynamically sized button. Draw a rectangle with rounded corners in a paint program and save it as a PNG. Add the code to build a border image, and you have a custom button.

Code Listing 12-5 shows the CSS that produced Figure 12-4. Notice that it includes the vendor prefixes for compatibility with older browsers. If this page is viewed in Internet Explorer, the border will be a dotted gray.

Code Listing 12-5   Using border-image around a div tag

```
<!doctype html>
<html lang="en">
<head>
<meta charset="utf-8">
<title>Chapter 12</title>
<style>
.imgBorder{
border:1em dotted gray;
width:400px;
```

```
text-align:center;
-webkit-border-image:url("images/border2.png") 30 30 round;
-moz-border-image:url("images/border2.png") 30 30 round;
-o-border-image:url("images/border2.png") 30 30 round;
border-image:url("images/border2.png") 30 30 round;}
</style>
</head>
<body>
<p>The image used for the border:
<img src="images/border2.png" alt="image for the border"
title="image for the border" /></p>
<div class="imgBorder"><h1>Bordered by an image</h1>
</div>
<br>
</body>
</html>
```

This example builds a border image by repeating elements in the image. Replacing the value `repeat` with `stretch` will make the image stretch to fit the border. This effect works well with a predrawn border, like a picture frame. Later in the chapter, Code Listing 12-7 demonstrates this technique.

Transformations

Property	Value
transform	A transformation function and its value

A *transformation* is a change in an object. CSS3 makes it possible to rotate, skew, or otherwise change how an object is rendered. You can create parallelograms, or twisted or mirrored sections on the page.

CSS3 offers both 2D and 3D transformations. The 2D transformations are supported in all modern browsers. Currently, only Chrome and Safari support the 3D transformations.

Table 12-3 lists the transformation functions to use with `transform`. When calling the transform functions, you need to specify the units. For example, when calling the skew method, you need to code `transform:skew(20deg, 15deg)`. The deg tells skew that the unit is in degrees. Similarly, for functions that take pixels, be sure to specify pixels.

CAUTION

Be careful using these transformations. Too many transformations can make your page look bad.

Code Listing 12-6 adds transformations to the wanted poster created earlier in Code Listing 12-1. It implements the skew, translate, and rotate methods. I used skew on the header, creating a backward italics effect. I translated the header 150 pixels to the right

Function	Description	Parameters
translate()	2D transformation that can move an element on the page	Pixel distance in X and Y from the current position
rotate()	2D transformation that angles the element clockwise	Angle in degrees or radians
skew()	2D transformation that turns the element on both the X and Y axes	Angle to rotate the X and Y axes
matrix()	Combines all of the 2D transformations into one effect	Rotate (use radians), scale, translate, and skew values
scale()	3D transformation that adjusts the size of the object	The X and Y values to shrink the object
rotateX()	3D transformation that spins the element around its X axis	Angle in degrees to spin the element
rotateY()	3D transformation that spins the element around its Y axis	Angle in degrees to spin the element

Table 12-3   Transformation Functions and Parameters

of the line. Finally, the rotate method angles the names in text, creating a taped-on effect. Figure 12-5 shows the results in Internet Explorer.

NOTE
Some odd interactions between dynamic fonts using @font-face and CSS transformations were observed in browsers at the time of writing. Check your browser for display quirks.

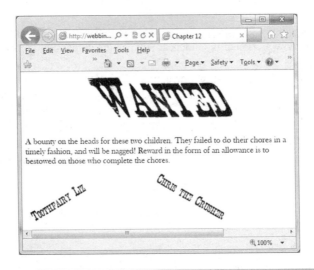

Figure 12-5   The transform function working in Internet Explorer

Code Listing 12-6   Transformations added to the wanted poster

```
@font-face {
    font-family: 'NashvilleRegular';
    src: url('fonts/nashvill-webfont.eot');
    src: url('fonts/nashvill-webfont.eot?#iefix')
        format('embedded-opentype'),
        url('fonts/nashvill-webfont.ttf') format('ttf'),
        url('fonts/nashvill-webfont.woff') format('woff'),
        url('fonts/nashvill-webfont.svg#NashvilleRegular')
            format('svg');
    font-weight: bold;
}
@font-face {
    font-family: 'BaskervilleOldFaceRegular';
    src: url('fonts/baskvill-webfont.eot');
    src: local('Baskerville Old Face Regular'),
        url('fonts/baskvill-webfont.eot?#iefix')
            format('embedded-opentype'),
        url('fonts/baskvill-webfont.woff') format('woff'),
        url('fonts/baskvill-webfont.ttf') format('truetype'),
        url('fonts/baskvill-webfont.svg#BaskervilleOldFaceRegular')
            format('svg');
}
h1, h2, h3{
    font-family:NashvilleRegular, sans-serif;
    font-weight:bold;
    font-variant:small-caps;
}
body{
    font-family:BaskervilleOldFaceRegular, serif;
}
h1.moved{
    transform:skew(30deg, 0deg);
    -ms-transform:skew(30deg, 0deg) translate(150px, 0px);
}
.leftName{
    width:200px;
    text-align:left;
    -ms-transform:rotate(-30deg);
    -moz-transform:rotate(-30deg);
    -webkit-transform:rotate(-30deg);
    -o-transform:rotate(-30deg);
    transform:rotate(-30deg);
}
.rightName{
    width:200px;
    text-align:right;
```

```
        -ms-transform:rotate(30deg);
        -moz-transform:rotate(30deg);
        -webkit-transform:rotate(30deg);
        -o-transform:rotate(30deg);
        transform:rotate(30deg);
}
div{
        float:left;
}
</style>
</head>
<body>
<h1 class="moved">Wanted</h1>
<p>A bounty on the heads for these two children.
They failed to do their chores in a timely fashion,
and will be nagged! Reward in the form of an allowance is
to bestowed on those who complete the chores.</p>
<div>
<h2 class="leftName">Toothfairy Liz</h2>
</div>
<div>
<h2 class="rightName">Chris the Crusher</h2>
</div>
</body>
```

Transitions

Property	Value
transition	A shorthand property for setting the four transition properties with a single property
transition-property	The name of the CSS property to which the transition is applied; no default
transition-duration	Number of seconds the transition lasts; defaults to 0
transition-timing-function	One of the timing functions (see Table 12-4); defaults to linear
transition-delay	Number of seconds until the transition starts; defaults to 0

CSS3 makes it easier for the developer to create animations on a web page without needing to use JavaScript or Flash. This is a very important development. Owners of the iPhone, iPod touch, and iPad are quite aware that their devices currently cannot play Flash, and may never play Flash if Apple keeps its current position. With a few lines of CSS code, really neat effects are possible.

The transition allows you to specify how an object changes over time. Prior versions of CSS made changes happen immediately. Table 12-4 lists the values for the transition-

Function	Description
`cubic-bezier(n,n,n,n)`	Define your own values from 0–1
`ease`	Slow transition start, fast middle, slow end; same as `cubic-bezier(0.25,0.1,0.25,1)`
`ease-in`	Slow transition start, fast end; same as `cubic-bezier(0.42,0,1,1)`
`ease-in-out`	Slow transition start and end; same as `cubic-bezier(0.42,0,0.58,1)`
`ease-out`	Fast transition start, slow end; same as `cubic-bezier(0,0,0.58,1)`
`linear`	Same transition speed from beginning to end; same as `cubic(0,0,1,1)`

Table 12-4   Transition Timing Functions

`timing-function` property. The change is typically triggered by one of the three dynamic action pseudo classes: `hover`, `active`, or `focus`. You need to specify what happens, over how much time, and the delay before the transition starts.

Table 12-5 lists the CSS properties that can be part of a transition. Unfortunately, you cannot animate the background image with a URL. You can change only the gradient.

`background-color`	`background-image`	`background-position`
`border-bottom-color`	`border-bottom-width`	`border-color`
`border-left-color`	`border-left-width`	`border-right-color`
`border-right-width`	`border-spacing`	`border-top-color`
`border-top-width`	`border-width`	`bottom`
`color`	`crop`	`font-size`
`font-weight`	`grid-`	`height`
`left`	`letter-spacing`	`line-height`
`margin-bottom`	`margin-left`	`margin-right`
`margin-top`	`max-height`	`max-width`
`min-height`	`min-width`	`opacity`
`outline-color`	`outline-offset`	`outline-width`
`padding-bottom`	`padding-left`	`padding-right`
`padding-top`	`right`	`text-indent`
`text-shadow`	`top`	`vertical-align`
`visibility`	`width`	`word-spacing`
`z-index`	`zoom`	

Table 12-5   Properties That Can Be Used in Transitions or Animations

Transitions are applied to divisions or other sections on your page. Start building the transition by creating the div style, in the manner it appears before the transition. In particular, you need to specify the original value of the properties you are going to transition. The next step is to define the transition properties. For simple transitions consisting of just a property change and duration, the shortcut will work fine. For complex transitions that modify multiple properties, you will need to specify each property explicitly.

After you specify this transition, you need to build another style for the div event. The three events are hover, focus, and active. Inside this style, you specify the value for the property after the transaction. Finally, you can specify code for the transitionEnd event, which calls a programmer-specified JavaScript function whenever the transition is finished.

Code Listing 12-7 is a complex chunk of code. It creates two transitions and another border image. The border image takes the image of a picture frame I drew in Photoshop and extends it around the image of the all-stars athletes page from Chapter 10.

The first transition creates a div.box that when clicked and held will eventually reveal directions for the picture frame. Clicking and holding an object makes it active. The directions are revealed simply by changing the background color.

The second transition slowly displays the figure within the frame. The figure:hover setting slowly sets the opacity to 0, making the figure visible. The second transition also demonstrates the transitionEnd event, which fires when a transition finished. The event is set up in the onload event of the page. The text above the picture changes when the transition is complete. Visit www.webbingways.com to view the full effects.

Code Listing 12-7   Specifying the transitions

```
<!doctype html>
<html lang="en">
<head>
<meta charset="utf-8">
<title>HTML5 Figures</title>
<style>
div.box{
     width:100px;
     height:100px;
     background-color:black;
     -webkit-transition-property:background-color;
     -webkit-transition-duration:5s;
     -webkit-transition-timing-function:ease-in;
     -webkit-transition-delay:2s;
}
div.box:active{
      background-color:yellow;
}
.picFrame{
     border:50px solid brown;
     width:490px;
```

```
        height:568px;
        -webkit-border-image:url("images/frame.png") 57 57 stretch;
        -o-border-image:url("images/frame.png") 57 57 stretch;
        -moz-border-image:url("images/frame.png") 57 57 stretch;
        border-image:url("images/frame.png") 57 57 stretch;
}
figure{
        padding:0px;
        opacity:0;
        -moz-transition: opacity 3s;
        -webkit-transition: opacity 3s;
        -o-transition: opacity 3s;
        transition: opacity 3s;
}
figure:hover{
        opacity:1;
}
div{
        float:left;
}
</style>
<script>
function displayMessage(){
        document.getElementById("thank").innerHTML=
            "Thank you for hovering!";
}
function setHandlers(){
        document.getElementById('transit').addEventListener(¬
            "webkitTransitionEnd", function(){displayMessage()}, false);
        document.getElementById('transit').addEventListener(¬
            "oTransitionEnd", function(){displayMessage()}, false);
        document.getElementById('transit').addEventListener(¬
            "mozTransitionEnd", function(){displayMessage()}, false);
        document.getElementById('transit').addEventListener(¬
            "transitionend", function(){displayMessage()}, false);}

        window.onload = function () { setHandlers(); };
</script>
</head>
<body>
<p id="thank">Click and hold on the black box for 7
seconds to receive directions.</p>
<div class="picFrame">
<figure id="transit">
<img src="images/kids.jpg" alt="Image of all star athletes"
width="409" height="512">
<figcaption>All Star Athletes</figcaption>
</figure>
```

```
</div>
<div class="box">
<p style="left:120px;">Hover in the frame to see the best
athletes in Elliott.</p>
</div>
</body>
</html>
```

Animations

Property	Value
`@keyframes`	Rule that defines the individual frames in the animation. Requires an animation name.
`animation`	A shorthand property for all the animation properties. Minimum parameters are an animation name and duration. Expected order of attributes is `animation-name`, `animation-duration`, `animation-timing-function`, `animation-delay`, `animation-iteration-count`, and `animation-direction`.
`animation-name`	Specifies the name of the `@keyframes` animation.
`animation-duration`	Number of seconds the transition lasts; defaults to 0.
`animation-timing-function`	Uses the same timing functions as the transition (see Table 12-4); defaults to `ease`
`animation-delay`	Creates a delay before the animation starts; defaults to 0.
`animation-iteration-count`	Lists the number of times an animation is played; defaults to 1. Values from 1 to infinite are supported.
`animation-direction`	Specifies whether or not the animation should play in reverse on alternate cycles; defaults to `normal`. Accepts `normal` or `alternate`.
`animation-play-state`	Stops or starts an animation; defaults to `running`. Accepts `paused` or `running`. (May be dropped in the final CSS3 version.)

The animation properties allow you to create a simple animation directly in HTML. You can change multiple animation properties at a time. The animation will be smooth. Changes in color will happen gradually, rather than abruptly. Moving objects across the screen will result in motion, rather than jumping from one place to another place.

TIP

Transitions and animations are similar. In the transition, the object will remain in the final state. In animations, by default, the object will return to its original state.

Building an Animation

Building an animation requires a few steps:

1. Select the object and properties to animate. Not all properties can be animated. Table 12-5 lists the CSS properties that can be animated. In CSS, set the initial values for the properties. If you are going to move the object, you should use `position:absolute`. Although not required, creating a CSS class for the animated object will make it easier for you to test and debug the animation.

2. Create the animation properties. You need to set the name of the animation and its duration. The other properties are optional. The shortcut property is quite useful with animations. It takes what could be many CSS properties and rolls them into one property. For complete compatibility, you need to use the `animation`, `-webkit-animation`, and `-moz-animation` properties.

3. Build the `@keyframes` rule. This is the most complicated part. The keyframes rule will have a name, which matches the animation name you specified in the CSS properties for your object. Inside the rule, you create several lines. Each line describes the value of your animated properties after a percentage of your duration has elapsed. For complete browser compatibility, include `0%` and `100%` in your lines. `0%` will match your object's initial values. `100%` will contain the values for the end of your animation.

Code Listing 12-8 shows a simple animation. This code will change the color of a body from red to yellow to orange, and then back to red. I set a 20-second duration and specified keyframe rules for 0%, 33%, 66%, and 100%. The body background color starts at red. This is reflected both in the body element and the 0% keyframe. After 6 seconds, or 33% of the time, has elapsed, the body is orange. Between 6 and 12 seconds, the body will slowly change from orange to yellow. By the end of the 20 seconds, the page will become red. For clarity, I left out the compatibility `webkit` and `moz` vendor prefixes here.

Code Listing 12-8	A sample animation

```
body{
width:50px;
height:50px;
background:red;
animation:colorChange 20s;}
@keyframes colorChange{
0%    {background: red;}
33%   {background: orange;}
66%   {background: yellow;}
100% {background: red;}
}
```

Code Listing 12-8 is neither overly exciting nor unique. Nearly every page on the Internet that describes animation changes an object's color. Code Listing 12-9 provides a better example. It displays two classic EGBDF music scales. I animated an arrow moving from one note to another as an indication for which note to play. Since the five notes are repeated, the entire animation will take ten seconds. There is a two-second delay on the animation to allow the musician time to get ready.

Code Listing 12-9   Animating an image's position on the screen

```
<!doctype html>
<html lang="en">
<head>
<meta charset="utf-8">
<title>Chapter 12</title>
<style>
img.scale{
     position:absolute;
     left:100px;
     top:100px;
     z-index:10;
}
img.arrow{
     position:absolute;
     z-index:2;
     animation:moveArrow 10s linear 2s;
     -moz-animation:moveArrow 10s linear 2s;
     -webkit-animation:moveArrow 10s linear 2s;
}
@-webkit-keyframes moveArrow{
0%     {left:100px;top:100px;}
10%    {left:155px;top:180px;}
20%    {left:207px;top:165px;}
30%    {left:253px;top:140px;}
40%    {left:300px;top:115px;}
50%    {left:351px;top:90px;}
60%    {left:409px;top:180px;}
70%    {left:457px;top:165px;}
80%    {left:507px;top:140px;}
90%    {left:555px;top:115px;}
100%   {left:606px;top:90px;}
}
@-moz-keyframes moveArrow{
0%     {left:100px;top:100px;}
10%    {left:155px;top:180px;}
20%    {left:207px;top:165px;}
30%    {left:253px;top:140px;}
```

```
40%    {left:300px;top:115px;}
50%    {left:351px;top:90px;}
60%    {left:409px;top:180px;}
70%    {left:457px;top:165px;}
80%    {left:507px;top:140px;}
90%    {left:555px;top:115px;}
100%   {left:606px;top:90px;}
}
@keyframes moveArrow{
0%     {left:100px;top:100px;}
10%    {left:155px;top:180px;}
20%    {left:207px;top:165px;}
30%    {left:253px;top:140px;}
40%    {left:300px;top:115px;}
50%    {left:351px;top:90px;}
60%    {left:409px;top:180px;}
70%    {left:457px;top:165px;}
80%    {left:507px;top:140px;}
90%    {left:555px;top:115px;}
100%   {left:606px;top:90px;}
}
</style>
</head>
<body>
<h1>Every Good Burger Deserves Fries</h1>
<img src="images/music.png" class="scale">
<img src="images/arrow.png" class="arrow">
</body>
</html>
```

Multiple Animations

The examples in Code Listings 12-8 and 12-9 have one keyframe, animating one item at a time. CSS animations can support multiple keyframes and many simultaneous animations. Unfortunately, too many animations are difficult to track in your code. Additionally, it is unclear how well browsers will handle many animations at one time.

Code Listing 12-10 provides a sing-along example for a song I sang when I was a kid. One lyric line at a time is displayed on the screen. The current sung word is rendered in red. While the animation is rendering, music is playing. The lyrics are synchronized to the music. Code Listing 12-10 shows the two keyframe rules and two simultaneous animations.

Code Listing 12-10   Multiple animations

```
<!doctype html>
<html lang="en">
<head>
```

```
<meta charset="utf-8">
<title>Chapter 12</title>
<style> <style>
#line1{
      position:absolute;
      font-size:0em;
      z-index:1;
      -moz-animation:showline 2s ease-in-out 0s;
      -webkit-animation:showline 2s ease-in-out 0s;
      animation:showline 2s ease-in-out 0s;
}
#word1-1{
      color:black;
      -moz-animation:wordColor .5s ease-out 0s;
      -webkit-animation:wordColor .5s ease-out 0s;
      animation:wordColor .5s ease-out 0s;
}
@keyframes wordColor{
      0% {color:black;}
      1% {color:red;}
      99% {color:red;}
      100% {color:black;}
}
@keyframes showline{
0% {font-size:0em;z-index:1;}
1% {font-size:1em;z-index:10;}
99% {font-size:1em;z-index:10;}
100% {font-size:0em;z-index:1;}
}
</style>
<body>
<div id="line1">
<p><span id="word1-1">Pain</span>
<span id="word1-2">Pain</span>
<span  id="word1-3">go away</span></p>
</div>
<div id="line2">
<p><span id="word2-1">Come</span>
<span id="word2-2">again</span>
<span id="word2-3">no other</span>
<span id="word2-4">day</span></p>
</div>
<div id="line3">
<p><span id="word3-1">Pain</span>
<span id="word3-2">Pain</span>
<span  id="word3-3">go away</span></p>
</div>
<div  id="line4">
```

```
<p><span id="word4-1">Come</span>
<span id="word4-2">again</span>
<span id="word4-3">no other</span>
<span id="word4-4">day</span></p>
</div>
</body>
</html>
```

Code Listing 12-10 is rather complicated. It shows that multiple animations on multiple elements can occur at one time. The code was abbreviated for publication (the entire code is available from www.webbingways.com). I removed the additional vendor-prefixed keyframe rules and each individual word's style. Given the amount of code, I am unsure whether CSS is strong enough to handle complicated animations.

CSS Animation Caveats

The future of CSS animations is unclear. It looks like they will be in the final standard. It is not clear whether they will replace JavaScript and Flash as the animation tools of choice. It took me several hours to get this animation right, using only tools freely available online. I repeated the same exercise in Flash, and it took less than an hour. In the absence of CSS animation tools, Flash and JavaScript will remain the preferred animators.

In addition to the complexity, there is some doubt whether CSS actually should handle animations. W3C prefers separating content from format and functionality. It is not clear if animation is format or functionality. If animation is defined as functionality, then it should not be in CSS at all.

My recommendation on this point is to use CSS animations for small animations. Changing a color and moving an object are good candidates. For more advanced animations, such as the one in Code Listing 12-10, it's better to use other tools.

Summary

This chapter covered many different emerging CSS properties. I tried to emphasize those properties I feel will best benefit the multimedia developer. We explored the user-interface enhancements in the previous chapter. This coverage is by no means complete. Other properties exist. Multicolumn support and modifiable boxes are other areas you could explore. An entire book could be written about CSS3 (hmm, perhaps my editor will be generous?).

CSS3 has made great strides. Borders and boxes have become simpler to implement. An unlimited number of fonts are now at your disposal. Animation of screen objects no longer requires Flash or JavaScript. In general, you have many more tools at your disposal. I look forward to seeing what the community does with the new tools.

Chapter 13

Editable Regions and Offline Sites

HTML5 introduced many technologies for the multimedia developer. Audio, video, CSS, and container tags have improved. HTML5 also offers many other enhancements. We will explore two of the new technologies in this chapter: editable content, which is an attribute of a region that allows the user to add comments to a web page, and taking your pages offline. Although neither technology is directly related to multimedia development, with a little thought, both editable content and offline files can be applied by multimedia developers.

Editable Content

Editable content, a feature first introduced by Microsoft, turns your HTML pages into text editors. With a little code work, you can make the Web a full, rich text editor.

Editable content allows the developer to create a region on the page in which users can type text. This region, typically a div or other section, can accept any text the user wishes to type. You, as the developer, can control some of the final markup of the user-generated text. The user simply clicks within the region and starts typing. Any of the text within this region can be edited by the user. The text entered by the user will be stored within the region's `innerHTML` property. This can be accessed later in JavaScript code.

Creating an editable region in your code is simple. You need to add the attribute and value `contenteditable="true"` to the section. On Chrome, the editable region is clearly identified on the screen with an orange border. Unfortunately, other browsers do not identify the region. For consistency across browsers, use a CSS style on the `:focus` pseudo class.

Creating an Editable Region

Code Listing 13-1 shows a simple editable region and a JavaScript function that reads the `innerHTML` region and deposits it into a paragraph. Additionally, Code Listing 13-1 uses local storage to store the edits placed in the object.

Code Listing 13-1   An editable region

```
<!doctype html>
<html lang="en">
<head>
<meta charset="utf-8">
<title>Chapter 13</title>
<style>
.wall{
     width:25em;
     margin:0em;
}
.wall:focus{
     border:thin solid orange;
}
</style>
<script>
```

```
function readWall(){
     var content = document.getElementById("wall").innerHTML;
     content = "Thank you for posting <br />"+ content ;
     document.getElementById("walloutput").innerHTML = content;
}
function storewall() {

   var walldetail = document.getElementById("wall").innerHTML;
     localStorage.setItem("wall", walldetail);
}
function getwall() {
     var walldetail = localStorage.getItem("wall");

     if(walldetail == null){
        document.getElementById("wall").innerHTML = "Replace this text";
     }
     else{
        document.getElementById("wall").innerHTML=walldetail;
     }
}
</script>
</head>
<body onload="getwall('wall');">
<h1>Write on my wall</h1>
 <section id="wall" class="wall" contenteditable="true">
Replace this text.
 </section>
 <img src="images/button.png" alt="button to click"
onclick="readWall();storewall();">
 <br><br>
 <section id="walloutput" class="wall">
 
 </section>
</body>
</html>
```

Figure 13-1 shows the region being edited by a user. The coolness factor of Code Listing 13-1 is that the screenshot clearly shows the region was edited by the user.

When the page loads, the wall section holds either the phrase "Replace this text" or the last edit by the user. The figure shows that "Replace this text" was replaced with my own text. When clicked, the image called `readWall()`, which read the `innerHTML` from the first section called `wall`, added a thank you, and then changed the `innerHTML` for the second section titled `walloutput`. Clicking the button also wrote the edits into the local storage for the browser. When the page loads, local storage is read and placed into the section.

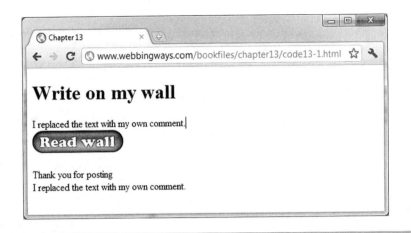

Figure 13-1 The changed region

Code Listing 13-1 also shows an important item to remember about editable areas. You need to inform the user that the region is editable. All editable regions should have some placeholder text with instructions. Without this text, the user will need to click to find the region.

A Game with Editable Content

Let's see how editable content can be put to good use by a multimedia developer. The example in this section is a simple game called Name That Wav. The site plays a medley of four songs. The user types the names of the songs in order in a content-editable region. To begin, the region has an ordered list for structure. As long as the user does not completely remove the ordered list from the area, the edited text will remain in an ordered list. The code to check the correctness of the answers depends on the ordered list remaining intact.

TIP
I used the freeware program Audacity to merge and convert the sound file.

Code Listing 13-2 shows the complete code for the game. The HTML code uses the `<audio>` tag introduced in Chapter 6. I added the `preload="auto"` attribute to speed up the loading of the music files.

When ready, the user clicks the Play button. The audio player will then play the songs. The user can type the names of the songs into the ordered list. The Score button will call the function `readList`, which will strip the `<li>` and `</li>` from the song names. It will then compare the songs in the order typed to the correct order.

To simplify the game, the song names are converted to lowercase. For every song, the user gets right, the `right` variable is incremented. If the user gets four correct, a congratulatory message appears. If the user gets fewer than four right, a consolation message with the number of correct answers appears, as shown in Figure 13-2.

Figure 13-2 A sample run of Name That Wav

Code Listing 13-2 Name That Wav

```
<!doctype html>
<html lang="en">
<head>
<meta charset="utf-8">
<title>Chapter 13</title>
<style>
.wall{
     width:25em;
     margin:0em;
}
ol{
     margin:0em;
}
.wall:focus{
     border:thin solid orange;
}
</style>
<script>
function readList(){
     var content =
        document.getElementById("list").innerHTML.toLowerCase();
     var songs = content.split("<li>");
```

```
        var rightSongs =
new Array("taps","beethoven\'s fifth","beethoven\'s ninth","dixie");
        var right=0;
        var ltp;
        for(var s in songs){
                ltp= songs[s].indexOf("<");
                songs[s] = songs[s].substring(0,ltp);
                if(songs[s] == rightSongs[s-1]){
                        right ++;
                }
        }
        if(right == 4){
                document.getElementById("correct").innerHTML =
                  "Good job! You got them all right!";
        }
        else{
                document.getElementById("correct").innerHTML =
                  "OOOH So close, you got " + right + " right!";
        }
}
function playmusic() {
 document.getElementById("audio1").play();
}
</script>
</head>
<body>
<h1>Name That Wav!</h1>
 <audio id="audio1" preload="auto">
  <source src="music/medley.ogg" type="audio/ogg">
  <source src="music/medley.mp3" type="audio/mpeg">
  <source src="music/medley.wav" type="audio/wav">
Your browser does not support the audio element
  </audio>
  <br><br>
</div>
<img src="images/play.png" alt="Click to play" onclick="playmusic();">
<p>Click the play button to start the medley.
In the box below, type the names of the songs you hear.
Choose from Beethoven's Fifth, Beethoven's Ninth, Dixie, Taps.
<br><br>
<strong>Please be sure to leave the list numbers in with your
answers.</strong></p>
 <section id="list" class="wall" contenteditable="true">
<ol>
<li>Song</li>
<li>Song</li>
<li>Song</li>
```

```
<li>Song</li>
</ol>
</section>
<img src="images/score.png" alt="click to score"
    onclick="readList();">
<br><br>
<div id="correct">
  
</div>
</body>
</html>
```

Name That Wav is one use of a content-editable region. The same effect could have been accomplished with a form. However, the numeric list is harder to achieve with forms than it is with the editable regions. I like the results of the program. You can see the choices you made and the number you got right.

Offline Sites

We are becoming more and more connected every day. Wireless Internet is available over 98% of the United States. In other countries, the level of coverage is actually higher. It is becoming difficult for us to unhook and come offline. However, there are still times when we are not connected to the Web. Traditional HTML meant that your web site was unavailable without a connection. The new offline feature of HTML5 changes this.

HTML5 now allows your pages to be available offline. You specify which portions of your web site are available offline. When users visit these portions, the content is downloaded to their device. Depending on the browser, they may not even know that the content is being downloaded. Once users have visited the site, they can still access the offline material, even without a web connection.

The challenge to developers is how to handle this offline capability. For a simple static HTML page, the process is straightforward: List the items to offload on the device, and your site is available offline. For sites that depend on user interaction or that gather user input, the process is trickier. You need to not only offload the site to the device, but you also need to handle the interaction both offline and online.

For a site that gathers user input and posts it to a server, one strategy is to hold the user input using local storage, and then post the data once the user is back online. For a multimedia site, you must decide what multimedia content can be offline. There may be several legal ramifications of offloading video and audio.

Manifest Files

Making pages available offline requires building a cache manifest file. The cache manifest file tells the web server that hosts your page which items are to be downloaded to the client device.

It lists those items that will be downloaded, which items are to be available online, and what to do if your user attempts to access an element offline that is not available.

Manifest File Preparations

Before the cache manifest file will work, you need to add a MIME type to your web server. Specifically, you need to add `text/cache-manifest .manifest` to the list of document types your web server will download. If you do not add this MIME type, your manifest file will not download. If you are paying for hosting, an e-mail message to your host provider may solve the problem. If you host your own web page, you will need to talk to your network administrator to add the MIME type.

You may have a hard time getting the manifest file to work from your web host or locally. To test the examples, you will need a web server that you control. Here, I discuss how to add the MIME type to an Apache server installed on a Windows machine. For help with Internet Information Services (IIS) on a Windows server, visit http://technet.microsoft.com/en-us/library/cc725608(WS.10).aspx.

If you do not have one, download a WAMP, LAMP, or MAMP stack. These programs load working copies of Apache, MySQL, and PHP on a computer. The *W* stands for Windows, *L* for Linux, and *M* for Mac. In Windows, save your files into the c:\wamp\www folder that is created on your system. Once the files are ready, you will need to edit the httpd.conf file and add the following line, with the rest of the `AddType` lines.

```
AddType text/cache-manifest .manifest
```

Once this line is added, restart the service, and you can visit the site as 127.0.0.1/yourfile .html. The files will then download and be available for offline viewing. You can turn the Apache service off, and the site will work offline.

A Simple Manifest File

The cache manifest file is a plain text file with up to three sections, as shown in the example in Code Listing 13-3.

Code Listing 13-3   A sample manifest file

```
CACHE MANIFEST
#version 42
CACHE:
style.css
page.html
images/image.png
FALLBACK:
notAvailable.html
NETWORK:
post.cgi
```

Code Listing 13-3 lists all of the possible portions of a manifest file. The first line is required. All manifest files must start with CACHE MANIFEST. The offline API very clearly lists this requirement.

The second line is a comment listing the version number. This comment serves two purposes:

- It allows you to track the number of times you have changed the document.

- It allows you to signal a change to your web server to download a new copy of the files to the client device.

To clarify the version number issue, imagine that you visit www.webbingways.com and download the Name That Wav game to your device. After this file is downloaded, I make a change in my code. You now revisit the game online. Your browser and the web server will communicate that the file has already been downloaded. The offline files will not reflect the change. If I adjust the revision line, the web server will signal to the browser that a new offline version is available, and will download the new content to your device.

The first header in the manifest file is CACHE:. The CACHE section, also called the *explicit section*, indicates the resources that are to be downloaded to the client. Any files in this section will be downloaded to the device. You may use a relative path, as in the example, or a fully qualified domain name (FQDN) to the file. Any files listed in the manifest file not in a section are considered to be in the explicit section and will be downloaded.

NOTE

The CACHE section in Code Listing 13-3 lists the HTML file. Technically, this is not required unless you have multiple pages for offline use. I included it simply for completeness.

The FALLBACK section lists the file that will be opened if the user attempts to access a resource that is not listed in the explicit section. This section is optional; include it only when you have a NETWORK section.

The NETWORK section lists the files and resources that are to remain online. Several candidates will appear here. Any copyrighted content should remain on the network. Scripts that post to remote servers must remain online. Any resources that you do not own also must remain online.

An Offline Application

Now, let's look at a complete application. This example takes the Name That Wav page (Code Listing 13-2) offline. All portions of the page will be available offline.

To build the offline file, I wrote a manifest file and told the HTML page about the file, which is done in the <html> tag at the top of the page.

Code Listing 13-4 lists the short manifest file, called offline.manifest. Since all files are available offline, I did not specify CACHE, FALLBACK, or NETWORK. The server will treat all of the files listed as offline files to cache.

Code Listing 13-4   The manifest file for Name That Wav

```
CACHE MANIFEST
#Version 6
code13-5.html
music/medley.wav
music/medley.ogg
music/medley.mp3
images/play.png
images/score.png
```

Code Listing 13-5 shows the beginning of the HTML file. The only change to the HTML file is the addition of manifest property in `<html manifest="code13-4 .manifest">`.

Code Listing 13-5   The offline-capable HTML file

```
<!doctype html>
<html lang="en" manifest="offline.manifest">
<head>
<meta charset="utf-8">
<title>Chapter 13</title>
<link rel="stylesheet" href="offline.css">
</head>
<body>
<h1>This page is viewable offline</h1>
<img src="images/kids.jpg" alt="My kids" title="My kids" />
</body>
</html>
```

You need to be careful to include all files in the manifest file. If you forget a file, then your page will not work properly offline. Figure 13-3 was generated by forgetting to include the play.png file in the manifest. Notice that the play image is missing. Additionally, failing to list a file in the manifest file may cause the page to fail online as well.

Detecting Offline Code

Code Listing 13-4 is the manifest for a very simple offline site. Every part of the file is to be available offline. There is no difference in functionality between offline and online. This will not always be the case. Quite often, your sites will need to know when they are online or offline. The DOM provides a number of methods to determine this status.

According to the W3C specifications, `navigator.onLine` is supposed to return `true` when online and `false` if offline. Unfortunately, this property is handled differently across

Figure 13-3   A forgotten image in the cache manifest file

browsers. Firefox and Internet Explorer require a switch to offline mode before this property works. Chrome and Safari do not consistently detect your offline status.

Another choice for detecting the online or offline status is to set event handlers. The events fire whenever the status of the browser changes. Again, this functionality is not yet consistent in the browsers. Code Listing 13-6 shows the creation of these event viewers and a call to `navigator.onLine`.

Code Listing 13-6   Offline detection

```
<!doctype html>
<html lang="en" manifest="offline.manifest">
<head>
<meta charset="utf-8">
<title>Chapter 13</title>
<link rel="stylesheet" href="offline.css">
<script>
function setupListeners(){
window.addEventListener("offline", function(e) {
  alert("offline");
}, false);
window.addEventListener("online", function(e) {
  alert("online");
}, false);>
}
```

```
</script>
</head>
<body onload="setupListeners()">
<h1>This page is viewable offline</h1>
<p onclick="alert(navigator.onLine);">
Click me to determine online status.</p>
</body>
</html>
```

Caching Multiple Pages

The previous examples cache only one page. Your offline application may cache several pages. For this to work, you need to list all objects in the CACHED section. Items that should not be cached are left in the NETWORK section.

Let's see how to extend the Name That Wav page. Instead of one page, this example has five pages. The first four pages allow you to hear the song prior to taking the test. It can be considered training. The fifth page is the current Name That Wav page.

Whenever you finish the training portion of the page, the app tracks your scores in a database. This database can be handled only when online. The nameThatWav.html page and medley files will be listed in the NETWORK section of the manifest file. If the user attempts to access nameThatWav.html while offline, the goOnline.html page will be accessed instead. Code Listing 13-7 shows the cache manifest file for this site.

NOTE
The cache manifest file must be listed in every HTML file that is available offline.

Code Listing 13-7   A manifest file for the entire Name That Wav game

```
CACHE MANIFEST
#Version 8
NETWORK:
nameThatWav.html
music/medley.wav
music/medley.ogg
music/medley.mp3
FALLBACK:
goOnline.html
CACHED:
beethovensfifth.html
beethovensninth.html
dixie.html
taps.html
images/play.png
images/score.png
```

```
music/dixie.wav
music/dixie.ogg
music/dixie.mp3
music/taps.wav
music/taps.ogg
music/taps.mp3
music/beethovensfifth.wav
music/beethovensfifth.ogg
music/beethovensfifth.mp3
music/beethovensninth.wav
music/beethovensninth.ogg
music/beethovensninth.mp3
```

Summary

This chapter discussed two unrelated technologies. It started with editable content, which allows you to build a section that interacts with the user without building a form. The technology simplifies the creation of rich text areas and can make the user interface more elegant.

The second topic was offline site support. The ability to download portions of a web site allows you to build a page that is available at all times. You are capable of controlling which portions of the web site are available when offline. Unfortunately, the technology for detecting when you are offline has not yet matured.

Chapter 14

Advanced Topics: Taking It All a Little Further

This book has covered quite a bit, from basic HTML5 elements through how to animate and interact with those elements, to even determining your location. This last chapter covers a few topics to put a bit of icing on the cake.

This chapter features three distinct sections. First is a treatise on JavaScript. JavaScript has been shown throughout the book, but here it is covered generally as a subject of its own, and not about interaction with HTML5 elements.

Next is a section on math (no, it's not boring and there is no test!). In particular, geometry and a bit of (shudder) trigonometry are reviewed. Why cover math in a book like this? Because shapes and animation are often based on a handful of principles and functions of these mathematical areas. Right off the bat, any rectangle or oval, by its very nature, is a product of some aspect of geometry (think back to what you've learned about angles and such). Trigonometry functions often serve as the basis for animation. Therefore. the coverage of these specialties is really focused on how they come into play in creating visual elements on the HTML5 canvas.

Finally, the third section of this chapter offers a bit of a surprise. So far, all of the examples of the canvas have been two-dimensional. The canvas is a two-dimensional platform. Or is that really so? A technique known as *parallax processing* (not to be confused with parallel processing) allows the impression of three-dimensional visuals put on the canvas.

JavaScript

JavaScript's early usage was mostly to validate form entries or do a few tricks on the screen, but that is just what they were considered: tricks and cutesy "ooh-aahs."

As web development in general got more sophisticated, so did JavaScript, or more to the point, its purpose and place in the scheme of web site interaction. Numerous JavaScript frameworks (libraries) became popular, among them Prototype, Scriptaculous, Dojo, MooTools, Yahoo User Interface (YUI), and the 800-pound gorilla: jQuery. Many web developers have come to rely on such frameworks, and that's a good thing, since they offer much help and make scripting easier.

Still, it's a subjective necessity to know how to deal with raw JavaScript. The coverage here focuses on a few main areas that are common to any programming language: loops, conditional tests, and reusable code. These are shown here without the use of a framework.

Looping

Looping serves to iterate over items and count to a certain value, and also has quite a number of other uses—essentially for any situation in which repetition is needed. The two main looping methods are the `for` loop and the `while` loop.

A `for` loop works by setting an initial value to start counting from, a number at which to stop counting, and the value by which to increment the counter (usually by one, making a sequential loop). Here is a code block of a `for` loop:

```
for (i=0;i<=5;i++) {
  document.write("The number is " + i);
  document.write("<br>");
}
```

TIP

Using a lowercase i as the variable in a loop is just an accepted practice. The variable name can be anything that doesn't violate JavaScript naming rules. You might find it easier to give your variables more meaningful names.

The for statement encloses, in parentheses, the three pieces needed to make the loop work:

- A variable, i in this example, is initialized to 0. Consider i to be the counter.

- Next, the statement indicates to keep looping as long as i is less than or equal to 5.

- Finally, the statement indicates how to increase i—in this case, by 1, represented by i++. (The two plus signs are a shortcut to count up by 1.) Incrementing the counter is vital to the loop completing. If i were not incremented, it would stay equal to 0 and the loop would never end, which, in practical terms, would appear as though your computer had gone haywire.

The full code block starts with the for statement and then uses a set of curly braces to show what happens while the loop is running. The ending curly brace is the end of the loop structure.

In the example, the code block simply writes out "The number is 1," "The number is 2," and so on. Note that since the for statement was set up to run to 5 (less than or equal to 5), the final output does indeed say "The number is 5."

The part of the for statement that sets the increment can just as well set the counter to decrement. The statement could look like this:

```
for (i=5;i>=0;i--) {
  document.write("The number is " + i);
  document.write("<br>");
}
```

Note the reversal of the items in the for statement. The counter, i, starts with a value of 5. The loop runs as long as i is greater than or equal to 0, and with each iteration of the loop, the counter is lowered by 1, using the i-- operator. Just as using two plus signs (++) is a shortcut to count up by 1, using two negative signs, or dashes (--), is a shortcut to count down by 1.

Code Listing 14-1 puts the two for loops together. Between them is an HTML line break to separate them in appearance.

Code Listing 14-1   Looping with the for statement

```
<!doctype html><html lang="en">
<head>
<meta charset="utf-8">
<title>JavaScript</title>
```

```
</head>
<body>
<div style="margin-left:30px;">
<h1>JavaScript</h1>
<script>
var i=0;
for (i=0;i<=5;i++) {
  document.write("The number is " + i);
  document.write("<br>");
}
document.write("<br>");
for (i=5;i>=0;i--) {
  document.write("The number is " + i);
  document.write("<br>");
}
</script>
</div>
</body>
</html>
```

Figure 14-1 shows the output of the code in Code Listing 14-1.

JavaScript also has the while and do...while loops. These are quite similar, but have a distinct difference: a while loop tests the counter at the start of the loop, and a do...while loop tests at the end of the loop. The most discernable difference is that using do...while guarantees at least one pass through the loop, since the test is at the end of the loop. Code Listing 14-2 shows a while loop followed by a do...while loop.

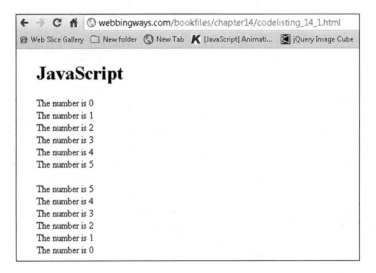

Figure 14-1 Output of the JavaScript for loop

Code Listing 14-2   Looping with the while statements

```html
<!doctype html>
<html lang="en">
<head>
<meta charset="utf-8">
<title>JavaScript</title>
</head>
<body>
<div style="margin-left:30px;">
<h1>JavaScript</h1>
<script>
var i=0;
while (i<=5)
  {
  document.write("The number is " + i);
  document.write("<br>");
  i++;
  }
document.write("<br>");
do
  {
  document.write("The number is " + i);
  document.write("<br />");
  i--;
  }
while (i>=0);
</script>
</div>
</body>
</html>
```

Figure 14-2 shows the output of the code in Code Listing 14-2.

The output shown in Figure 14-2 demonstrates a pertinent point of following the value of a variable. The variable i begins initialized to 0. The while loop increments i until it is equal to 6. Even though the output from the while statement shows counting up to 5, looking at the code, you can see that the block of the while statement runs when i equals 5, and within the block, i is incremented to 6. It doesn't appear from this loop as 6 because at the start of the loop, the test is to see if it is less than or equal to 5. It isn't; it's equal to 6.

```
while (i<=5)
{
  document.write("The number is " + i);
  document.write("<br>");
  i++;
}
```

Figure 14-2 Output of looping with while statements

The second loop, the do...while loop, starts by showing an output of i equals 6 because the write statement occurs before the test. In this loop, the test is at the end of the loop structure. The test is to see if i is greater than or equal to 0, which is true.

```
do
   {
   document.write("The number is " + i);
   document.write("<br />");
   i--;
   }
while (i>=0);
```

Conditional Branching

JavaScript has two mainstay conditional test structures: the if statement and the switch statement. In both statements, a test is performed and an action is taken (a branch) based on the results of the test. Here is an example of a simple if test:

```
var a = (Math.floor(Math.random()*20));
if (a>10) {
   document.write("The variable a is greater than 10, it equals " +
a);
   } else {
   document.write("The variable a is less than or equal to 10, it
equals " + a);
   }
```

The variable a is assigned a random number between 0 and 20. Sometimes it is greater than 10, and sometimes it is equal to or less than 10. The appropriate message is written depending on what a is.

The `if` structure can be enhanced to test more than two outcomes by using `else if`, which allows multiple tests. This structure shows how the testing now takes into account if a is greater than 10, if a is equal to 10, or if a is less than 10:

```
var  a=(Math.floor(Math.random()*20));
if (a>10) {
    document.write("The variable a is greater than 10, it equals " + a);
} else if (a==10){
    document.write("The variable a is equal to 10");
} else {
    document.write("The variable a is less than 10, it equals " + a);
}
```

The inclusion of `else if` in the middle of the code block allows the block to be extended to include an additional test.

Another way to use `if` statements is to just have a number of them follow each other. Each is a separate block; however, the inclusion of more than one allows multiple testing, as follows:

```
var a = (Math.floor(Math.random()*20));
if (a>15) {
    document.write("The variable a is greater than 15, it equals " + a);
}
if (a<=15 && a>=10) {
    document.write("The variable a is between 10 and 15, it equals " + a);
}
if (a<=9 && a>=5) {
    document.write("The variable a is between 9 and 5, it equals " + a);
}
if (a<5) {
    document.write("The variable a is less than 5, it equals " + a);
}
```

TIP

In a test structure such as if (a<=9 && a>=5), the double ampersands represent the operator for the logical AND. Similarly, two pipe characters (||) form the operator for the logical OR.

The `switch` statement is another way of implementing multiple tests, which is more efficient than using multiple `if` statements. Here is an example:

```
var a = (Math.floor(Math.random()*10));
switch (a) {
 case 0:
   document.write("The variable a equals 0");
 break;
 case 1:
   document.write("The variable a equals 1");
```

```
break;
case 2:
  document.write("The variable a equals 2");
break;
case 3:
  document.write("The variable a equals 3");
break;
default:
  document.write("The variable a is greater than 3");
}
```

The switch statement, sometimes referred to as the switch...case statement, presents numerous tests within one large code block. The construct starts with the variable being tested placed directly after the switch statement, in parentheses, followed by an opening curly brace:

```
switch (a) {
```

The tests follow. Each begins with the case keyword, the value that is being tested for, and then a colon. Following that, you put in any code needed to run when the condition is true. Then the break statement ends the block of code that runs if the test is true. A final default catch is put in, to use if none of the other tests were true. The entire switch construct ends with a closing curly brace.

Code Listing 14-3 demonstrates the various conditional tests and branching.

Code Listing 14-3   A combination of conditional tests and branching

```
<!doctype html>
<html lang="en">
<head>
<meta charset="utf-8">
<title>JavaScript</title>
</head>
<body>
<div style="margin-left:30px;">
<h1>JavaScript</h1>
<script>
var  a=(Math.floor(Math.random()*20));
if (a>10) {
   document.write("The variable a is greater than 10, it equals " + a);
   } else {
   document.write
   ("The variable a is less than or equal to 10, it equals " + a);
   }
   document.write("<br><br>");
```

```
var  a=(Math.floor(Math.random()*20));
if (a>10) {
   document.write("The variable a is greater than 10, it equals " + a);
   } else if (a==10){
   document.write("The variable a is equal to 10");
   } else {
   document.write("The variable a is less than 10, it equals " + a);
   }
document.write("<br><br>");
var  a=(Math.floor(Math.random()*20));
if (a>15) {
   document.write("The variable a is greater than 15, it equals " + a);
}
if (a<=15 && a>=10) {
   document.write("The variable a is between 10 and 15, it equals " + a);
}
if (a<=9 && a>=5) {
   document.write("The variable a is between 9 and 5, it equals " + a);
}
if (a<5) {
   document.write("The variable a is less than 5, it equals " + a);
}
document.write("<br><br>");
var  a=(Math.floor(Math.random()*10));
switch (a) {
 case 0:
   document.write("The variable a equals 0");
 break;
 case 1:
   document.write("The variable a equals 1");
 break;
 case 2:
   document.write("The variable a equals 2");
 break;
 case 3:
   document.write("The variable a equals 3");
 break;
 default:
   document.write("The variable a is greater than 3");
}
</script>
</div>
</body>
</html>
```

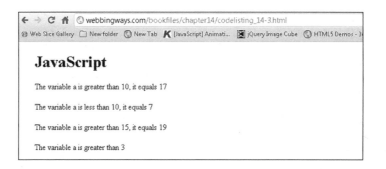

Figure 14-3 Tests and branching output

Figure 14-3 shows the output of the various tests shown in Code Listing 14-3.

Functions

When a web page is rendered, any JavaScript not in a function is run. JavaScript that is in a function runs only when some event calls the function.

Code Listing 14-4 contains JavaScript code both in and out of functions.

Code Listing 14-4 JavaScript functions

```
<!doctype html>
<html lang="en">
<head>
<meta charset="utf-8">
<title>JavaScript</title>
</head>
<body>
<div style="margin-left:30px;">
<h1>JavaScript</h1>
<script>
document.write("I'm run as soon as the page is in the browser");
document.write("<br><br>");
document.write("Me too!");
document.write("<br><br>");
function one(){
  document.write("<br><br>I run only when the Run Function One is
clicked");
}
function two(number){
  document.write("<br><br>I run only when the Run Function Two is
clicked");
  document.write("<br><br>The number passed to me is " + number);
}
</script>
```

```
</div>
<br><br>
<input type="button" value="Run Function One" onclick="one();">
<br><br>
<input type="button" value="Run Function Two" onclick="two(7);">
</body>
</html>
```

Figure 14-4 shows how the page initially appears in the browser. The lines of text are from the `document.write()` method calls that are at the beginning of the script section, but not inside a function.

TIP

Running Code Listing 14-4 may be surprising. When you click a button, the entire page is replaced with what is found in the `document.write` statement. That's a side effect of the point of the lesson: how functions don't run upon loading.

Functions can take arguments—values sent to the function, for the purpose of the function doing something with the passed value(s). Not all functions need arguments, so passing data to a function depends on the type of function. Code Listing 14-4 includes two functions. The first has no arguments, and the second has an argument (a number) passed to it. When the second function is run, it displays the number, as shown in Figure 14-5.

Math Made Visible

Lines, shapes, movement, and animation—we often look at these visual entities and think someone drew this, or used Photoshop to make that, or … what? The fact is whatever method is behind making any visual element, except those that are utterly freehand (illustrating, for example), has some basis of math working in the wings.

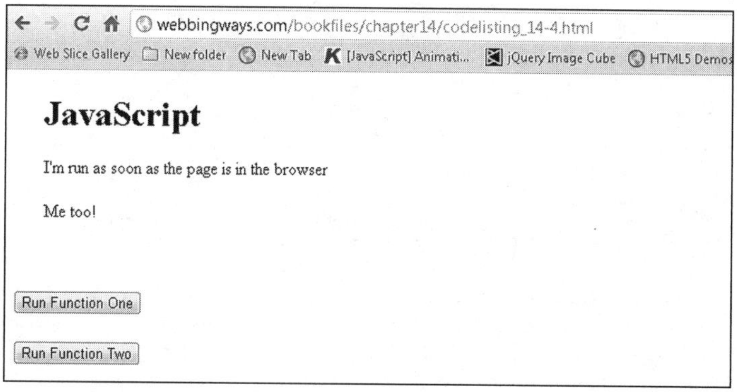

Figure 14-4 JavaScript not in a function runs immediately.

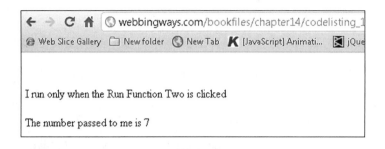

I run only when the Run Function Two is clicked

The number passed to me is 7

Figure 14-5 A JavaScript function displays its passed-in argument.

Geometry is the area of focus behind visual creation. Pick up a text on geometry, and you'll see a discussion of lines, circles, angles, triangles, and so on. The material here is not meant to reproduce the information you can learn from mathematical-based material; rather, it's intended to show some of the geometric items involved in computer-based art, such as the images that appear on the canvas.

Trigonometry, calculus, and other mathematical subjects also can be turned into visual representations. It's rather fascinating, or boring, or above your head, or under your feet. Perhaps you don't know a circle from an oval, or know the fine distinction of what makes an isosceles triangle, well, an isosceles triangle.

Let's consider lines first. Any two lines that touch form an angle. Nearly everyone is familiar with the 90-degree angle, as in the letter *L*. Another type of angle—the acute—is one in which the two lines make an angle that is less than 90 degrees; that is, the lines are closer in the same direction. To give a sense of perspective, a 0-degree angle is like a single line.

So what can be done with acute angles? A popular effect is that of a flock of birds in the distance. As a bird's wings flap, most of the wing movement is in the acute. Figure 14-6 shows a scene of a flock of birds in the distance, flying over a hill. The hill is created using the sine wave function of JavaScript, as discussed shortly. Code Listing 14-5 shows the coding to make the randomly placed acute angles and hill.

Code Listing 14-5   Geometry makes nature

```
<!doctype html>
<html lang="en">
<head>
<meta charset="utf-8">
<title>Geometry and Trigonometry</title>
<style>
body { background-color:#eeeeee; }
#canvas1 {background-color:white;
          border: 5px blue solid; }
#outer {margin-left:40px;
        margin-top:20px;
        }
</style>
```

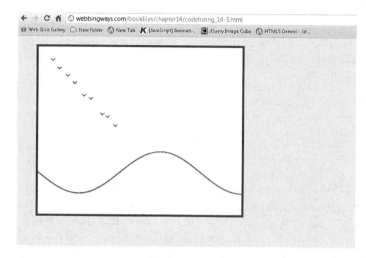

Figure 14-6 Angles and a sine wave simulate nature.

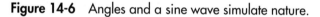

```
</head>
<body>
<div id="outer">
<canvas id="canvas1" width="500" height="400">
Your browser doesn't support the canvas! Try another browser.
</canvas>
<br>
</div>
<script>
var mycanvas=document.getElementById("canvas1");
var cntx=mycanvas.getContext("2d");
mycanvas.width = mycanvas.width; //clears canvas
cntx.lineWidth="2";
// draw birds
for (a=10; a<100; a=(a+10)) {
   b=a+(Math.random()*10);
   c=a+(Math.random()*6);
   d=a+(Math.random()*12);
   cntx.beginPath();
   cntx.moveTo(b+c,b+d);
   cntx.lineTo(b+c+5,b+d+5);
   cntx.lineTo(b+c+10,b+d);
   cntx.strokeStyle="rgb(50,80,80)";
   cntx.stroke();
   cntx.closePath();
}
// draw hill
cntx.strokeStyle="rgb(0,128,0)";
```

```
cntx.beginPath();
for (i=0; i<= 500; i=(i+10)) {
    i2=(Math.sin(i * ((2 * Math.PI) / 400)) * 50 + 300);
    cntx.lineTo(i,i2);
    cntx.stroke();
}
cntx.closePath();
</script>
</body>
</html>
```

Of note in Code Listing 14-5 are the two snippets used for the birds and the hill. Here, the birds are displayed as pairs of lines, assembled within a loop, with some randomness thrown in to have the birds appear in flight in loose formation. The loop uses the variable a as the counter. Within each iteration, it uses other variables—b, c, and d—to add randomness to the line placement and length. Not much randomness is used; it's just enough to give a visual impression of birds a bit closer and farther when viewed as a flock (a little imagination helps!).

```
for (var a=10; a< 100; a=a+10) {
    b=a+(Math.random()*10);
    c=a+(Math.random()*6);
    d=a+(Math.random()*12);
    cntx.beginPath();
    cntx.moveTo(b+c,b+d);
    cntx.lineTo(b+c+5,b+d+5);
    cntx.lineTo(b+c+10,b+d);
    cntx.strokeStyle="rgb(50,80,80)";
    cntx.stroke();
    cntx.closePath();
}
```

In any rendering of a set of lines creating an angle from this code, the angle is acute. None of the angles representing the birds is at or near 90 degrees.

The hill is created with the drawing of a sine wave. The loop counts up to 500, as this is the width of the canvas. Other values affect the curve by setting how wide it is (a value of 400 makes it barely longer than a single cycle), how tall the cycle is (value of 50), and the placement toward the bottom of the canvas (value of 300).

```
cntx.beginPath();
for (i=0; i<= 500; i=(i+10)) {
i2=(Math.sin(i * ((2 * Math.PI) / 400)) * 50 + 300);
cntx.lineTo(i,i2);
cntx.stroke();
 }
cntx.closePath();
```

Code Listing 14-6 shows a mini-application in which variations of the frequency of the sine (or cosine) wave is adjustable, as well as the amplitude (height).

Code Listing 14-6   Sine and cosine frequency and amplitude

```
<!doctype html>
<html lang="en">
<head>
<meta charset="utf-8">
<title>Geometry and Trigonometry</title>
<style>
body { background-color:#eeeeee; }
#canvas1 {background-color:white;
        border: 5px blue solid; }
#outer {margin-left:40px;
        margin-top:20px;
        }
</style>
</head>
<body>
<div id="outer">
<canvas id="canvas1" width="500" height="400" onclick="create_image()">
Your browser doesn't support the canvas! Try another browser.
</canvas>
<br>
<form>
Shape:  
<select id="shapetype">
 <option value="sine" >sine</option>
 <option value="cosine" >cosine</option>
</select>
   Frequency  
<select id="frequency">
 <option value=50 >50</option>
 <option value=100 >100</option>
 <option value=150 >150</option>
 <option value=200 >200</option>
 <option value=300 >300</option>
 <option value=400 >400</option>
 <option value=500 >500</option>
</select>
   Amplitude  
<select id="amplitude">
 <option value=50 >50</option>
 <option value=100 >100</option>
 <option value=150 >150</option>
 <option value=200 >200</option>
```

```
  <option value=300 >300</option>
  <option value=400 >400</option>
  <option value=500 >500</option>
</select>
</form>
<br><br>
select a shape from the dropdown, then click once on the canvas
<br><br>
<div id="description">
</div>
</div>
<script>
var mycanvas=document.getElementById("canvas1");
var cntx=mycanvas.getContext("2d");
function create_image() {
 mycanvas.width = mycanvas.width; //clears canvas
cntx.strokeStyle="rgb(0,0,0)";
cntx.lineWidth=2;
var shapetype=document.getElementById("shapetype").value;
var frequency=document.getElementById("frequency").value;
var amplitude=document.getElementById("amplitude").value;
switch (shapetype) {
case "sine":
 for (var i=0; i< 500; i++) {
  i2=(Math.sin(i * ((2 * Math.PI) / frequency)) * amplitude + 200);
  cntx.lineTo(i,i2);
  cntx.stroke();
 }
 document.getElementById("description").innerHTML="The Sine Function";
break;
case "cosine":
 for (var i=0; i< 500; i++) {
   i2=(Math.cos(i * ((2 * Math.PI) / frequency)) * amplitude + 200);
   cntx.lineTo(i,i2);
   cntx.stroke();
 }
 document.getElementById("description").innerHTML="The Cosine Function";
break;
default:
// nada
} // end switch
} //function
</script>
</body>
</html>
```

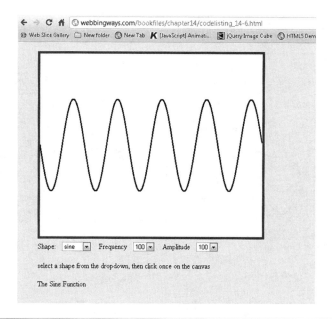

Figure 14-7 Testing variations of the sine and cosine functions

The sine and cosine methods produce the same results, other than they are out of phase with each other. Getting into the finer details of trigonometric functions is not the focus here. The cosine is included simply to point out that JavaScript supports all the standard trigonometry functions (even though they aren't all used in this example). Figure 14-7 shows how Code Listing 14-6 appears in a web browser. It is available to try out at www.webbingways.com.

With a little creative ingenuity (and some JavaScript, of course), you can achieve some interesting visuals. Figure 14-8 shows how a handful of sine waves combined together can make a complex image (unfortunately, the sine wave colors don't show in the printed book). Code Listing 14-7 shows the code used to produce the image in Figure 14-8.

Code Listing 14-7   Sine waves of varying height and color

```
<!doctype html>
<html lang="en">
<head>
<meta charset="utf-8">
<title>Geometry and Trigonometry</title>
<style>
body { background-color:#eeeeee; }
```

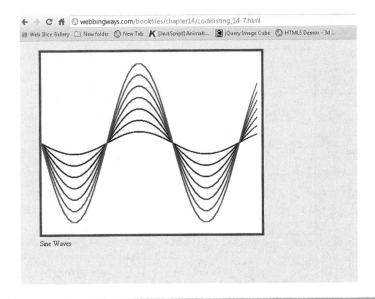

Figure 14-8 Stacked sine waves

```
#canvas1 {background-color:white;
        border: 5px blue solid; }
#outer {margin-left:40px;
        margin-top:20px;
        }
</style>
</head>
<body>
<div id="outer">
<canvas id="canvas1" width="500" height="400">
Your browser doesn't support the canvas! Try another browser.
</canvas>
<br>
Sine Waves
</div>
<script>
var mycanvas=document.getElementById("canvas1");
var cntx=mycanvas.getContext("2d");
mycanvas.width = mycanvas.width; //clears canvas
cntx.strokeStyle="rgb(0,0,0)";
cntx.lineWidth="2";
for (var a=25; a< 200; a=a+25) {
   cntx.beginPath();
   for (var i=0; i< 500; i=i+10) {
      i2=(Math.sin(i * ((2 * Math.PI) / 300)) * a + 200);
```

```
        cntx.lineTo(i,i2);
        cntx.strokeStyle="rgb(" + a + "," + a/10 + "," + a + ")";
        cntx.stroke();
    }
    cntx.closePath();
}
</script>
</body>
</html>
```

Not to leave geometry out of the mix, Figure 14-9 shows an assembled matrix of right triangles. The right-angle construction here ends by coloring in two triangles for an artistic effect. Code Listing 14-8 shows the code used to create the overall visual shown in the figure.

Code Listing 14-8   Right triangles patterned to perfectly fit the canvas

```
<!doctype html>
<html lang="en">
<head>
<meta charset="utf-8">
<title>Geometry and Trigonometry</title>
<style>
```

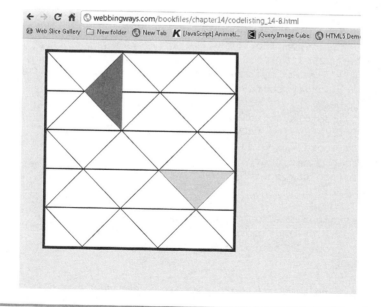

Figure 14-9 A canvas full of right angles

```
body { background-color:#eeeeee; }
#canvas1 {background-color:white;
border: 5px blue solid; }
#outer {margin-left:40px;
margin-top:20px;
}
</style>
</head>
<body>
<div id="outer">
<canvas id="canvas1" width="375" height="375" onclick="create_image()">
Your browser doesn't support the canvas! Try another browser.
</canvas>
<br>
</div>
<script>
var mycanvas=document.getElementById("canvas1");
var cntx=mycanvas.getContext('2d');
makelines(0,0,75,75,150,0,225,75,300,0,375,75);
straightline(0,75,375,75);
makelines(0,150,75,75,150,150,225,75,300,150,375,75);
straightline(0,150,375,150);
makelines(0,150,75,225,150,150,225,300,150,375,225);
straightline(0,225,375,225);
makelines(0,300,75,225,150,300,225,300,300,375,225);
straightline(0,300,375,300);
makelines(0,300,75,375,150,300,225,375,300,300,375,375);
// fill in a couple of triangles
triangle(0,150,75,75,150,150,0,150,255,0,255);
triangle(225,225,300,300,375,225,225,225,0,255,255);
function makelines(mx,my,coord1x,coord1y,coord2x,coord2y,coord3x,coord3y,
        coord4x,coord4y,coord5x,coord5y) {
cntx.moveTo(mx,my); // move to
cntx.lineTo(coord1x,coord1y);
cntx.lineTo(coord2x,coord2y);
cntx.lineTo(coord3x,coord3y);
cntx.lineTo(coord4x,coord4y);
cntx.lineTo(coord5x,coord5y);
cntx.stroke();
}
function straightline(mx,my,coord1x,coord1y) {
cntx.moveTo(mx,my); // move to
cntx.lineTo(coord1x,coord1y); // draw one line
cntx.stroke();
}
function triangle(mx,my,coord1x,coord1y,coord2x,coord2y,
        coord3x,coord3y,r,g,b) {
  cntx.beginPath();
```

```
      cntx.moveTo(mx,my);
      cntx.lineTo(coord1x,coord1y);
      cntx.lineTo(coord2x,coord2y);
      cntx.lineTo(coord2y,coord3x);
      cntx.closePath();
      cntx.fillStyle="rgb(" + r + "," + g + "," + b + ")";
      cntx.fill();
    }
</script>
</body>
</html>
```

The main part of the code makes use of functions to manage the repetitive drawing. Two functions, `makelines` and `straightline`, are used.

The `makelines` function takes 6 sets of double arguments (12 arguments all together), with each set setting a marking point. The first two arguments set where the `moveTo` method places the "pen," and the next five sets are used in `lineTo` methods to draw. You might be wondering why five lines are drawn to create a triangle, which has three lines. That's a good observation. The five lines draw triangular shapes (more than one triangle) across the width of the canvas. Each `makelines` function call is followed by a `straightline` function call, which simply draws a straight, horizontal line underneath the sequence of triangles just drawn by the `makelines` function.

```
makelines(0,0,75,75,150,0,225,75,300,0,375,75);
straightline(0,75,375,75);
```

Finally, a third function, `triangle`, is called. The passed arguments indicate which triangle to draw over again. However, this time, the single triangle is closed up by using the `beginPath` and `closePath` methods. Also, three arguments are used for the red, green, and blue values for the `rgb` function, which sets the color that the triangle will be filled with.

```
function triangle(mx,my,coord1x,coord1y,coord2x,coord2y,
    coord3x,coord3y,r,g,b) {
  cntx.beginPath();
  cntx.moveTo(mx,my);
  cntx.lineTo(coord1x,coord1y);
  cntx.lineTo(coord2x,coord2y);
  cntx.lineTo(coord2y,coord3x);
  cntx.closePath();
  cntx.fillStyle="rgb(" + r + "," + g + "," + b + ")";
  cntx.fill();
}
```

Closing out this treatise on geometry and trigonometry is one more mini-application. This one provides a drop-down list of various angles, triangles, arcs, and trig functions from which

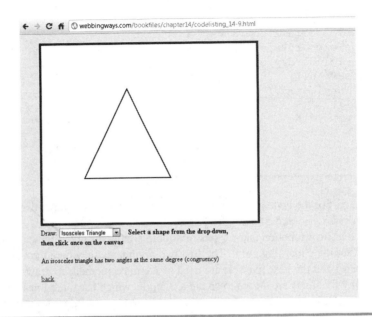

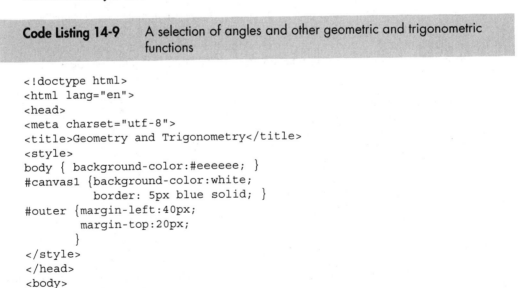

Figure 14-10 A review of angles, triangles, and other shapes

to select. Once you select a shape, a click on the canvas shows the shape, along with a brief description underneath, as shown in Figure 14-10. Code Listing 14-9 shows how the canvas and functionality it uses run.

Code Listing 14-9 A selection of angles and other geometric and trigonometric functions

```
<!doctype html>
<html lang="en">
<head>
<meta charset="utf-8">
<title>Geometry and Trigonometry</title>
<style>
body { background-color:#eeeeee; }
#canvas1 {background-color:white;
          border: 5px blue solid; }
#outer {margin-left:40px;
        margin-top:20px;
        }
</style>
</head>
<body>
<div id="outer">
```

```
<canvas id="canvas1" width="500" height="400" onclick="create_image()">
Your browser doesn't support the canvas! Try another browser.
</canvas>
<br>
<form>
Draw:
<select id="shapetype" name="shapetype">
 <option value="obtuseangle">Obtuse Angle</option>
 <option value="acuteangle">Acute Angle</option>
 <option value="rightangle" >Right Angle</option>
 <option value="obtusetriangle">Obtuse Triangle</option>
 <option value="acutetriangle">Acute Triangle</option>
 <option value="righttriangle" >Right Triangle</option>
 <option value="isoscelestriangle" >Isosceles Triangle</option>
 <option value="equiangulartriangle" >Equiangular Triangle</option>
 <option value="scalenetriangle" >Scalene Triangle</option>
 <option value="circle" >Circle</option>
 <option value="arc" >Arc</option>
 <option value="sine" >Sine</option>
 <option value="cosine" >Cosine</option>
</select>
</form>
   Select a shape from the drop-down,
    then click once on the canvas
<br><br>
<div id="description">
</div>
</div>
<script>
var mycanvas=document.getElementById("canvas1");
var cntx=mycanvas.getContext("2d");
function create_image() {
 mycanvas.width = mycanvas.width; //clears canvas
cntx.strokeStyle="rgb(0,0,0)";
cntx.lineWidth=2;
var shapetype=document.getElementById("shapetype").value;
switch (shapetype) {
case "obtuseangle":
 angle(50,50,50,200,200,280);
 document.getElementById("description").innerHTML=
    "An obtuse angle is one of less than 90 degrees";
break;
case "acuteangle":
 angle(50,50,50,200,200,120);
 document.getElementById("description").innerHTML=
    "An acute angle is one of less than 90 degrees";
break;
case "rightangle":
```

```
 angle(50,50,50,200,200,200);
 document.getElementById("description").innerHTML=
    "A right angle is two lines set at an angle of 90 degrees";
break;
case "acutetriangle":
 triangle(50,50,50,200,200,120);
 document.getElementById("description").innerHTML=
    "Angles in an acute triangle are all less than 90 degrees";
break;
case "obtusetriangle":
 triangle(50,50,50,200,200,280);
 document.getElementById("description").innerHTML=
    "An obtuse triangle has one >90 degree angle
    and two that are <90 degrees";
break;
case "righttriangle":
 triangle(50,50,50,200,200,200);
 document.getElementById("description").innerHTML=
    "A right triangle has one angle that is 90 degrees";
break;
case "isoscelestriangle":
 triangle(100,300,300,300,200,100);
 document.getElementById("description").innerHTML=
    "An isosceles triangle has two angles at the same degree
(congruency)";
break;
case "equiangulartriangle":
 triangle(100,300,300,300,200,200);
 document.getElementById("description").innerHTML=
    "All angles are congruent (at 60 degrees) in an equiangular
triangle";
break;
case "scalenetriangle":
 triangle(100,100,100,240,160,40);
 document.getElementById("description").innerHTML=
    "All three angles are different in a scalene triangle";
break;
case "circle":
cntx.beginPath();
cntx.arc(200, 200, 100, 0, Math.PI * 2, true);
cntx.closePath();
cntx.stroke();
document.getElementById("description").innerHTML=
    "Circles are created with the Arc method - use Math.PI *2";
break;
case "arc":
```

```
cntx.beginPath();
cntx.arc(200, 250, 100, 0, Math.PI, true);
cntx.closePath();
cntx.stroke();
document.getElementById("description").innerHTML=
    "Semicircles are created with the Arc method - use Math.PI";
break;
case "sine":
 for (i=0; i< 500; i++) {
  i2=(Math.sin(i * ((2 * Math.PI) / 500)) * 200 + 200);
  cntx.lineTo(i,i2);
cntx.stroke();
 }
document.getElementById("description").innerHTML="The Sine Function";
break;
case "cosine":
 for (i=0; i< 500; i++) {
  i2=(Math.cos(i * ((2 * Math.PI) / 200)) * 200 + 200);
   cntx.lineTo(i,i2);
cntx.stroke();
 }
document.getElementById("description").innerHTML="The Cosine
Function";
break;
default:
// nada
}  // end switch
} //function
function angle(mx,my,coord1x,coord1y,coord2x,coord2y) {
 cntx.moveTo(mx,my);
 cntx.lineTo(coord1x,coord1y);
 cntx.lineTo(coord2x,coord2y);
 cntx.stroke();
}
function triangle(mx,my,coord1x,coord1y,coord2x,coord2y) {
 cntx.beginPath();
 cntx.moveTo(mx,my);
 cntx.lineTo(coord1x,coord1y);
 cntx.lineTo(coord2x,coord2y);
 cntx.closePath(); // the closePath method completes the triangle
 cntx.stroke();
}
</script>
</body>
</html>
```

Code Listing 14-9 contains the basic snippets of code to create the shapes provided in the drop-down box. A `switch` statement is used throughout to tap the correct code block based on the drop-down selection. For example, here is the piece of the `switch` statement for the obtuse triangle:

```
case "obtusetriangle":
 triangle(50,50,50,200,200,280);
 document.getElementById("description").innerHTML=
    "An obtuse triangle has one >90 degree angle
    and two that are <90 degrees";
break;
```

Within this snippet, a custom function, `triangle`, is called.

```
function triangle(mx,my,coord1x,coord1y,coord2x,coord2y) {
 cntx.beginPath();
 cntx.moveTo(mx,my);
 cntx.lineTo(coord1x,coord1y);
 cntx.lineTo(coord2x,coord2y);
 cntx.closePath(); // the closePath method completes the triangle
 cntx.stroke();
}
```

Parallax Processing

The canvas is a two-dimensional, on-screen drawing tablet. No matter how fancy the examples throughout the book have seemed—be it drawing, shape manipulation, or animation—everything has been two-dimensional. It's time to take the canvas to the next level, or rather, the next dimension. Enter 3D.

TIP
One dictionary listing (from www.dictionary.com) for parallax is "The apparent displacement of an observed object due to a change in the position of the observer." Here, something similar is achieved. You, the observer, are not changing positions. However, in the canvas, objects are apparently displacing themselves from each other.

The basis behind this technique is movement. To be more precise, it's a matter of the movement of objects relative to where they are being observed. Something close to us—say a cat running across the room—appears to move fast. In the sky, clouds appear to move more slowly. With an objective measure of speed, the clouds are moving much faster than the cat, but the distance of the clouds makes their movement appear slower. That is the principle applied here to the canvas.

Figure 14-11 shows a scene with trees in the back and rocks up front. When you press the left or right arrow key, the trees and rocks move appropriately toward the left or right. However—and this is the key point—the trees move slower than the rocks. The result is the rocks seem closer and the trees appear farther away. Essentially, it's a 3D visual experience.

Figure 14-11 Nearby rocks and farther away trees

You do need to see this in action to appreciate the effect. Visit www.webbingways.com and try it out for yourself.

How is this done? First, images are needed, and they must be sized in a certain way. The canvas is sized to 400 pixels wide by 300 pixels high. While an arrow key is pressed, a graphic of trees and a graphic of rocks are effectively scrolled. Thus, these graphics must be larger than the canvas. The movement is horizontal. Therefore, the graphics must be wider than the canvas, while the graphics stay at the same 300-pixel height. Figure 14-12 shows the two graphics seen as assembled in a graphics program.

The rocks and greenery graphics are sized at 800 pixels wide—twice that of the canvas on which they are displayed. The code running the moving effect shows a slice of the overall graphic at any one time. Code Listing 14-10 shows the full set of functions behind the moving effect.

Code Listing 14-10   How parallax processing is coded

```
<!doctype html>
<html lang="en">
<head>
<meta charset="utf-8">
<title>Parallax Processing</title>
<style>
body { background-color:#eeeeee; }
#canvas1 {background-color:dddddd;
          border: 5px blue solid; }
```

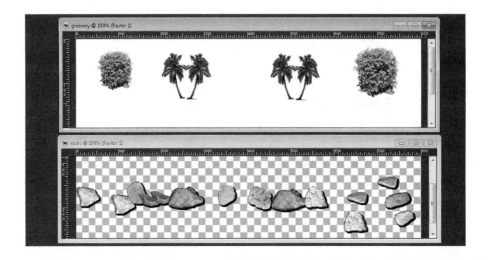

Figure 14-12 Rocks and greenery graphics

```
#outer {margin-left:40px;
       margin-top:20px;
       }
</style>
</head>
<body>
<div id="outer">
<canvas id="canvas1" width="400" height="300">
This text is displayed if your browser does not support HTML5 Canvas.
</canvas>
<br><br>
<b>Use the Left and Right Arrow Keys</b>
<br><br>
</div>
<script>
var greenery = new Image(); // background image (greenery)
var greenerydx = 2;  // Amount to move greenery image
var greeneryx = 0;  // x coord to slice greenery image
var rocks = new Image(); // rocks image
var rocksdx = 5;  // Amount to move rocks image
var rocksx = 0;  // x coord to slice rocks image
canvas1 = document.getElementById("canvas1");
cntx = canvas1.getContext("2d");
greenery.src = "greenery.png";
rocks.src ="rocks.png";
setInterval(draw, 10);
```

```
window.addEventListener('keydown',doKeyDown,true);
function doKeyDown(evt){
  switch (evt.keyCode) {
   case 37:  /* Left arrow was pressed */
    if ((greeneryx + greenerydx) >2) {
      greeneryx -= greenerydx;
    } else {
      greeneryx = 400;
    }
    if ((rocksx + rocksdx) >5) {
       rocksx -= rocksdx;
    } else {
      rocksx = 398;
    }
  break;
   case 39:  /* Right arrow was pressed */
    if ((greeneryx + greenerydx) < (400 - greenerydx)) {
       greeneryx += greenerydx;
    } else {
      greeneryx = 0;
    }
    if ((rocksx + rocksdx) < (400 - rocksdx)) {
      rocksx += rocksdx;
    } else {
      rocksx = 0;
    }
break;
} // switch (evt.keyCode) {
}  // function doKeyDown(evt)
function draw() {
cntx.drawImage(greenery, greeneryx, 0, 300, 300, 0, 0, 400, 400);
cntx.drawImage(rocks, rocksx, 0, 300, 300, 0, 0, 400, 400);
}
</script>
</body>
</html>
```

When the page opens, some variables are set, as well as an event listener for the keyboard, and a setInterval statement is set to call the draw function every 10 milliseconds.

Note the variables greenerydx and rocksdx. These variables establish what appears as the scrolling speed. The greenery has a value of 2; rocks have a value of 5. These are not actually scrolling speeds, but rather indicate where in the larger-than-canvas graphics to pluck out the area that is shown. The rocks value of 5 is larger, and the result is the appearance that the rocks are scrolling faster. The action appears smooth, as the refresh speed is rather fast (10 milliseconds).

```
var greenery = new Image(); // background image (greenery)
var greenerydx = 2;  // Amount to move greenery image
var greeneryx = 0;   // x coord to slice greenery image
var rocks = new Image(); // rocks image
var rocksdx = 5;  // Amount to move rocks image
var rocksx = 0;   // x coord to slice rocks image
canvas1 = document.getElementById("canvas1");
cntx = canvas1.getContext("2d");
greenery.src = "greenery.png";
rocks.src ="rocks.png";
setInterval(draw, 10);
window.addEventListener('keydown',doKeyDown,true);
```

The draw function applies the constantly updated values to the drawImage method.

```
function draw() {
cntx.drawImage(greenery, greeneryx, 0, 300, 300, 0, 0, 400, 400);
cntx.drawImage(rocks, rocksx, 0, 300, 300, 0, 0, 400, 400);
}
```

It is within the keyboard listener that the portion of the graphic to display is updated. When the position reaches 400 (the width of the canvas), the counter is reset to 0.

```
  case 39:  /* Right arrow was pressed */
    if ((greeneryx + greenerydx) < (400 - greenerydx)) {
      greeneryx += greenerydx;
    } else {
      greeneryx = 0;
    }
    if ((rocksx + rocksdx) < (400 - rocksdx)) {
      rocksx += rocksdx;
    } else {
      rocksx = 0;
    }
break;
```

This is admittedly a bit intimidating code to get your head around. Careful review of the code (as well as trying out the example on the Web) is the best way to grasp how this works.

The preceding example has two moving graphics, which are traveling at different speeds. In the next example, another feature is introduced: a third graphic is placed in the canvas. This one behaves a bit differently. It does not appear to scroll, although it seems to be in motion. It stays stationary, but in the way the larger graphics described earlier have only a portion appear at a time, this graphic does the same. In this example, the background is the night sky (a field of stars), the closer graphic is a skyline, and the third graphic is a wagon.

The wagon is really three views of the wagon that are cycled through, as shown in Figure 14-13. You might notice that the wheels appear turned in each segment, as well as the handle coming out of the top of the wagon.

Figure 14-13 A wagon in three views, of which only one is seen at a time

The code for this example is quite similar to that in Code Listing 14-10, but with more included to handle the visual representation of the wagon, and a few more lines to take care of clearing the canvas and setting the color. Code Listing 14-11 shows the full set of routines that run the 3D effect.

Code Listing 14-11 Parallax processing, with an added step

```
<!doctype html>
<html lang="en">
<head>
<meta charset="utf-8">
<title>Parallax Processing</title>
<style>
body { background-color:#eeeeee; }
#canvas1 {background-color:dddddd;
          border: 5px blue solid; }
#outer {margin-left:40px;
        margin-top:20px;
        }
</style>
</head>
<body>
<div id="outer">
<canvas id="canvas1" width="400" height="300">
This text is displayed if your browser does not support HTML5 Canvas.
</canvas>
<br><br>
<b>Use the Left and Right Arrow Keys</b>
<br><br>
</div>
<script>
var w = 400; // Canvas width
var h = 300; // Canvas height
var sky = new Image();  // Sky image
var skydx = 2;  // Amount to move sky image
```

```
var skyx = 0;  // x coord to slice sky image
var skyline = new Image(); // skyline image
var skylinedx = 5; // Amount to move skyline image
var skylinex = 0; // x coord to slice skyline image
var wagon = new Image(); // wagon image
var wagonx = 150; // x coord of wagon image
var wagony = 250; // y coord of wagon image
var wagonslice = 0; // x coord to slice wagon image
canvas1 = document.getElementById("canvas1");
cntx = canvas1.getContext("2d");
sky.src = "sky.png";
skyline.src ="skyline.png";
wagon.src =" wagon.png";
setInterval(draw, 10);
window.addEventListener('keydown',doKeyDown,true);
function rect(x,y,w,h) {
cntx.beginPath();
cntx.rect(x,y,w,h);
cntx.closePath();
cntx.fill();
cntx.stroke();
}
function doKeyDown(evt){
switch (evt.keyCode) {
  case 37: /* Left arrow was pressed */
    if ((skyx + skydx) >2) {
      skyx -= skydx;
    } else {
      skyx = 400;
    }
    if ((skylinex + skylinedx) >5) {
      skylinex -= skylinedx;
    } else {
      skylinex = 398;
    }
    if (wagonslice > 0) {
      wagonslice -= 45;
    } else {
      wagonslice = 90 ;
    }
  break;
  case 39:  /* Right arrow was pressed */
    if ((skyx + skydx) < (400 - skydx)) {
      skyx += skydx;
    } else {
      skyx = 0;
    }
    if ((skylinex + skylinedx) < (400 - skylinedx)) {
```

```
      skylinex += skylinedx;
    } else {
      skylinex = 0;
    }
    if (wagonslice < 90) {
       wagonslice += 45;
    } else {
       wagonslice = 0 ;
    }
  break;
} // switch (evt.keyCode) {
}  // function doKeyDown(evt)
function draw() {
  cntx.fillStyle = "black";
  rect(0,0,w,h);
  cntx.drawImage(sky, skyx, 0, 300, 300, 0, 0, 400, 400);
  cntx.drawImage(skyline, skylinex, 0, 300, 300, 0, 0, 400, 400);
  cntx.drawImage(wagon, wagonslice, 0, 45, 39, wagonx, wagony, 32, 32);
}
</script>
</body>
</html>
```

The width and height of the canvas are stored in the w and h variables. Initialization of the sky and skyline graphics is similar to that for the greenery and rocks graphics in Code Listing 14-10. New here are variables holding information about the wagon. The variables wagonx and wagony are coordinates of where the wagon is seen on the canvas. These do not change. The wagonslice variable changes to show which of the three wagon views to use.

```
var w = 400; // Canvas width
var h = 300; // Canvas height
var sky = new Image();  // Sky image
var skydx = 2;  // Amount to move sky image
var skyx = 0;  // x coord to slice sky image
var skyline = new Image(); // skyline image
var skylinedx = 5; // Amount to move skyline image
var skylinex = 0; // x coord to slice skyline image
var wagon = new Image(); // wagon image
var wagonx = 150; // x coord of wagon image
var wagony = 250; // y coord of wagon image
var wagonslice = 0; // x coord to slice wagon image
```

The wagon graphic is 135 pixels wide, which means each view of the wagon is 45 pixels wide ($45 \times 3 = 135$). Therefore, the testing of the wagonslice variable is based on a multiple of 45. When the left arrow key is pressed, wagonslice is tested to see if it is greater than 0. If so, then 45 is subtracted from its value. When it is 0, it is reset to 90.

```
    if (wagonslice > 0) {
      wagonslice -= 45;
    } else {
      wagonslice = 90 ;
    }
```

When the right arrow key is pressed, `wagonslice` is tested to see if it is less than 90. If so, then 45 is added to the value; otherwise, it is reset to 0.

```
    if (wagonslice < 90) {
       wagonslice += 45;
    } else {
       wagonslice = 0 ;
    }
```

Regardless of direction, 45 pixels of the overall 135 pixels are shown—in other words, one slice of the overall 135-pixel graphic.

As the `draw` function is chugging away every 10 milliseconds, the canvas is filled with black, and the images are redrawn.

```
function draw() {
  cntx.fillStyle = "black";
  rect(0,0,w,h);
  cntx.drawImage(sky, skyx, 0, 300, 300, 0, 0, 400, 400);
  cntx.drawImage(skyline, skylinex, 0, 300, 300, 0, 0, 400, 400);
  cntx.drawImage(wagon, wagonslice, 0, 45, 39, wagonx, wagony, 32, 32);
}
```

Some type of clearing is necessary because the wagon is not moving. Filling the background of the canvas with black takes care of that, as well as following the nighttime theme; the background is a field of stars. Figure 14-14 shows the canvas filled with the background stars, foreground skyline, and stationary wagon.

Summary

This closing chapter of the book presented some techniques that are beyond the basics. The JavaScript overview was intended as a reference for the common programming needs of looping and branching, and reusable code efficiency via functions as well. Geometry and a touch of trigonometry were covered to serve as a basis of future graphics you might create. There is quite a bit more that can be accomplished with math—simulations of gravity, elasticity, and more. Even rocket science (calculus) can be made visual. Finally, you learned about parallax processing, both the technique and perhaps as a demonstration of how you can often find a way around a limitation. The canvas, two-dimensional in all respects, was used in such a way to show depth—the third dimension.

We hope this book provides inspiration in addition to a reference of techniques. Multimedia is the sugar of web page use. Seeing something always has an instant response,

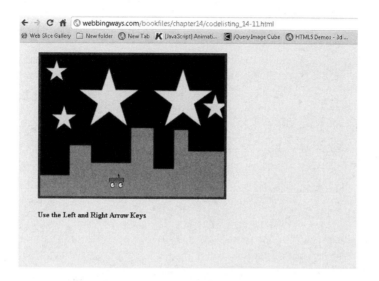

Figure 14-14   Left or right movement provides a 3D experience.

or at least invokes an emotion in most of us. And that is the point to much of the Web: to get a rise out of your viewers.

HTML5 is not brand-new in its design, but is evolving in its implementation. Being on top of browser nuances has always been a blessing and a curse (mostly a curse) of web developers and designers. It comes with the territory and is no reason not to push the envelope.

Thanks for reading, and best wishes with your web projects!

Appendix

Quick Reference

The appendix is designed as a quick reference for all of HTML5 and earlier versions. You will find a barebones HTML5 template, HTML attribute definitions, and HTML tag definitions. This appendix is intended to summarize the HTML5 landscape and provide quick facts at a glance.

HTML5 Template

All HTML documents start from the same humble beginnings. You can save yourself some time by creating and using a template with your standard layout. Code Listing A-1 shows a template that my students develop over the course of our class.

Code Listing A-1   A simple HTML5 template

```
<!doctype html>
<html lang="en">
<head>
<meta charset="utf-8">
<title>HTML5 Template</title>
<style>
.mastHead{

}
.mainContent{

}
.pageFooter{

}
</style>
<script>
</script>
</head>
<body>
<header id="masthead">
<h1>Page Title Here</h1>
</header>
<div id="mainContent">
<p>Your page contents here</p>
</div>
<footer id="pageFooter">
<p>Your footer legal disclaimers here</p>
</footer>
</body>
</html>
```

HTML Global Attributes

Global attributes are shared by every HTML tag. For Boolean attributes, HTML5 supports simply listing the tag as setting a true value; omission suggests false. If you want to set a value or are using XML style syntax (XHTML5), you should use the syntax and set `attribute="attribute"`.

The following table lists the attributes in HTML5. Not all of these attributes are covered in this book, but each has its use.

Attribute	Description	Possible Values
accesskey	Creates a shortcut keystroke combination to access the element.	Any letter on the keyboard (user needs to press ALT plus the key to access the element); not supported by Opera
class	Use to apply a CSS class to an HTML element.	Name of a CSS class
contenteditable	A Boolean attribute that determines if the user can change the content of the HTML element to which the attribute is applied.	Empty string, `false`, `true`
contextmenu	Links a context menu to an element.	ID of a DOM menu element
dir	Sets the direction of the text.	`ltr`, `rtl`
draggable	A Boolean attribute used to set draggable content on a page.	Empty string, `auto`, `false`, `true`
hidden	A Boolean attribute that hides text from the user. HTML5 allows empty attributes or you can set the value of `hidden`, similar to HTML4.	Empty string, `false`, `true`
id	The name of the element. The name can be associated with a CSS class, a JavaScript function, or both.	Name of the element
lang	Sets the language code to be used.	A valid RFC 3066 language code or an empty string
spellcheck	A Boolean attribute that sets if the edited content is to be spell checked. You need to implement the spell checking; it is not included in your browser.	Empty string, `false`, `true`
style	Sets in-line style rules for the element.	CSS property and value pairs
tabindex	Suggests the tabbing order on a page. User choice or browsers can override this attribute. Every object the user can tab into will have a value indicating the order in the tab progression.	An integer from 1 to 32,767
title	Sets a tooltip entry for an element. Certain screen readers read this element to the user.	Text for the tooltip

HTML Tag-Specific Attributes

The following table defines the attributes used by some tags supported by HTML5. Not all tags will support all of these attributes. See the table in the next section to determine which tags support an attribute.

Attribute	Description	Possible Values
accept	Lists the MIME type the object will receive	A valid MIME type
action	URL to which a form is sending its data	A URL to a script
alt	Alternate text; use in addition to the title	A string
async	Boolean attribute used to instruct the browser to run a script as soon as it is available	Empty string, true, false
autocomplete	Specifies whether a browser can autocomplete entries in this box	Empty string, true, false
autofocus	Determines which form element receives the focus when the page is loaded	Empty string, true, false
autoplay	Boolean attribute that determines if the media object plays when loaded	Empty string, false, true
checked	Preselects elements in a check box or radio button	Empty string, true, false
cite	Source of the content inside the element	Valid URL
controls	Boolean attribute for audio and video players that shows or hides the object controls	Empty string, true, false
coords	Coordinates of the hotspot in the image map	Pixel coordinates
datetime	A date and time stamp for an element	Date and time in the format *YYYY-MM-DDHH:mm:ss*
defer	Boolean attribute used to instruct the browser to run a script once the page has finished loading	Empty string, true, false
disabled	Makes an object unable to be used by the user	Empty string, true, false
form	Specifies the ID of a form to which the object belongs	Form ID
formaction	Allows an object to override the action of its parent form	URL
formmethod	Allows an object to override the method of its parent form	get, post
formnovalidate	Boolean attribute that is used to instruct the browser to submit data without checking for validation	Empty string, true, false

Attribute	Description	Possible Values
formtarget	Allows an object to override the target of its parent form	_blank, _self, _parent, _top, ID of a location
height	Height of the element (better to set using CSS)	Height in pixels, ems, or percentage
href	Holds the URL to a web page or file	String holding a URL
hreflang	Language of the URL (works only when an HREF is present)	A valid RFC 3066 language code or an empty string
icon	URL for an image	URL
list	ID of a list object that is used to populate a form object	DOM ID of a list object
loop	Boolean attribute that tells the media player to repeat the song	Empty string, false, true
max	Largest value allowed in a form object	Number
maxlength	Maximum number of characters allowed in a text box	Number
media	Media or device for which the object is optimized	Media name
method	Command that a form uses to send data to the action	get, post
min	Smallest value allowed in a form object	Number
multiple	Boolean value that can allow the user to select many objects from a list object	Empty string, true, false
open	Boolean attribute that tells the browser to render a section as open and readable	Empty string, false, true
pattern	Holds a regular expression used in form validation	Regular expression formatted as a string
placeholder	Text that appears in the text box prior to user editing	String
preload	Instructs the web server to download the file as the web page is loaded—if auto, the media loads with the web page; if metadata, the page loads only the metadata of the media	auto, metadata, none
radiogroup	Name of a group of radio buttons	String name
readonly	Boolean attribute specifying if the user can edit the form element	Empty string, false, true

Attribute	Description	Possible Values
rel	Relationship between the current document and the URL	alternate, archives, author, bookmark, external, feed, first, help, index, last, license, next, nofollow, noreferrer, prev, search, sidebar, stylesheet, tag, up
required	Boolean value describing if a form object must be completed by the user	Empty string, false, true
reversed	Boolean attribute that indicates the ordered list is in reverse order	Empty string, true, false
sandbox	Creates a set of restrictions on the nested content, with several subattributes: allow-forms Blocks form submission allow-same-origin Blocks the nested content from retrieving mode content from the source; links and database lookups can be blocked allow-scripts Blocks script execution allow-top-navigation Controls whether nested content can navigate to the top-level browsing context	
seamless	Boolean attribute that removes the border from the nested content	Empty string, true, false
shape	Describes the geometric shape of an area	circle, circ, poly, polygon, rect, rectangle
size	Width of the input field	Number
span	Number of <td> or <tr> tags to include in the span	Number
src	Path to file used by the attribute	Path or URL to a file
srcdoc	Content of the page that will be nested	
start	Numeric position where an ordered list should start counting	Number
step	Intervals for the input field	Number indicating the interval
target	Location on the screen where a followed URL will appear	_blank, _self, _parent, _top, ID of a location

Attribute	Description	Possible Values
type	Determines which version of an element is used; most commonly used by the `<input>` tag	`button`, `checkbox`, `color`, `date`, `datetime`, `datetime-local`, `email`, `file`, `hidden`, `image`, `month`, `number`, `password`, `radio`, `range`, `reset`, `search`, `submit`, `tel`, `text`, `time`, `url`, `week`
type	MIME type of the URL, used by a link or a tag	MIME type
value	Holds contents of the object; commonly used with the `<input>` tag	String or numbers
width	Width of the element (better to set using CSS)	Width in pixels, ems, or percentage

HTML5 Tags

The following table lists the tags supported in HTML5 and their associated attributes.

Tag	Description	New to HTML5?	Attributes
`<!--...-->`	Builds a comment		None
`<!doctype>`	Builds the document type		
`<a>`	Creates a hyperlink		`href`, `hreflang`, `media`, `rel`, `target`, `type`
`<abbr>`	Identifies an abbreviation		
`<address>`	Builds an address element		
`<area>`	Creates an area inside an image map; must be associated with an `img` with the `usemap` attribute	Yes	`cords`, `href`, `hreflang`, `rel`, `shape`, `target`, `type`
`<article>`	Builds an article	Yes	
`<aside>`	Builds content aside from the page content	Yes	
`<audio>`	Builds sound content	Yes	`autoplay`, `controls`, `loop`, `preload`, `src`
`<b>`	Builds bold text		
`<base>`	Sets the base URL for all the links in a page; must be within the head section		`href`
`<bdo>`	Sets the direction of the contained text		`dir`
`<blockquote>`	Builds a long quotation		`cite`

Tag	Description	New to HTML5?	Attributes
`<body>`	Builds the body element		
` `	Inserts a single line break		
`<button>`	Builds a push button		`autofocus, disabled, form, formaction, formenctype, formmethod, formtarget, name, type, value`
`<canvas>`	Defines a graphic area on a web page	Yes	`height, width`
`<caption>`	Creates a table caption		
`<cite>`	Semantic tag that creates a reference citation		
`<code>`	Semantic tag that describes computer code text		
`<col>`	Defines different attributes for columns of `<td>` tags		`span`
`<colgroup>`	Creates groups of table columns with the same formatting	Yes	`span`
`<command>`	Creates a command button within a menu element	Yes	`checked, disabled, icon, label, radiogroup, type`
`<datalist>`	Builds an autocomplete drop-down list	Yes	
`<dd>`	Builds a definition description		
`<del>`	Highlights deleted text		`cite, datetime`
`<details>`	Builds details of an element	Yes	`open`
`<dfn>`	Semantic tag that creates a definition		
`<div>`	Builds a section in a document		
`<dl>`	Builds a definition list		
`<dt>`	Builds a definition term		
`<em>`	Semantic tag that marks emphasized text	Yes	
`<embed>`	Places an external object into an HTML page	Yes	`height, src, type, width`
`<eventsource>`	Creates a target for events sent by a server	Yes	`src`
`<fieldset>`	Builds a fieldset in a form		`disabled, form, name`

Tag	Description	New to HTML5?	Attributes
`<figcaption>`	Adds a caption for the figure element	Yes	
`<figure>`	Creates a section on your page designated to hold a picture, drawing, or video	Yes	
`<footer>`	Builds a footer for a section or page	Yes	
`<form>`	Builds a form		
`<h1>`	Creates a heading level 1		
`<h2>`	Creates a heading level 2		
`<h3>`	Creates a heading level 3		
`<h4>`	Creates a heading level 4		
`<h5>`	Creates a heading level 5		
`<h6>`	Creates a heading level 6		
`<head>`	Creates the first portion of a web document, the head		
`<header>`	Creates a header for a section or page	Yes	
`<hgroup>`	Creates a grouping of headers or navigational aids	Yes	
`<hr>`	Renders a horizontal rule		
`<html>`	Starts an HTML document		`manifest`
`<i>`	Builds italic text		
`<iframe>`	Creates nested content on the web page		`sandbox, src, srcdoc, seamless`
`<img>`	Builds an image		`alt, src, ismap, usemap`
`<input>`	Builds an input field		`accept, alt, autocomplete, autofocus, checked, disabled, form, formaction, formenctype, formmethod, formnovalidate, formtarget, list, max, maxlength, min, multiple, pattern, placeholder, readonly, required, size, type, value, width`

Tag	Description	New to HTML5?	Attributes
`<ins>`	Semantic tag that marks inserted text		`cite, datetime`
`<kbd>`	Semantic tag that marks keyboard text		
`<keygen>`	Generates a key/value pair on a form	Yes	`auto, challenge, disabled, form, keytype`
`<label>`	Associates a label with a form control		`for, form`
`<legend>`	Applies a title to a fieldset		
`<li>`	Adds an item to an ordered or unordered list		`value`
`<link>`	Creates a link to another document		`href, hreflang, media, rel, type, sizes`
`<mark>`	Marks text as though a highlighter passed over it	Yes	
`<map>`	Builds an image map		`name`
`<menu>`	Creates a menu list		`type, label`
`<meta>`	Adds meta information to a page		`content, charset, http-equiv`
`<meter>`	Creates a visual gauge for displaying a scalar measurement	Yes	`high, low, max, min, optimum, value`
`<nav>`	Creates navigation links	Yes	
`<noscript>`	Builds a no script section		
`<object>`	Builds an embedded object		`data, form, name, height, type, width`
`<ol>`	Builds an ordered list		`reversed, start`
`<optgroup>`	Groups related options in a drop-down list		`disabled, label`
`<option>`	Builds an option in a drop-down list		`disabled, label, selected, value`
`<output>`	Creates an area in which output from a program can appear	Yes	`for, form`
`<p>`	Creates a paragraph		
`<param>`	Creates a parameter to pass in to an object		`value`
`<pre>`	Builds preformatted text		
`<progress>`	Creates a progress bar	Yes	`value, max`

Tag	Description	New to HTML5?	Attributes
`<q>`	Creates a short quotation		`cite`
`<ruby>`	Includes a ruby annotation (used in East Asian typography)	Yes	
`<rp>`	Used for the benefit of browsers that don't support ruby annotations	Yes	
`<rt>`	Builds the ruby text component of a ruby annotation	Yes	
`<samp>`	Semantic tag that marks sample computer output		
`<script>`	Builds a script		`async, defer, src, type, charset`
`<section>`	Builds a section	Yes	
`<select>`	Builds a selectable list		`autofocus, disabled, form, multiple, size`
`<small>`	Builds small text		
`<source>`	Builds media resources	Yes	`src, media, type`
`<span>`	Builds a section in a document		
`<strong>`	Semantic tag that marks strong text		
`<style>`	Creates a style definition		`media, type, scoped`
`<sub>`	Creates subscripted text		
`<summary>`	Builds a summary/caption for the `<details>` element	Yes	
`<sup>`	Renders superscripted text		
`<table>`	Builds a table		
`<tbody>`	Groups body content in a table		
`<td>`	Builds a table cell		`colspan, headers, rowspan`
`<textarea>`	Builds a text area		`autofocus, cols, disabled, form, maxlength, placeholder, readonly, required, rows, wrap`
`<tfoot>`	Groups footer content in a table		
`<th>`	Builds a column header in a table		
`<thead>`	Groups header content in a table		

Tag	Description	New to HTML5?	Attributes
`<time>`	Renders a date/time	Yes	`datetime`
`<title>`	Creates the document title		
`<tr>`	Creates a table row		
`<ul>`	Builds an unordered list		
`<var>`	Semantic tag that marks a variable		
`<video>`	Builds a video	Yes	`autoplay, controls, loop, preload, src`
`<wbr>`	Builds a line-break opportunity for very long words and strings of text without any spaces	Yes	

Index

C

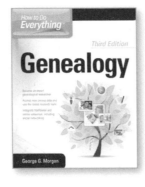